John Bridcut has directed and produced television documentaries for the past twenty years or so, specializing in contemporary history, current affairs and the arts. For the Golden Jubilee in 2002, he produced BBC1's four-part series *Queen and Country*. He has recently profiled Hillary Clinton and Roald Dahl, and has also directed a film about the realisation of Elgar's piano concerto. He has had a lifelong enthusiasm for the music of Benjamin Britten; his documentary, *Britten's Children*, won the Royal Philharmonic Society Award 2005 for Creative Communication.

Britten's Children

JOHN BRIDCUT

faber and faber

First published in 2006
by Faber and Faber Limited
3 Queen Square London WC1N 3AU

This paperback edition first published in 2007

Photoset by RefineCatch Limited, Bungay, Suffolk
Printed in England by Mackays of Chatham, plc

A CIP record for this book
is available from the British Library

ISBN 978-0-571-22840-9
ISBN 0-571-22840-2

Contents

Illustrations

Photographs 1–3, 6–7, 9, 12 and 18 are reproduced by permission of the Trustees of the Britten-Pears Foundation

Preface

I was lucky enough to work with Benjamin Britten across one long weekend in July 1971. As a member of the London Symphony Chorus, I took part in Decca's recording of Elgar's oratorio *The Dream of Gerontius*, which Britten conducted at The Maltings in Snape. The previous month, we had worked with Sir Michael Tippett, who was conducting his own oratorio *The Vision of Saint Augustine*. As conductors, there was no contest. Britten won hands down. During the rehearsal in London, and the sessions in Suffolk, he proved to be methodical, efficient, crystal-clear – but also electrifying. With Peter Pears singing the part of Gerontius, it was an extraordinary experience. Few would have presumed any sympathy between the musical languages of Elgar and Britten, yet Britten was deemed to have been closer in spirit to Elgar's own interpretation than any of the famous conductors (Boult and Barbirolli included) for whom *Gerontius* was a repertoire work. That Suffolk weekend gave me a direct insight into the physicality of his music-making which has never left me.

Later that year I had the memorable experience of singing in what was apparently the first student production of *Curlew River*, Britten's extraordinary cocktail of medieval mystery play and Japanese Noh-drama. The story describes a madwoman's search for her missing son: she is finally released from her torment when she finds his grave, and hears his voice. Most of this vivid and haunting score is still embedded in my memory 35 years later, entirely due to the intensity of those performances in the Oxford University Church.

There have been many other unforgettable Britten experiences: standing in the Royal Opera House to see *Peter Grimes* for the first time, in Elijah Moshinsky's production in 1975; being gripped by concert performances at the Proms of *Billy Budd* and *The Prince of the Pagodas*; and singing in the 60th birthday performance of his *Spring Symphony* at the Royal Albert Hall, just before which the conductor, André Previn, read out a telegram of thanks from the composer, still recovering from his heart operation earlier in the year.

But there is no obligation on those who admire, even adore, the music to feel the same about the man. As with many other composers during their lifetime, Britten's powerful magnetic field could repel as well as attract. Sometimes the polarity changed mid-career. But in his dealings with children Britten was at his most engaging and lovable – the adult friend and collaborator we would all like to be. In many cases, their parents were surprisingly trusting, and through their children they loved him too.

Although Britten wrote extensively for children, and about children, this aspect of his work has received surprisingly little attention, perhaps out of concern that, if too many stones were dislodged, something nasty might crawl out. So I am most grateful to Colin Matthews, chairman of the Britten Estate, for suggesting that this aspect of Britten might lend itself to a television documentary, and for his trust and encouragement as the film was made. The result, *Britten's Children*, was shown on BBC 2 in June 2004.

This book substantially extends the scope of that film with further exploration of the Britten archive (much of it never previously published), and fresh testimony from hitherto unknown children whom Britten befriended. It cannot pretend to be a comprehensive account: there are others more deeply versed in Britten's life and music who are far better qualified to provide that. But one of the great pleasures of making a television programme is to see and hear witnesses setting down their evidence as they recall it, rather than simply to read a written memoir. That allowed me to experience the visceral delight that most of Britten's boys took in his memory and continued to feel about their friendship with him. This was for me the most powerful evidence that, whatever shadows may have lurked in Britten's mind, his effect on these boys was benign, wholesome and inspiring.

We do come laden with preconceptions. Every time we read about the young Britten doing this or that, the use of his surname immediately conjures up the eminence and gravitas that properly adhere to one of the greatest composers of the twentieth century. This is misleading and unhelpful. In the years immediately before the Second World War, he was not yet a national figure, he was quite unselfconscious about the reputation he had begun to earn, and he was just a young man in his twenties. I have therefore tended to restrict my use of his surname to the occasions where his role as composer or musician is paramount: when his personality or character is to the fore, I have preferred to call him 'Benjamin' or 'Ben'. This is not out of a presumption of familiarity, but because I want to emphasise that, at the time, he was relating to his friends as an engaging and energetic young man (whatever his actual age), not as a grand composer. That is certainly how his young companions perceived him.

I have listed separately the books from the considerable Britten literature which I have found of particular help. But I should here acknowledge the central importance of the first three selections of his letters, edited by Donald Mitchell, Philip Reed and (latterly) Mervyn Cooke. Their erudition is invaluable to any student of Britten. Following their example, I have retained Britten's spelling and punctuation in any of his letters or diary entries that I have quoted. Humphrey Carpenter's biography remains controversial in its approach, but I have found it indispensable. And the catalogue of Britten's published works, compiled and edited by Paul Banks, has always been at my side.

I owe a considerable debt to the staff of the Britten-Pears Library under its Librarian Chris Grogan, for their patience with my persistent enquiries, particularly to its Curator for Reader Services, Nicholas Clark, and to Anne Surfling and Pamela

Wheeler. I am also grateful for the understanding of my erstwhile colleagues at Mentorn, the production company which made the documentary; and to the BBC for commissioning it, in particular to Peter Maniura (Head of Classical Music) whose support was staunch. I was fortunate to have contributors with such vivid recall: my thanks to them too – particularly to the late David Hemmings and to John Woolford (*alias* Wulff Scherchen), who has now agreed, for this book, to the unrestricted publication of his correspondence with Britten and of his poems. The documentary was the work of many hands, each with his or her distinctive contribution: my assistant producer Adam Lively, my cameraman Dirk Nel, my sound recordist Paul Vigars, my film researcher Alex Cowan, and my film editor David Richards, let alone the camera crew during my flying visit to Australia, Steve Hider and Maurice Carvajal. Annie Dinner, Julian Hamlin and Alex Thiele played essential roles in managing the production throughout, along with others during parts of the journey: they ensured that the film hit the screen.

I am also indebted to Donald Mitchell, Paul Kildea and Philip Reed for their wise guidance (though any mistakes herein are entirely mine); to my editor at Faber, Belinda Matthews, her assistant Elizabeth Tyerman and my production editor Lesley Felce, for their faith and encouragement in this my first book; and above all to my wife Suzanne and our family – Jonathan, Julia and Holly – for their patience and support which were sorely tested during the gestation of both film and book. I should also thank Benjamin Britten for music which continues to entrance, fascinate and thrill me, and without which there would have been no point in writing this book.

John Bridcut
Liss
December 2005

Chronological table of Britten's works mentioned in the text

1937	*Variations on a Theme of Frank Bridge* for strings, op. 10
	On This Island, song cycle to words by W. H. Auden, op. 11
1938	*Tell me the Truth about Love*, setting of poem by W. H. Auden, later published in *Cabaret Songs* (1937–9)
	Piano Concerto, op. 13
	On the Frontier, incidental music to play by Auden & Isherwood
1939	*Not to you I sighed. No, not a word*, setting of poem by Stephen Spender
	Young Apollo for piano & strings, op. 16
	Violin Concerto, op. 15
	Les Illuminations for high voice & strings, op. 18
1940	*Sinfonia da Requiem*, op. 20
	Seven Sonnets of Michelangelo for tenor & piano, op. 22
1941	*Paul Bunyan*, operetta, op. 17
1942	*A Ceremony of Carols* for trebles & harp, op. 28
	The trees they grow so high, arrangement of Somerset folk song
1943	*Serenade* for tenor, horn & strings, op. 31
	Rejoice in the Lamb, cantata, op. 30
	The Ballad of Little Musgrave and Lady Barnard for male voices & piano
1944	*Festival Te Deum*, op. 32
1945	*Peter Grimes*, opera, op. 33
	The Young Person's Guide to the Orchestra, op. 34
1946	*The Rape of Lucretia*, chamber opera, op. 37
1947	*Albert Herring*, chamber opera, op. 39
	A Charm of Lullabies, song cycle for mezzo-soprano & piano, op. 41
1948	*The Beggar's Opera*, op. 43
	Saint Nicolas, op. 42

1969   *Children's Crusade*, ballad for children's voices &
          percussion, op. 82
          Five Walztes (Waltzes), for piano, originally written
          1923-5
          Who are these Children?, song cycle to words by
          William Soutar, op. 84
1970   *Owen Wingrave*, opera, op. 85
1973   *Death in Venice*, opera, op. 88
1974   *Suite on English Folk Tunes*, 'A time there was ...'
          for orchestra, op. 90
1975   *Phaedra*, cantata for mezzo-soprano &
          orchestra, op. 93
          String Quartet no. 3, op. 94
1976   *Welcome Ode* for young people's chorus &
          orchestra, op. 95

CHAPTER I

It's because I'm still thirteen

A swarm of friends and admirers was jostling for position outside Britten's dressing room at the Royal Albert Hall. It was 12th September 1963, and the forty-nine-year-old composer had just conducted a long Promenade concert of his own music. The door opened, and an assistant called out: 'Is there someone called Robert Saxton here?' The whole queue turned round in surprise as a nine-year-old boy was carried past them on the shoulders of his violin teacher, and deposited – tiny and tongue-tied – at the feet of Benjamin Britten, whom he had never met or even seen before. The great man bent down over him (Saxton says he can still smell the after-shave to this day), and said, with a twinkle in his eye: 'My, aren't we tall?!'

Britten had invited him 'to come & say "hullo"' at the Proms, after receiving an unsolicited letter from Robert, who wanted advice about writing music. Even after conducting the British première of his *Cantata Misericordium*, followed by the *Sinfonia da Requiem*, and then the *Spring Symphony*, the first thing in the composer's mind was that out there in the crush was a small boy who wanted to meet him. It led to several years' correspondence, as Robert sent in his manuscripts, and Britten replied with practical suggestions and criticism. Saxton went on to become a professional composer in his own right. But that first September evening he was just a small boy. And Britten relished the company of children.

Among the treasures in the archive of the Britten–Pears Library in Aldeburgh, which covers Britten's whole life, is a series of Letts Schoolboy's Pocket Diaries, in which he noted his engagements. Each volume came complete with lists of Latin and

French verbs, logarithms, Morse code, kings and queens of England, athletics and swimming records, and an explanation of the Metropolitan-Vickers gas turbine locomotive. In one particular diary his Personal Memorabilia are completed in full detail. They begin with his name, given simply as 'BRITTEN'. His height is recorded as it was when he was thirteen: 5 ft 2 in, and his weight as 7 stone 9. Then come his bicycle number (4652), his season ticket number (6390), his National Savings Registration number (6755), and the train or bus service: 'To School: 7.55 From School: 4.22', with the addition: 'via Knodishall [a village near Aldeburgh]'. Further inside, he has filled out his weekly timetable. At the top of the frontispiece, the words 'SHALL WE?' have been written in pencil. Immediately below, the publisher's name, Letts, has been amended to read: 'LET'S!'

The anomaly is that opposite the Personal Memorabilia is a photograph of the newly crowned Queen Elizabeth II. The year of this well-thumbed pocket diary is 1954. Its proud owner was Benjamin Britten, Companion of Honour, illustrious composer the previous year of the Coronation opera *Gloriana*, and of *Peter Grimes* and *Billy Budd* before that. He was forty years old.

E. B. Britten never completed his schooldays. After five years at South Lodge preparatory school on the Suffolk coast, he moved to Gresham's public school in north Norfolk. But he was whisked away at the age of sixteen to specialise (and be frustrated) at the Royal College of Music in London. He never reached the point where he had outgrown his school, and so he seems to have spent the rest of his life unconsciously hunting for those three missing scholastic years. Although he never professed particular nostalgia for his schooldays, the pattern of Britten's daily timetable, his physical exercise, his food – all harked back to the comforting rhythms of school and the companionship of schoolboys.

After leaving South Lodge, he kept in touch by organising (as captain) the Old Boys' cricket team and even dropped into the school in March 1933 for an unseasonal game of cricket with the boys, in which he made 'a quick 25 not out'. He also invited the new generation of senior boys round to tea at his family home, which was only a few minutes' walk away on the Lowestoft seafront. He took a photograph of one such occasion in June 1934, when he was twenty: his mother appears a rather bored chatelaine in the background, while four boys sitting on deckchairs in grey flannel suits look towards the camera (see plate 1). One of them was the thirteen-year-old Piers Dunkerley, a strikingly good-looking boy whom Benjamin described as 'disconcertingly witty'. He was the first of a virtually unbroken chain of favourites threaded through Britten's busy life.

The friendship with Piers became much closer during his years at Bloxham public school in the mid to late 1930s. At the same time, Benjamin also took under his wing a young chorister from north London, Harry Morris, and gave him treats which his impoverished parents could never have contemplated. Just before the war, he became infatuated with an older German schoolboy, Wulff Scherchen, whose long interview with me sixty-five years later marked the first time he had spoken publicly about their intense relationship, explored in detail in these pages. During Britten's American years in the early 1940s, he was briefly captivated by the teenaged son of friends on Long Island, Bobby Rothman. Back in England, he became close to the children of other friends of his, John and Jean Maud, in particular to their son Humphrey during his years at Eton. At the same time, he championed the cause of a budding schoolboy composer, James Bernard, who went on to write the scores for many of the Hammer horror films.

In the late 1940s it was the turn of Jonathan Gathorne-Hardy, his siblings and cousins (who gave their names to the child characters in *The Little Sweep*), and he felt protective of David Spenser, the thirteen-year-old treble who created the role of Harry in his opera *Albert Herring*. Photographs during the gestation of *Billy Budd* show Britten and his librettist, E. M. Forster, aboard a fishing boat, with a young boy

3

nestling beside him, holding the tiller: this was Robin Long, or 'Nipper' as he was known. He corresponded affectionately with David Bedford and his brother Steuart, delighting in the colourful ties they gave him, and nurturing their early musical skills, which were to develop professionally as composer and conductor respectively.

He went out of his way to help another musician destined for the conductor's podium, Benjamin Zander, who was just a schoolboy in the early 1950s. He had an intense, even poignant, friendship with the adolescent Paul Rogerson, who was about to become a monk. He was also the first to spot the young David Hemmings, who created the role of Miles in *The Turn of the Screw*, which launched his stage and screen career. Some of those working with Britten at the time were worried that his infatuation with Hemmings might result in a scandal. In the later 1950s he was devoted to Roger Duncan, whom he treated almost as his own son: indeed he persuaded his father Ronnie to 'share' Roger with him. Humphrey Stone was another teenaged son of a friend of Britten's who was given favoured treatment.

Britten invited many of the boys who performed his music to stay with him in Aldeburgh, such as John Hahessy, the first boy to sing the alto part in his second canticle *Abraham and Isaac*; John Newton, who sang in early performances of his church parable *Curlew River*; and Stephen Terry, who played the parts of Harry in *Albert Herring* and Puck in *A Midsummer Night's Dream*. The early encouragement he gave to Adrian Thompson, just as to Robert Saxton, played a part in his decision to become a professional musician. He had a soft spot for Charles Tait, the son of his doctor, and, while he was writing his last opera *Death in Venice*, in deteriorating health, he devoted many hours that he could ill afford to a wild and passionate music student, Ronan Magill.

Even this extraordinary list of Britten's children is far from complete. There were the Lascelles boys – children of his close friends George and Marion Harewood – quite apart from his nephews Alan, John and Sebastian, and nieces Sally and Roguey. He also befriended a local boy, Richard Kihl, and his sister Alys. This gives some idea of the important part that children played in Britten's existence as a creative artist. But it has cast a long shadow over his reputation. The paradox is that, if this aspect of Britten the man is his most dubious, it is also his finest.

In many respects he treated adults in a cavalier way. They would often demand too much from him in time and affection. He found this hard to handle, and, instead of managing the difficulty, he would simply withdraw himself. The deliberate rupture of relationships caused hurt and offence. But, as far as boys were concerned, his time and affection were a bottomless well from which both he and they drew in full measure. He was at his most generous and natural when engaging with adolescents: through them he re-encountered and re-charged himself. When he turned back to adults 'a kind of frown came over his face as the world had to be confronted again'.

Almost without exception, his tenderness brightened the lives of these teenaged boys, and today their faces light up as they recall a unique friendship. Humphrey Stone remembers him as alert, sporty and funny: 'he made you laugh: for a boy who enjoyed larking about, he was fun to be with, and totally unpompous'. Humphrey Maud recalls his boyishness, as exemplified in his curly brown hair. For Ronan Magill, he was kind and patient, but also 'incisive and demanding'. Robert Saxton regarded him as 'a youngish grandfather' in cardigan and 'neat shoes', a figure of 'great safety, comforting and very polite'. Roger Duncan's sister, Briony Lawson, says he was 'so sweet with children. We were just so happy with him, that's all.' Many of their father's friends were above their level as children, 'but he was with us. That was what was so lovely about him. He kept us amused the whole time.' For Roger Duncan himself, it was 'a very close, loving relationship. I was very aware that he loved me. I wasn't in love with him, but I was very affectionate to him.'

Britten was aware, of course, of his own weakness for boys. His friend W. H. Auden taunted him about his 'attraction to thin-as-a-board juveniles', while his homosexual partner, Peter Pears, knew it was a part of Britten beyond the reach of their own enduring relationship. There were some overlapping areas of enthusiasm: Pears spoke of Britten's twenty-two-year-old former schoolfriend Francis Barton as 'just the sort of person I should hopelessly lose my heart to'. In the early 1950s, Britten wrote to Pears in some excitement about a concert invitation that had arrived from a contact in Germany: 'You remember the glamorous German youth who visited us in the Summer – Lederhosen & all? – well, he's just written the sweetest letter, presents of sweets & a tie, & lots of love to you.' Twenty years later, they had a shared interest in the Adonis-like son of the Maltings caretaker. But Britten's delight in the company of younger boys was different. Pears recognised that when he reported from his Amsterdam hotel that 'the sweet pageboy asked tenderly after you'. On another occasion he tried to cheer Britten up with the words: 'remember there are lovely things in the world still – children, boys, sunshine, the sea, Mozart, you and me'. The deliberate distinction between children and boys is significant.

Britten assumed an openness and transparency in his dealings with boys that prevented any secret desire devouring him through repression and denial. It was a sublimation which enabled him to control his weakness – perhaps even to transform it into something wholesome and good, as it emerged in his friendships and his music. That is why he always needed to have a favourite of the moment: it was an essential part of his creativity, and of his knowledge and understanding of himself. But his unabashed association with boys set tongues wagging, even among his own friends and family. No one was ever quite certain whether some of his boy friends were not boyfriends.

These friendships did not prevent him forming close adult relationships with musical colleagues. Nor did they supplant them. But Britten's world stopped for his children. According to the singer John Elwes, 'When we, the boys, were around, Peter Pears definitely took second place. We were very much at the forefront. Ben was the boy, the lad. Peter wasn't – he was an adult and never joined us in Ben's fast cars, ripping around the Suffolk countryside.' Elwes says he can visualise Ben only with the 'huge, crinkly grins' he had on his face as they 'zoomed along'. These occasions gave Ben the chance to 'indulge in that time of life that he missed or remembered with joy. He was happy. I don't really think that we could do wrong.' One of Britten's librettists, Eric Crozier, observed these relationships at first hand.

It was almost a return to his own youth, but a kind of idealised image of himself at the age of ten or twelve, the gay, attractive, charming young Lowestoft boy, unerringly skilful in his use of a cricket bat or a tennis racquet, and being able to do things with a ball that no other child of his age could do. It was like a flirtation that he carried on with any child that he met, particularly of course young boys, trying to dazzle them and astonish them by his virtuosity and his charm, making them his undying friends.

Crozier's analysis rings true in every particular except one. The 'idealised image' did not relate to E.B. Britten at the age of ten or twelve: it was most definitely at the age of thirteen, as he was entering his final year at South Lodge prep school. Thirteen was *the* age for Britten, the age that crops up again and again when boys began their friendships with him, the age when, as an adolescent, a boy first found himself on the threshold of experience and knowledge. It was the age the inner man in Britten felt himself to be throughout his life. We have this on good authority from Imogen Holst, his music assistant and daughter of the composer Gustav Holst. In February 1953, she was working with Britten on his forthcoming opera *Gloriana*, and keeping a journal about all her meetings with him – an invaluable insight into Britten's working methods, domestic rhythm and conversation. One evening, emboldened by rum before supper and sherry during it, and feeling 'completely lightheaded by halfway through the soup', she talked to him about the second scene of the opera's third act. She told him how much she enjoyed the effect of the quaver rest he had written at the end of each line in the boys' song 'Now Rouse Up All the City'. In a revealing flash of self-knowledge, Britten replied: 'It's because I'm still thirteen'.

CHAPTER 2

Britten's at it again!

The boy Benjamin was of course a special thirteen-year-old. He was the fourth 'B' in the Britten family, born in 1913 after his siblings Barbara, Bobby and Beth. But his mother nursed a much higher claim to fame for him, as the fourth 'B' in the musical pantheon: Bach, Beethoven, Brahms, and then Britten. His childhood friend in Lowestoft, Basil Reeve, remembers her making the point as she escorted the two of them back from Morling's music shop, where Benjamin was often allowed to demonstrate his prowess informally on one of the pianos for the delectation of Mr Morling's customers. But Beth Britten never realised the extent of her mother's ambitions for Benjamin. When Reeve told her the 'fourth B' story many years later, she was astonished. ' "Mother never said that in the family", she said. "If my father had heard that, he'd have laughed them out of the house." '

Basil Reeve first met the boy Benjamin in 1925. His father had just arrived in Lowestoft as vicar of St John's Church, which Mrs Britten and her children attended. When Basil first visited his new friend's home in Kirkley Cliff Road, the eleven-year-old Benjamin struck the dinner-gong in the hall before taking him upstairs to the drawing room, where he proceeded to replicate the sound of the gong on the piano, note by note, until he had built up a cluster of twenty. Basil was then thirteen, and 'staggered' by the younger boy's brilliance at picking out the harmonics. 'He had this incredible ear and sense of pitch. I could only hear two notes at a time, but he could hear twenty or more. His brain must have taken apart the sounds he heard, and so he could put them together again.'

Basil was an untrained pianist, but was swept along by Benjamin's enthusiasm and knowledge. He soon found himself playing and studying all Beethoven's piano sonatas, some of the piano concertos, the symphonies of Beethoven and Brahms (in four-hand piano arrangements), and then Schubert chamber music. Together with Charles Coleman, son of the church organist, they played trios day after day. Basil's young friend was 'the Pope of music. He decided what we should do, and he explained what the music meant.' At one point they tackled the new viola concerto by William Walton, at another pieces by Delius and Frank Bridge. It was musical education in the fast lane, boy to boy, and in the process Britten was discovering his craft as a composer. Reeve remembers how excited Britten was to realise that Schubert often began pieces with an upbeat: they did not have to start at the beginning of the bar. He was also thrilled by long pedal notes in Brahms.

Their joint musical adventures were always under the supervision of Mrs Britten. 'She was the queen bee that controlled the outfit', he says, 'and you were allowed in and out. It was almost absurd – like being at boarding-school, where everything is controlled.' When the boys went for walks, the departure and arrival times were dictated by Benjamin's mother. She did the same when they wanted to play tennis or go swimming. This continued until they were fifteen or sixteen. 'She was really possessive of Benjamin, so being too close to him really wasn't encouraged.' Although Basil became a good friend, he did not find much warmth or fun in the larger household: he was never invited to stay to lunch, and his offers to take Benjamin sailing on the Norfolk Broads were rebuffed. But then most days Edith Britten required her son to play Wagner's *Siegfried Idyll* to her as she rested in the drawing room in the early afternoon – which he did at the piano, from the miniature full score.

Apart from the regular excursions to Morling's music shop, Benjamin's precocity was on display at Mrs Britten's musical soirées. Her husband remained sceptical that Benjamin's talents were sufficient to provide him with a livelihood, but he dressed up formally for these occasions, at which ten or fifteen invited guests listened to Benjamin playing solo, or accompanying his mother's soprano. One such evening would be devoted to Beethoven, another to Brahms, another to 'modern music' – featuring Schönberg and Skryabin. His piano teacher, Miss Astle, would add her party piece (always the same bit of Chopin), and a terrified Basil Reeve was sometimes drafted to perform, but the purpose 'was really to hear Benjamin – *pro bono Benjamini*!' When, almost thirty years later in *The Turn of the Screw*, Britten portrayed the boy Miles giving a virtuoso display of his piano practice, it was familiar ground for him and no wonder that the mother-figure (the Governess) exclaimed: 'Oh, what a clever boy!'

Reeve remembers that Edith Britten had 'a pleasant singing voice', but she sang with 'an unusual sound'. Many years later he heard Peter Pears sing, and the particular quality of Pears's tenor reminded him immediately of Mrs Britten's soprano. He mentioned this to Britten's sister Beth some while after Britten had died. She was so startled by the acuity of his observation that 'she stopped, looked at me and said that it had never occurred to her. It was a revelation to her.' Reeve deduces from this that Pears was, in effect, a surrogate mother to Britten. He first met the composer only a month after Edith Britten's death in 1937, and later adopted her role, by providing a reassuring and stable domestic environment in which Britten's composing genius could flourish. In Reeve's opinion, Pears would have remained an indifferent singer without the influence of Britten, and he knew it. Similarly, he reckons Mrs Britten knew that her son had transformed her existence: without him, it would have been quite humdrum.

The adult Basil Reeve lost contact with Britten for many years, after emigrating to America. But their reunion in Colorado in 1964, when Britten was given the first Aspen Award, seemed to confirm his thesis. Reeve complimented his old friend by saying how proud of him his mother would have been, and was amazed when Britten replied that he could not remember a thing about his mother. Reeve took this to mean that Britten's loving relationship with Pears had not just replaced that with his mother, but had displaced it – perhaps because she would never have countenanced his homosexual lifestyle.

Basil and Benjamin met only in school holidays, because Basil was at boarding-school in Norwich, while Benjamin was at South Lodge, in walking-distance of his home. Britten later purported to be dismissive of it. He said there was 'no music at all – that's not *quite* true: at the end of each term, on the last evening, we sang some songs – but that was the limit of our music.' Yet somehow, by the time he left aged fourteen and a half, he had a stream of compositions to his credit, all neatly catalogued with opus numbers. He said he learnt about writing music from reading scores, even if it made the masters and mistresses 'a bit cross. They thought I was showing off – they always do. The boys themselves made no trouble at all. They thought it was rather amusing. I used to sit up in bed writing music, and they took that for granted: "Britten's at it again!" '

The photographic record of his years at South Lodge suggests a keen sportsman, rather than a musician. It was perhaps the one beneficent influence of his father: he may have been a rather unimaginative Lowestoft dentist, but he defied his wife's mollycoddling instincts and insisted their son should take part in sport. In so doing, he unwittingly secured one of the main-springs of Britten's music, its competitive, athletic physicality. Each year Benjamin was in the cricket team, ending up as vice-captain and also the school's top athlete after winning the title of *victor ludorum*. His headmaster, however, was under no illusions about what really counted for the boy in his charge: when a cricket ball hurtled towards Benjamin, he would bellow from the boundary: 'Britten, you're not to catch it!' He knew that the boy's hands (as pianist rather than composer at this stage) were even more precious than his own vicarious wish to triumph on the cricket field, and that he dare not risk Mrs Britten's wrath.

Britten himself took great pride in the way he had 'managed to do all the other things at school as well'. As an adult, he would sometimes refer to himself as 'E.B. Britten (minor)'. On one such occasion, when he was twenty-nine, he boasted of his five credits in School Certificate at his senior school, and went on to add:

> It might interest you to know I was also a valuable member of all the elevens, Victor Ludorum, held record for several years for Throwing the Cricket Ball (until broken by a beastly little boy in a gale), apart from my highly distinguished career in the Junior Tennis World*. So now you know the stature of the composer you're dealing with – !

His abiding regard for South Lodge was evident not only in the old boys' cricket matches he enjoyed, but in the exuberant setting of *Psalm 150* he wrote in 1962. He was marking the centenary celebrations of the school, now reincarnated as Old Buckenham Hall†, and although he called it 'a minor work', he gave it the distinction of an opus number (67), and said it had given him 'great pleasure' to write it. He added that it was 'a bribe to make his old school take music a little more seriously'.

The setting is tailored for children (two-part choir and simple orchestra), in C major, the first key that most children encounter. Britten did not prescribe particular instruments for the ensemble: he suggested pitch-ranges, so that schools could perform it with whatever resources they had. The only essentials were a treble instrument, some sort of drum, and a keyboard player. 'The more instruments there are', he said, 'the merrier'. My own first, hugely enjoyable, experience of it was as a thirteen-year-old schoolboy pianist, when the other instruments taking part were: clarinet, two recorders, triangle, tambourine, cymbals and drums.

---

* Both Wulff Scherchen and Humphrey Maud remember him saying he had been junior tennis champion of Suffolk.
† During the stewardship of his headmaster, Captain Thomas Sewell, South Lodge had burned down twice. Some former pupils regarded this as neither unfortunate nor careless, but suspicious.

The piece is strikingly physical. It belongs to the energetic world of the football pitch or the playground, particularly in the *marcato* chords of the opening, each syllable of 'O praise God, praise God: praise God in his holiness' separated by a characteristic quaver rest, which therefore imposes fresh impetus for each note. If the rests were not there, the energy (and the essence) would evaporate. Britten the conductor made the same point to the London Symphony Orchestra strings when rehearsing Purcell's *Chacony* in G minor at around this time: 'Not too long on these chords,' he said: 'off on the fourth quaver'.

He jotted down a sketch of the opening of *Psalm 150* as it occurred to him, in the back of his 1962 Schoolboy's Pocket Diary. The second section ('Praise Him in the sound of the Trumpet, Praise Him upon the Lute and Harp') is sung, as it is spoken, to an irregular 7/8 rhythm – a dance with a hint of the Arab *souq*, building to the climax of 'Praise Him upon the loud Cymbals', when the final word is shouted.

The particular genius of this straightforward piece is that, as in *Noye's Fludde*, his children's opera of a few years earlier, it achieves its full effect only if it is performed, as Britten intended, by children. One recent professional recording is crisply accurate and hard-driven – and consequently sterile: it needs occasional imprecisions of pitch and rhythm to work. When the Oldham Boys' Choir sang the piece recently for my television documentary *Britten's Children*, the bright-eyed, vigorous response from many of the boys, straining at the leash in their eagerness, would doubtless have delighted Britten: it was a world away from the sedate, ethereal sound of the cloister.

In his last year at South Lodge, Britten was Head Boy, and was certainly no slouch academically – he 'adored Mathematics, got on all right with History', even if 'scared by Latin Unseen'. He had sufficient familiarity with French to compose the first of *Quatre chansons françaises* just before he left the school, a work of extraordinary self-confidence in its writing for soprano and full orchestra, with a vivid understanding (appropriately enough) of the musical world of Ravel and

Debussy, as well as Wagner. He completed it in the summer holidays. The four poems by Victor Hugo and Paul Verlaine were chosen from his copy of *The Oxford Book of French Verse*. His use of what came to hand was an early instance of his practical approach to composition. He happened to light upon the two shortest poems of either author in the anthology, but his choices – and his response to the unease beneath their romantic surface – presaged his later mastery of the song-cycle form.

By now he was travelling regularly to London for composition lessons with Frank Bridge and piano lessons with Harold Samuel. This was bound to mean that, when in 1928 he arrived at Gresham's, his Norfolk boarding-school, the music department headed by Walter Greatorex would suffer in Britten's esteem. When Greatorex ventured a perhaps kindly-meant opening gambit, 'So you're the boy who likes Stravinsky', the fourteen-year-old Benjamin took it amiss. His best friend at Gresham's, David Layton, recalls how irritated he was by playing duets with Greatorex, who was 'incapable of playing *staccato*' because he played the piano 'as if it were the organ'. There was no abatement of Britten's fury, to judge by *A Poem of Hate*, a startlingly dissonant 50-second paroxysm on the piano, 'written at W.G.' in 1930. The hapless music-master ranked higher in the estimation of one of Britten's predecessors at Gresham's: W.H. Auden, no great respecter of persons, regarded him as a first-rate musician, who set out to be a friend first and schoolmaster second. But young Britten, of the 'long delicate fingers and protuberant misty eyes', was implacable.

Later in life, he put his Greatorex grievance down to mutual suspicion, and acknowledged that Gresham's was 'for those days a progressive and enlightened Public School'. He gave it credit for the way it dealt with his burgeoning pacifism. He and David Layton both refused to take part in the School's OTC army training, which resulted in a 'considerable battle with authority'. He said there were 'many hours of strenuous argument and close questioning of motives', but in the end they were permitted to opt out. They would play cricket in the nets while the rest of the school marched up and down the parade ground, with the sound of the military band echoing off the surrounding buildings. Layton is convinced that those echoes planted the seed of the bugle flourishes in *Noye's Fludde* thirty years later.

The two boys sat side by side in the same class in their first year. They both scored well in languages (German, French and Latin). 'Britten was good at everything. He was very bright. He was top, and I was second.' Layton remembers him as tall and slender, 'not a robust person at all – but he was physically stronger than you might have expected'. They went on walks and played tennis together. They had a shared musical interest as well, as members of that rare breed in school orchestras, viola-players. 'He played well', says Layton, 'and I had a good viola'. They spent hours in the music school, rifling through its supply of sheet music in the practice rooms or monopolising the big radiogram, with Britten sharing all his knowledge and discoveries with Layton, just as he did with Basil Reeve at home. Both Layton and Reeve remember Brahms's 4th Symphony as a particular enthusiasm. Layton was struck by the way Britten would readily improvise music in the style of other composers while confessing he found it much more difficult to write his own. One visitor to Gresham's at that time overheard a boy asking the headmaster if he could be excused rugger, because he wanted 'to go and hear Britten practise'.

Britten left Gresham's after only two years, with a composition scholarship to the Royal College of Music in his pocket. In his diary he had talked of suicide or running away rather than having to face another term at Gresham's, which he seemed to regard with venom. He felt it was 'rather a waste of time, my going on with general schooling'. But in later years he came to see that that feeling had been wrong. He said that he was grateful to Gresham's in many ways, he remembered it with 'great affection' and on the whole he had been 'very happy there'. At the moment of leaving in July 1930, he had indeed found it a wrench.

I spend all the afternoon with David Layton in music rooms, & walk. Walk with Willcock after tea. I am terribly sorry to leave such boys as these. [. . .] I didn't think I should be so sorry to leave.

He was still feeling the loss a few weeks later, and wrote a *Sketch* for strings to capture David Layton in music.*

It must have come as a surprise to discover that the school was also sad to lose him. His housemaster paid tribute to 'a most excellent boy . . . His quiet capacity has always impressed me. I am sorry he must go and I wish him a brilliant career.' The headmaster was equally fulsome: 'a thoroughly sound & very high-principled & delightful boy [. . .] His music has been a great joy to us all.' He sent his congratulations on the scholarship, and said he felt some reflected glory: 'He is such a dear boy & so modest about all his brilliant performances!'

As an adult, he perhaps tried to recover those missing years at Gresham's by pressing the thirteen-year-old David Hemmings to go there, and even fixing him up with a place. When the school celebrated its quatercentenary in 1955, distinguished alumni were asked to mark the occasion. Britten was by then the renowned composer of *Billy Budd, Gloriana* and *The Turn of the Screw*, and it would have been easy to plead pressure of work, but he responded readily with a charming, simple and apposite song, to which he gave the title *Farfield 1928–30* (the boarding-house he belonged to, and his dates). It set lines by an East Anglian contemporary of Chaucer, John Lydgate, the Monk of Bury. Britten added in a footnote that the words may have dated from the 15th century, 'but they still apply . . .' They speak of the wilful, irrational behaviour of the schoolboy, and the musical instruction to the performers is 'gently reminiscing'. Despite the occasional caning (three strokes audible in the accompaniment),

---

* This was published posthumously in 1997 as the first of *Two Portraits*.

Like a young colt that ran without bridle,
Made I my friends their good to spend in idle.

At the time of writing *Farfield*, Britten was working with David
Hemmings, and following Roger Duncan's progress through his
last year at prep school. His own time as a schoolboy was much
on his mind, so his response to the Gresham's anniversary was
born of sentiment, not censure.*

The boarding-school rhythm that *Farfield* encapsulated had
come to dominate his life. That was where he had become such
a consistent and methodical letter-writer: he first kept his head
above water by writing what were almost love-letters to his
mother, and, although he often decried his own epistolary skill,
he must have known how effectively he could captivate his
friends with the elegance and eloquence of his written word.
However busy he became, he never stopped writing letters: his
surviving correspondence amounts to the astonishing total of
84,000 items, which means he wrote an average of three letters
every day of his adult life, many of them of considerable length.

Boarding-school also secured the daily routine of keeping a
diary which lasted for eleven years, and now illuminates his
youth. His lifelong favourite meals, often called 'nursery food',
had more to do with school: steak and kidney pudding, mashed
potatoes, kedgeree, trifle, milk puddings, steamed puddings,
queen of puddings – these were more to his taste than the *haute
cuisine* which Pears enjoyed. His passion for sport, his addic-
tion to swimming, and the fierce timetabling of every working
day – this was all part of a school routine he never shed. While
he was writing his church parable *The Burning Fiery Furnace*,
his long-serving music assistant Rosamund Strode helped him
plan his schedule for the period after its completion: she was

---

* Gresham's did not exactly respond in kind. *Farfield*'s first known performance
there was not for another thirty-four years (1989), by which time Gresham's was
co-educational. So the earliest 'young colt' to sing it was in fact female. It was
first performed professionally for the film *Britten's Children*, by Philip Langridge
and David Owen Norris: this recording was not in the end included in the film,
but was broadcast on *In Tune* on BBC Radio 3 on 31st May 2004.

amazed to find that he even built in time for illness. 'I'm always ill after a big piece', he told her. But then there had always been something comforting (and productive) about being unwell at school, as he frequently was: it won him individual attention. *Quatres chansons françaises* were begun in the 'san' at South Lodge, while his anthem for unaccompanied choir *A Hymn to the Virgin* was tossed off one day in the sick bay, shortly before he left Gresham's, at a time when he had the 'absolute wind up' over his School Certificate exams.

Schoolboy slang and jokes came readily to him all through his life. If he was impressed at hearing about a double century at cricket, or taken aback by the tale of a rider falling from his horse, the word that sprang naturally to his lips was 'Coo!'. He would write 'Boo-hoo!' in his letters when he was appealing for sympathy. He used 'old thing' as a term of endearment, whether for his sisters, for Pears or for one of the boys he had befriended. He delighted in reciting a suburban version of the Lord's Prayer ('Thy Kingston come, Thy Wimbledon'). He always wrote 'abit' and 'alot' as single words. As a Tchaikovsky fan, he found Humphrey Maud's awful pun about a place being hard to find because of a *lac de cygnes* 'colossally funny'. One of his composer protégés, Arthur Oldham, remembered Britten saying 'I *one* a dead rat in the road', to which others had to respond in turn, with 'I *two* a dead rat in the road' and so on, until Oldham found himself saying 'I *eight* a dead rat in the road', whereupon Britten 'laughed his head off'.

In the early 1950s, he was enamoured of the affectionate caricature of prep school life in the Molesworth books. He would joust with the twelve-year-old David Hemmings in Molesworth catchphrases. When collecting him from Saxmundham station, Britten would say, 'Chiz, chiz, trane late!' Hemmings's thank-you letters slipped easily into the same language. But Britten had entered this world six years before Geoffrey Willans and Ronald Searle published the first Molesworth book, to judge by a note in the back of his pocket diary in 1947. He had faithfully scribbled down a boyhood gem he had collected from a

Surrey prep school (Hazelwood, in Oxted), under the heading 'If I were a Headmaster':

> I would have a skoule: Down in a derstid part of Cormwole along way away from aney one. It would bein a wood on the clife.

> If I onde a school, the ferst rool I would mace. I would mace this one is the boys must not rag in the dormertris. And anuther rool would be that they should not goon the cricit pitch with thire shooson. But they could goon it if they had primselson. The necst rool would be that they should not bring anyeattabols. The eattaboel they had they had a joint every week and rabitstue.

Britten himself had closer links with Molesworth than Hemmings ever guessed. One of his schoolfriends at Gresham's was David Molesworth, who had earlier been at prep school with Willans and was later a prisoner-of-war with Searle. So he may have unwittingly given his name to the books. Molesworth always said that at school Britten had written him a song for his birthday, which thereafter he carried with him in his wallet.

He delighted in childhood games well into middle age: he introduced 'Dover Patrol' to David Hemmings, and played 'Pick Up Sticks' and 'Jenga' with Paul Rogerson. 'Happy Families' was an unmissable part of his Christmas Day ritual, but the cards were brought out on other occasions too. His close friend, the artist Mary Potter, gave him a special set, which she had painted herself, entitled 'Aldeburgh Happy Families', and marked 'very secret' and 'very private'. Bones the Butcher, Bung the Brewer, Cure the Chemist and Nibs the Newsagent represented thinly-disguised local families. They engaged the cruel side in Britten's childlike nature, and could be used only in the most discreet company. Imogen Holst recorded a game of 'Happy Families' during a 'frivolous' evening with him in October 1952. It came four days after one of the regular meetings of the Aldeburgh Music Club, in which Britten played the viola. She was conducting, but did not want to tackle one particular piece because she had not prepared it. 'But he made such a fuss, like a small boy, scraping his bow on his open strings, so I had to.'

He continued to de-construct sounds, as young Benjamin had done with the gong in the hall. Sometimes it was with professional intent (as with the bell in 'Would I might be hanged!', the penultimate number in his exhilarating realisation of *The Beggar's Opera*), sometimes it was just a party trick. But both were for fun. One of his conceits was to assemble the ingredients for a 'really fruity sneeze. Everyone round the table was allotted a "hish", a "hosh", a "hash" and a "rats". Ben's conductor's arm fell and this giant's sneeze shook the kitchen.'

He spoke a private language with Roger Duncan. This involved putting the letters *arp* before any vowel, which resulted in complete gobbledygook, so 'I want to play tennis' became '*Arp*I w*arp*ant t*arp*o pl*arp*ay t*arp*enn*arp*is'. They had long conversations in the car in this language, which amused Britten both because of its childish absurdity and because of the challenge of speaking it at speed without tripping up. It was a code in their letters too: 'arpI harpavarpn't farporgarpottarpened [*sic*] tharpe LARPIST', he wrote when Roger was twelve. Years later he was still doing it. He would sometimes tell Peter Pears: 'ArpI larpove yarpou!'

Roger and his sister would play 'pub cricket' with Ben (in which runs were scored according to the number of legs visible on pub signs they passed, and wickets were taken when a head was spotted) during their long drives to and from the family home in Devon. On one cliff-top walk with the children, Ben ran to the edge and apparently jumped off. As they gasped, unaware there was a ledge a few feet below, he reappeared as if by magic, with a childish grin on his face. At other times he would play hopscotch on the squares in a hotel corridor carpet, or try (and fail) to keep his balance walking along railway lines with his friend, the cellist Mstislav Rostropovich.

Roger Duncan, like Ben, was a keen mathematician, so it was perhaps with Roger in mind that he jotted down in the back of his 1957 pocket diary an algebraic absurdity, or maybe he collected it from him. Either way, its conclusion must have brought him a delicious sense of triumph.

$$\text{Let } a = b$$
$$\therefore a^2 = ab$$
$$\therefore a^2 - b^2 = ab - b^2$$
$$\therefore (a+b)(a-b) = b\,(a-b)$$
$$\therefore a+b = b$$
$$\therefore 2a = a$$
$$\therefore 2 = 1$$

This love of mathematical conundrums infused much of his music. He liked to set himself challenges, and proceed to overcome them. He had little time for the twelve-tone music that so many composers around him were embracing. For him, the idea of overthrowing the key system by giving all the semitones in the scale equal importance and repeating them throughout a piece in the same order resulted in desiccated music. But he was happy to play with the serial method, and apparently beat its practitioners at their own game – it attracted the mathematician in him. He did this in his opera based on the Henry James ghost story *The Turn of the Screw*, which incorporated the twelve-tone principle, but in a way that emphasised and reinforced the key structure.* He had the last laugh: he turned the screw clockwise in the first act, by setting the key of each orchestral interlude one step higher than the last – and anti-clockwise in the second, by lowering the key each time. This scheme is more than just clever: it has a powerful musical and psychological result in increasing the claustrophobic intensity of the score, whether the listener is aware of the method or not.

Part of the fun of these musical games was when the performer, and the listener, could see and hear him winning, which appealed to his competitive streak. Canon was a device which enabled this transparency – a simple form which always fasci-

---

* Britten was an admirer of Berg, who used the serial method in an often tonal way.

nated him. Just as a child delights in the simplest rounds like 'London's Burning' or '*Frère Jacques*', so he loved to see how a tune could be superimposed on itself, several times if necessary, a few beats apart, and yield rich musical rewards. At home, he delighted in singing rounds and canons by his favourite composer, Beethoven. The first Britten pieces to be published (when he was eighteen) were *Three Two-Part Songs*, to words by Walter de la Mare and written with children in mind. Their original title (not one to make the pulse race) was 'Three Studies in Canon', each song using the device differently. He proudly sent a copy of these to the place where his competitive streak had been nurtured, South Lodge. His school songs *Friday Afternoons* culminate in a sonorous four-part canon, 'Old Abram Brown is dead and gone'. Driven by relentless drumbeats in the bass, it builds to a point where half the choir sings the tune at half speed – and still the canon works. This little *coup de maître* makes the funeral march great fun to sing. Forty years later, he returned to canon to round off his final work *Welcome Ode*, again with children in mind. It was no coincidence. He had never stopped using canon in between, whether in the *Spring Symphony*, the *Cantata Academica*, his operas *Noye's Fludde* and *Albert Herring*, or in *A Ceremony of Carols*. For many children, the favourite carol is 'This Little Babe', where the voices start in unison before splitting into two-part, then three-part, canon – all at a furious pace, with the ever more frantic harp accompaniment adding to the tension. The result is a shimmering blur of sound, and the canon seems so intricate as to be beyond rescue. Then, suddenly, with a flick of his pen, the parts are in unison again, and can reach their destination safely and in triumph. The final words 'then flit not from this heavenly Boy' seem almost a compliment to the skill of the composer. The countless children who have performed this piece can see and hear the conundrum, and contribute to its deft solution, though they do not always reach the end without some derailment along the way.

A few years later, in *Peter Grimes*, he managed to get a well-lubricated crowd in the Boar pub singing a canon (the round

'Old Joe has gone fishing') in the unconventional rhythm of seven in a bar. Yet such is the skill and *élan* of his writing that it feels as natural as a traditional community song. He devised canons with relish (almost as if he were constructing crossword puzzles), as he once admitted to Peter Pears: 'The work [his re-composition of *The Beggar's Opera*] goes well, & pretty fast [. . .]. But I must stop myself too much "canonizing" of the music, which is probably more entertaining to write than to listen to!'

He set himself another conundrum, when in 1964 he came across twin thirteen-year-old boys in Budapest, both brilliant musicians. As well as the piano, Zoltán Jeney played the flute, and Gábor the violin. Britten decided to write a 'quartet for two players' for them, and the result was the *Gemini Variations*. During the twelve movements, he kept varying the instrumentation (flute and piano, violin and piano, flute and violin, piano duet, as well as each instrument solo), and then – of course, because this was Britten – hey presto! all four elements came together in the final movement. Even the final bar began with a four-handed piano chord, and ended with a chord for flute and violin. To emphasise how special the Jeney twins were, he noted magnanimously in the score that subsequent performances might need four players, rather than two.

This element of showmanship, which manifested itself from the start, led to criticism of Britten as a young man for being too clever by half. Thanks to his technique, of which he was so proud, he was thought to be flashy, ingenious, brilliant – all in a pejorative sense – leaving his music shallow, purposeless and cold. The trouble Britten had in rebutting this was that his work was undeniably clever, and the gamesmanship was part of the cleverness. But this was not superficial: it came direct from his musical soul. He knew better than anyone how music fitted together, and had great fun taking it apart and reassembling it. That is what he did in his much more impressive set of variations *The Young Person's Guide to the Orchestra*. He did something similar in the little *Fanfare for St Edmundsbury*, in which three trumpets play, in turn, a minute-long solo flourish, each quite distinct in character and each in a different key. They then repeat it, but playing together – lo and behold, the jigsaw fits!

The Young Person's Guide was originally devised as a score for 'Instruments of the Orchestra', an educational film funded by the government (an inconceivable project in Britain today). Britten completed it on the last day of 1945, in the wake of his triumph with *Peter Grimes*. He mapped it out in his Schoolboy's Pocket Diary in a form surprisingly close to the eventual score. He envisaged the film's opening titles being accompanied by the sound of the orchestra tuning up, then the full orchestra would play the main theme [the Rondeau from Purcell's *Abdelazar*], followed by fourteen variations for different instruments, and then the main theme again. In the event there were thirteen: he shifted the string movements to a position between those for woodwind and those for brass, combined the tuba with the trombones, and the timpani with the rest of the percussion, and added a variation for harp. But the idea that elevates the piece into the realm of genius developed only during its composition: he devised a complicated fugue to follow the variations, and during its hectic career through the orchestra he magisterially superimposed the original theme in the brass. It is a moment of crowning glory. The composer Michael Berkeley, Britten's godson, is full of admiration: 'It lays out all the cogs of the engine, all the ball bearings, all the gearing, and then fits them together and says: "Now, this is what happens when you put the whole thing together and turn the ignition. Boom!" ' Britten himself was thrilled by the studio recording – the first time he had heard his creation. He was said to have been 'jumping about and laughing with pleasure at hearing what he'd done'. During what was intended as a spoken interview in 2003, a transported David Hemmings sang, hummed and groaned his way through the piece (which he remembered Ben playing to him the first time he visited Aldeburgh as a boy), and as he reached the triumphant return of the theme in the brass, he cried out: 'That's the champagne moment! Fucking great!'

CHAPTER 3

Towards a world unknown

As a young music student in London, Britten was deeply affected by a film he saw in March 1933. It was a reference-point, conscious or not, for the rest of his life, and came to demonstrate how the mature composer never left his boyhood behind. He became a fully-fledged musician and man, but he always carried his childhood – his boyhood – with him.

It was at the Cinema House, off Oxford Street, that he came across 'the most perfect & satisfying film I have ever seen, or ever hope to see. Acting as natural & fine as possible – magnificent & subtle photography – plot very amusing & imaginative – a collosal [sic] achievement.' Three days later he bought a copy of the book on which the film was based, and it remained (well-thumbed) on his bookshelves for the rest of his life. It was a children's book, and a children's film, but that did not deter the nineteen-year-old composer. Indeed, he cut out the film's publicity photographs from magazines, glued them inside the covers of the book, and wrote a caption for each one. Faithfully preserved inside the volume is a yellowing 1930s cutting from the *Radio Times* about a wireless dramatisation of the story, to which presumably Britten made a point of listening. He saw the film at least twice more, and started to conceive a musical suite to illustrate the story. The film that had so entranced him was *Emil and the Detectives*.

Erich Kästner's novel of the same name had made a great impact when it was published in 1929, with its distinctive line-drawings by Walter Trier. The screen version followed within two years, with an English-language version soon after. It was the original German film, with a screenplay by Billie

Wilder* and directed by Gerhard Lamprecht, which caught Britten's imagination – presumably with an English sound-track dubbed on for a London audience.

Britten's musical suite never materialised, although his plan was to include a piece he had already written, *Alla marcia*. A few years later he incorporated this into the setting of 'Parade' in his orchestral song-cycle *Les Illuminations*, in which the singer several times declaims *'J'ai seul la clef de cette parade sauvage'* ('I alone hold the key to this wild circus'). The film of *Emil and the Detectives* not only holds the key to all Britten's instincts and feelings about boyhood, it may have crystallised them.

He was right: it is indeed a remarkable film. The direction is meticulous, the camerawork and editing inspired. There is not a false note in it, and it is scarcely credible that it was made so early in the life of the 'talkies', in 1931. But one suspects that Britten's emotional reaction was stirred by more than mere technical accomplishment. It was a film about the triumph of children over adults, the strength of boyhood camaraderie and the power of mother-love. It also highlighted the ingenuity of children. Emil and the detectives (all boys) achieve results through mental application and bodily energy, which Britten, as a keen athlete and cricketer at Emil's age, fully understood.

Both the screenplay and the direction followed the thrust of the book quite closely, though Kästner felt Wilder had vulgarised it. Perhaps what he had in mind were several scenes not in the book which under Lamprecht's skilled direction layer the simple narrative with a complex psychological drama. This layering ensures that, while *Emil* remains a children's film, it is also one for adults – and that may well explain part of its enchantment for Britten. The overlapping of boy and man that was the key to his personality for most of his life was already characteristic of his music. In early 1933 he was still studying with John Ireland and

---

* This was how Wilder's name was spelled in the credits at this early stage in his career. Soon afterwards he changed 'Billie' to 'Billy'.

Arthur Benjamin at the Royal College of Music, which he found 'uncongenial, fundamentally unserious, & narrow-minded'. But he had already written his *Sinfonietta*, Op.1 – a work both of adult continental sophistication (far removed from his own parochial upbringing) and of precocious schoolboy brilliance. He was in the middle of writing his choral variations *A Boy was Born*, his first adult masterpiece, which for much of its course beguiles the ear through an apparently childlike simplicity.

The film's story is straightforward. Emil Tischbein is a young boy from Neustadt, a small town west of Berlin. He is the pride and joy of his mother, who runs a hairdressing business in their front room. She is a widow, so Emil is immediately one of those boys with an absent father, who so engaged Britten. The boy travels by train to Berlin to visit his grandmother, carrying some money for her from his mother. On the journey, he is robbed by another passenger, a sinister man in a bowler hat called Grundeis. Emil feels he cannot go to the Berlin police: he is afraid of being apprehended for a prank he had carried out at home. Instead he chases the villain himself in Berlin, with the help of a gang of street urchins, the Detectives. By dint of ingenuity and hard work, he gets more than his money back: he captures the criminal, wins a reward and becomes a celebrity.

Britten perhaps identified with the good-looking, blond Emil (played in the film by Rolf Wenkhaus). Emil is devoted to his mother (as Britten was) but wary of being called a milksop. When he describes his home life, one of the Berlin boys observes: 'You and your mother must love each other very much'. Emil's reply is almost involuntary: 'Hugely', but he quickly recovers himself by adding: 'But that's not to say I'm a Mummy's boy. And if you don't believe me I'll throw you against the wall!'

The effusive waving between Emil and his mother as the train pulled out of Neustadt station must also have reminded Britten of the time he had stayed with a friend during the school holidays, and took the train home: the schoolfriend kept waving to him from the platform until he was out of sight. 'That', he later told the opera producer Basil Coleman, 'was the first time I realised what love was.'

He certainly would have identified with Emil's train journey. Much of his travel as a boy had been done by train, not least when he was going to London for regular lessons with the composer Frank Bridge. It was no accident that twenty years later, when writing his Thomas Hardy song-cycle, *Winter Words*, he chose two songs about trains: 'At the Railway Station, Upway (or The Convict and the Boy with the Violin)' and 'Midnight on the Great Western (or The Journeying Boy)'. In the latter song, the quavers in the piano part create the almost cinematic effect of the chugging steam-train approaching from afar: with the flourish of semiquavers, the wheels clatter over uneven rails as they cross the points. But before we can even see the train in our mind's eye, we hear the three-note sound of its whistle, complete with Doppler effect, miraculously conjured up on the keyboard (another reprise of the eleven-year-old's mimicry of the dinner gong). It is perhaps more evocative of a locomotive, complete with cow-catcher, crossing the American prairie than of an engine on the Great Western Railway in Thomas Hardy's Wessex – but then Britten, far from home and sometimes lonely, had experienced the North American railroads between 1939 and 1942. The whistle is not just a clever effect: it instantly suggests the loneliness enveloping the boy, journeying solo in a third-class carriage,* his ticket stuck into his cap, and carrying valuables.

> In the third-class seat sat the journeying boy,
>   And the roof-lamp's oily flame
> Played down on his listless form and face,
> Bewrapt past knowing to what he was going,
>   Or whence he came.

* Hardy perhaps had in mind the third-class carriages described by Louis Hayes in his *Reminiscences of Manchester*: 'There was a general feeling of bare boards and cheerlessness as you entered them and if you were travelling in the winter time they gave you a kind of cold shiver. The seats were cushionless and the longer you sat on them the harder they seemed.'

In the band of his hat the journeying boy
  Had a ticket stuck; and a string
Around his neck bore the key of his box,
That twinkled gleams of the lamp's sad beams
  Like a living thing.

The song acquires a darker resonance after the listener has
shared Emil's unpleasant experience on the train to Berlin.
When Britten read this poem, who knows what memories it
brought back of his own experiences as a journeying boy, or
what unconscious echoes it sounded of the *Emil* film? Emil is at
first squeezed in between other passengers in his compartment,
who quiz him about the journey he is making: later we see his
'listless form and face' as he is left alone with the sinister man
in the bowler hat, nervously contemplating his options. In
Hardy's poem, the boy is not spoken to – just observed. His
situation is imagined, but not enquired about. (In the same way,
the man [Aschenbach] in Britten's final opera *Death in Venice*
contemplates and observes the boy, but does not speak to him.)

What past can be yours, O journeying boy
  Towards a world unknown,
Who calmly, as if incurious quite
On all at stake, can undertake
  This plunge alone?

The journeying boy and Emil are both travelling alone 'towards
a world unknown' – London (presumably) on the Great
Western service, Berlin in Emil's case, about which the sinister
man alarms (and perhaps excites) him with absurd fantasies. He
tells him that Berlin is full of buildings one hundred storeys high
(this was indeed still a fantasy at that time*), and that it takes
three months to climb the stairs. The lift contains a kitchen to

---

* Kästner's book was published in 1929, some months before a new record was
set for the tallest building in the world by the Chrysler Building in New York,
which even then could boast only 77 storeys. The 102-storey Empire State
Building was still on the drawing-board.

ensure the passengers do not starve during their journey. He also advises him on the quickest way of getting around Berlin: go to a post office, and get dispatched in a pneumatic tube to your destination. In a similar way, the young boy Miles in Britten's 1954 opera *The Turn of the Screw* is tantalised by Peter Quint with visions of an adult world beyond his experience.

> Knows your soul a sphere, O journeying boy,
>   Our rude realms far above,
> Whence with spacious vision you mark and mete
> This region of sin that you find you in,
>   But are not of?

The final lines of Hardy's poem encapsulate all that Britten understood about innocence and childhood: the boy does not belong to the sinful adult world, but he is aware of it, and has marked and measured it. Although Britten later railed against the assumption that most of his works were about innocence, he did confess on radio that unconsciously there was something 'in that rather obsessive subject which can and does excite me, or anyhow occupy me'.

After almost all Emil's fellow-passengers in the crowded compartment have disembarked at an intermediate station, the darker sub-text of the film begins to emerge, at least to modern eyes. But, with a director as skilled as Gerhard Lamprecht (producer of Thomas Mann's *Buddenbrooks*, and director of *Somewhere in Berlin*), it is hard to believe this is accidental. In those days, train compartments did not interconnect. Emil is trapped with Grundeis for the final run to Berlin. As we watch, we become aware of a miasma of sexual threat from the man. The fear is not only in Emil's mind. It is in ours too.

The first thing that Emil does is to retreat into the toilet within the compartment, and pin his banknotes carefully to the inside breast pocket of his jacket – just to be sure he does not lose his grandmother's money. In a similar way, Hardy's journeying boy tied round his neck the key to his box of valuables. In both cases, any attempt at theft must therefore involve violation of the boy's innocence by physical contact. When Emil emerges from the lavatory, the jolting train seems to make him stumble, so that he falls almost into Grundeis's lap. But in fact the man has deliberately moved his foot to trip the boy up. It is a sinister moment, which does not derive from the book. In Kästner's original story, Grundeis is asleep (or pretending to be) all the time.

In the film, he offers Emil a cigarette. As the boy is just ten or eleven years old, this is an overt attempt both to corrupt him with a narcotic, and to seduce him into the adult world by testing his manhood. Emil refuses the offer: like Benjamin, he is in no hurry to grow up. With an odious smile, the man then tempts him with something childish – a boiled sweet. Emil is caught in a Garden-of-Eden dilemma. If he accepts it, will he aggravate the threat from the man, or avert it? He clearly has no interest in the sweet itself. But he takes it. Once again, this episode (which neatly demonstrates Emil on the cusp of adolescence) is not in the book. If the sweet has been drugged, as the film implies, then Grundeis has corrupted the boy with a different narcotic.

Emil quickly falls asleep (the book hints that he could have been hypnotised by Grundeis). He has a dream about the man which is more frightening than funny, and has an undeniable sexual undertow. Emil sees the man sitting opposite him, and rocking back in his seat; he watches him filling the carriage with smoke as he puffs (almost inflates) a huge cigar, and showers the boy with sparks. Emil is at the mercy of the man, who seems to the boy to be in complete control. He wakes up on the carriage floor to find the man – and his grandmother's money – gone. The moment of loss of innocence on his journey to manhood is marked by a heart-rending cry as he realises he has been robbed. That must have caught Britten's breath.

The rest of the film is devoted to the pursuit of Grundeis by Emil and the team of boys he encounters on the streets of Berlin. The consequent battle for dominance between the man and the boys gradually unnerves the villain. In a car-chase through the city, Grundeis has a sense that he is being followed. On the pavement, he is intimidated by a pack of children walking behind him. The moment of his capture is a physical assault, principally by Emil, which repays him for the moment of contact in the train. But the dividing-line between boyhood and adulthood is not clear-cut for Emil and his friends. They are both thrilled and alarmed by the threshold of adolescence, which Lamprecht captures brilliantly in a campfire scene (original to the film) in which the boys self-consciously pass round a cigarette as a 'pipe of peace'. Britten had himself experimented unsuccessfully with smoking at school. Emil and most of his friends choke on the smoke. But Gustav, the ringleader, proves his authority by inhaling without difficulty. The innocent is again on the verge of experience, but this time Emil takes the proffered cigarette because it does not come from an adult. He lives, as did Britten, in a paedocratic world where problems often come from grown-ups and solutions from children.

The most unsettling scene in the film (once again it is not in the book) is played out at night in the villain's hotel bedroom. In the hunt for his missing cash, Emil has dressed up as a bell-boy, and manages to get inside the bedroom while Grundeis, in his night-clothes, has gone to the lavatory in the corridor. (This forms a neat counterpoint to Emil's visit to the toilet in the train carriage.) The boy hardly knows where to start looking. Just as he spots a wallet between the pillows in the bed, the door opens, and Emil dives for cover under the bed. He sees the pyjama-ed legs of the man approaching, and we see the man sit on the bed, in close-up from his waist down. As if this were not enough to demonstrate the man's dominance, he then gets into the bed, with Emil still underneath. If the film were stopped at that point, and a virgin audience were asked what would happen next, few among them would guess correctly. As the man lies in the bed reading, Emil's hand creeps up from underneath, and works its exploratory way between the sheets, trying to extract the wallet. At that moment, the man turns in the bed, and traps the boy's hand under the pillow beneath his head. Only when the man turns out the light, and goes to sleep, can Emil try again. He gingerly re-inserts his hand to retrieve the wallet. As he does so, the man seems to wriggle in his sleep. (The wallet then turns out to be empty – such a risk for so little!) In this scene, intricately observed and paced by Lamprecht, today's audience may for the first time question Emil's hitherto un-assailable innocence. The battle for dominance becomes am-biguous. How much is Emil an innocent, how much a knowing child? Is he both averse to the man, and in some unconscious way drawn to him? The pure milk of innocence seems to be on the turn.

Similar questions apply to Miles in *The Turn of the Screw*. The answer is given by the boy himself at the end of Act I: 'You see, I am bad, aren't I?' When the television documentary *Britten's Children* was in production, it was uncanny to find that the music which opens Act II of the opera was a perfect fit for the bedroom scene in *Emil*, in mood, pace and psycho-sexual tension. Such things, in Britten's music, are not accidental. He had, after all, developed his craft as a film composer in the mid-1930s. The resourcefulness required of him in his formative years in the cutting-rooms of the GPO Film Unit gave his music a visual dimension which endured long after he had stopped composing for the cinema: the *War Requiem, Owen Wingrave* and *Death in Venice* each demonstrate a taste for inter-cut and fast-changing scenes. But we know how deep an impression *Emil and the Detectives* made upon him, and it doubtless res-onated with him down the years, particularly when it touched on aspects of childhood that continued to preoccupy him, such as the choices and the complicity of the innocent. *The Turn of the Screw* may have been written twenty years after he had first seen *Emil*, but he had first encountered the Henry James story when he was only eighteen, back in June 1932, in a dramatisa-tion on the radio. He called it 'wonderful, impressive, but terribly eerie and scary'. Next he read the book in January 1933: for him it was 'glorious and eerie . . . an incredible masterpiece'. Its disturbing undercurrents must have informed his understanding of *Emil and the Detectives* when he saw the film two months later. The confluence of the two stories may have fed the psychological and musical torrent of the opera, nearly all of which was composed in just sixteen summer weeks of 1954.

Nine months after seeing *Emil* for the first time, the maturing composer consciously turned back to his childhood in his *Simple Symphony*. He reverted to piano pieces and songs he had written between the ages of nine and twelve, and re-worked them into a four-movement piece for strings. At the age of twenty, most artists are keen to strike out towards new horizons and dis-own (often destroy) their immature works along with other memories of childhood. But the Britten of that age boasted of going back to them.

Those childish manuscripts, like most of Britten's documents, had been carefully stored, and occasionally saw the light of day. The thirteen-year-old treble David Spenser, who had just sung the role of Harry in *Albert Herring* at Glyndebourne, helped Britten move house in summer 1947. He found himself carrying 'piles of manuscripts' down the spiral staircase at the Old Mill in Snape: 'I kept saying to him: "Have you written all this?" ' Behind the piano in Crag House, Britten's new home in Aldeburgh, Spenser remembers a curtain drawn across some shelves. 'One night, Ben said (all naughtily), "Well I'm going to let you have a treat", and he pulled out some of the manuscripts and started playing. He said, "Do you like that?" I said yes, and he said "Well, I wrote that when I was four!" '

These boyhood manuscripts did not merely languish on the shelves. They meant enough to him that he always kept them in order and, in later life, he started to catalogue them. Many of them bear a dating in pencil in his own hand. When Rosamund Strode took over as his music assistant in 1964, one of her first jobs was to complete the process. She was astonished at how many there were. Britten would help her, and would 'sit and laugh sometimes at that little boy and what he'd been doing'.

Her predecessor, Imogen Holst, had also been allowed to delve into his juvenilia. While working on his opera *Gloriana* one afternoon in 1953, he said he wanted to show her the first symphony he had written (at the age of thirteen), and disappeared to dig out the full score. After a while, she became concerned that they were losing valuable time on the opera, and went upstairs to find him. She said it was time to get back to work. 'But he was still depressed about Covent Garden and in the mood for playing me his early piano pieces (including the tunes he used in his Simple Symphony). And then he went on to songs. [. . .] Stacks and stacks of manuscripts written while he was at prep school: <u>immense</u> full scores with beautifully clear writing and everything written in detail. I asked him how he ever had time for his school work and piano practice and he said "I don't know – and there were all the elevens [sporting teams] as well – I wish I'd got as much energy now".' Britten went on to tell her, perhaps disingenuously, that 'the only value in the stuff he kept from those early years was the chance it gave of seeing how a child's mind worked'. While that was no doubt true, his behaviour showed there was more to it than that. He was proud of it.

One of the songs she admired was 'a <u>marvellous</u> one called "Beware!"'. She included a facsimile of it in her book on Britten*, and this caught the eye of Robert Saxton, who had graduated from the nine-year-old boy at the Albert Hall to a sixth-former at Bryanston School. He wrote to Britten to ask permission for it to be performed in his house singing competition. The composer's reply is revealing:

> Of course you can use my little song 'Beware' [. . .], but you must make it quite clear to the audience that I was <u>nine</u> when I wrote it! I am afraid you must be careful what happens to any copies that you might make of the facsimile because, as you know, it is not published, but still is very <u>copyright</u>!

His disclaimer was both bashful and boastful. *Beware!* is a simple, strophic setting of Longfellow for voice and piano,

---

* Imogen Holst *Britten* (The Great Composers), Faber & Faber 1966.

dating from 1922. But in the major-minor key change at the end there is a whiff of Mahler, even though the boy Britten had not heard any Mahler at that point*. The adult Britten was a shrewd businessman and knew the song had copyright value: indeed, he had recently prepared it for publication, although Saxton did not realise this. The readiness of the internationally-renowned composer of *Peter Grimes* and the *War Requiem* to let this juvenile piece be performed in public meant, as Saxton points out, that he still felt close to, and proud of, his childhood. 'He probably rather liked the idea of all these schoolboys, aged between about fourteen and seventeen in flannel shorts, in serried rows, singing about a maiden: "Beware the lady who will corrupt and seduce you!" He probably thought it was quite funny.'

Beware! was not the only childhood piece the mature Britten published. He kept combing the manuscripts, looking for nuggets of interest. He went back four decades for the 'five settings from boyhood' of poems by Walter de la Mare, which he published in 1969 under the title *Tit for Tat*. Most of them, he said, were 'of course very naïve'. But it had given him 'great pleasure to dig these old scraps out, to titivate them a little'. While disclaiming any importance or originality in the songs, he added:

> I do feel that the boy's vision has a simplicity and clarity which might have given a little pleasure to the great poet, with his unique insight into a child's mind.

There was some safety in the enchantment lent by forty years' distance. But, for the *Simple Symphony*, the exhumations were of much fresher boyhood material – all less than ten years old. The work was dedicated to his first viola teacher, Audrey Alston, whom he called his 'musical grandmother'. He described it self-deprecatingly to his fellow-composer Grace Williams as 'a dear little school suite for strings' in which he was 'dishing up some very old stuff' as a money-making venture (which paid

* A further Mahler connection is that the words of *Beware!* are a translation by Longfellow of a poem from *Des Knaben Wunderhorn*, the three-volume anthology of German folk poetry from which Mahler drew for his songs of the same name.

off handsomely over the years). From his early manuscripts, he chose as many as eight unconnected pieces to provide his raw material. He transposed them all from disparate keys, arranged them for strings, and made numerous revisions and additions. But much of his original music survived unscathed. He drew the third movement ('Sentimental Saraband'), for instance, from a piano suite (no. 3 in F sharp minor, written when he was eleven) and a Chopin-esque waltz in B written in 1923 – though the Saraband's languid opening melody was originally fast and furious.

In a schoolboyish flourish, the alliterated composer was not sufficiently content with the work's alliterative title, but called the movements 'Boisterous Bourrée', 'Playful Pizzicato', 'Sentimental Saraband' and 'Frolicsome Finale'. To our ears, these titles may sound a little twee. But Britten would have scorned such an idea: for him, they encapsulated his re-entry into the childhood world. He was not simply a magpie plundering old nests. As a composer who was now espousing Mahler, Schönberg and Berg, he was affirming his own immaturity as part of his personality. He even signed the work in the way he had all his boyhood pieces: 'E.B. Britten'. It produced an amused response from an old schoolfriend at South Lodge, John Pounder. He said he had noticed that 'you have only arranged the Simple Symphony, and that it was written by E. B. Britten. Now I wonder who that could be? Could it by any chance be the little boy who was once familiarly known as Little O'Cedar mop?'

Even twenty years later Britten was still proud of what 'the sins of my youth' (as he defined the piece to Pounder) meant to him. He wrote an extensive sleeve note for the Decca recording of 1955:

Once upon a time there was a prep-school boy. He was called Britten mi., his initials were E.B., his age was nine, and his locker was number seventeen. [. . .] He worked his way up the school slowly and steadily, until at the age of thirteen he reached that pinnacle of importance and grandeur never to be quite equalled in later days: the head of the Sixth, head-prefect, and Victor Ludorum. But . . . there was one curious thing about this boy: he wrote music [. . .], reams and reams of it. [. . .] And they are still lying in an old cupboard to this day – String Quartets (six of them), twelve piano sonatas; dozens of songs; sonatas for violin, sonatas for viola and cello too; suites, waltzes, rondos, fantasies, variations; a tone-poem 'Chaos and Cosmos'; a tremendous symphony, for gigantic orchestra including eight horns and oboe d'amore [. . .]; an oratorio called Samuel: all the opus numbers from 1 to 100 were filled (and catalogued) by the time Britten mi. was fourteen.

He did not catalogue his pieces in the conventional, chronological way. Nearly all his early piano music, for instance, was grouped together, whatever the dates of composition. Observing that music was often published in collections, the boy Britten believed they had to be composed that way as well. So he tabulated 10 Waltzs [sic], 6 Scherzos, 2 Etudes, 4 Bourrées, 7 Fantasias, 4 Sonatas, 5 Suites, 2 Fugue-Fantasias, 6 Themas, 2 Rondo Capriccios [sic], 24 Themes (Walzes [sic]) – one for each major and minor key – 3 Toccatas, 4 Etudes Symphoniques, a Mazurka, a Valse, a Grand Scherzo and two Scherzo-Tarantellas – and that was just for opus 1. The whole catalogue, which purports to cover the period August 1923 to December 1927 but is in fact incomplete,* runs to more than 160 pieces, including those he mentioned, plus two dozen songs, some of them decorated in Britten's own hand as if published under the popular Home Series label.

Of course they aren't very good, these works; inspiration didn't always run very high, and the workmanship wasn't always academically sound [. . .]; besides, for the sake of

---

* Some unlisted piano pieces from 1923–25 were revised in 1969 and published as *Five Walztes (Waltzes)*.

neatness, every piece had to end precisely at the bottom of the right-hand page* [. . .]; but when Benjamin Britten, a proud young composer of twenty [. . .] came along and looked in this cupboard, he found some of them not too uninteresting; and [. . .] turned them into a Simple Symphony, and here it is.

* Rosamund Strode recalls Britten in the 1960s bringing her a piece to copy out, with the tongue-in-cheek apology: 'I'm afraid it doesn't end at the bottom on the right. It ends halfway down on the left.'

CHAPTER 4

The wider world of man

The death of his parents propelled Britten into the adult world. At the age of twenty-three, he began to face up to questions about himself, and decisions about his life, that he had always deferred, thanks to the almost suffocating influence of his mother. By coincidence, he met the great love of his life within a month of his mother's death in January 1937. Peter Pears was three and a half years older than Britten, and at the start of a singing career. But their early association was a musical partnership and a straightforward friendship: it did not develop beyond that for several more years. In 1937, Britten was only just beginning to acknowledge his own sexuality.

In the last few years of his mother's life, their relationship had been difficult. A beach photograph of Benjamin and his elder sister Barbara with Edith Britten, taken in 1936, caught something of the difficulty (see plate 2). Barbara has her arms around her mother, and he is sitting on the sand beside them. He is half-turned away from them, his body awkwardly contorted as if to suggest a separation, and yet his shoulder is touching his mother's. He was still devoted to her, but was finding her dogmatic attitudes and religious observance constricting. He may have been twenty-two, but as queen bee she was still trying to dictate when and whether he went to church. His schoolfriend John Pounder remembered her as gentle but strait-laced. Attending a comedy at Lowestoft repertory theatre, she objected when one actor said: 'My God!' In a loud voice, she exclaimed from the stalls: 'I don't think that's very funny'. Britten himself was delighted that his mother disapproved of the song 'Rats Away!' in his contentious cycle *Our Hunting Fathers*: 'that is almost an incentive', he wrote, before adding quickly, 'no actual insult to her tho'.'

After his father's death three years earlier, the two-decades-old umbilical cord with Lowestoft had been severed. Britten based himself in London and made occasional forays to the Essex coast, where his mother had moved. In London, his musical horizons were broadening dramatically. His work at the GPO Film Unit gave him invaluable experience of writing at speed, to order and to picture, in the way that many television composers do today. It also taught him how much he could achieve with slender resources. This stood him in good stead when he developed his chamber operas ten years later (*The Rape of Lucretia* and *Albert Herring*) and his Church Parables in the 1960s. But his work on the GPO documentary films such as *Coal Face* and *Night Mail* also brought him into direct contact with the poet W. H. Auden, the author Christopher Isherwood, and the painter William Coldstream, who opened the window for him to a wider world view and a new intellectual landscape. Britten found this stimulating, but he often felt inferior, and he somehow always remained 'the boy'. Both Auden and Isherwood were unabashedly homosexual and watched with some amusement as 'Benjie' wrestled with his own sexual dilemmas.

A few weeks before his mother died, he took Pounder into his confidence. 'There's quite alot to talk about that one can't (or even daren't) write about in letters. [. . .] I'm changing my views on Life (with a capital S) abit.' In April, he met Pounder 'for a long walk and much "queer" talk', and also confided in his brother. He regarded Bobby as 'obstinately conservative', so he was surprised to receive an understanding response. 'We have had very intimate discussions & he hasn't been shocked by but even helped with sympathy & advice my "queerness".'

His mother's death allowed him at last to break out of her controlling shadow. For a long time afterwards, as he was to tell Imogen Holst, he felt sure he had been responsible for her death. Mrs Britten had contracted bronchial pneumonia after coming to London to nurse his sister Beth, who had influenza:

he perhaps felt he should have kept her away. He may also have felt guilty over his arguments with her, and over his homosexuality, which he had never acknowledged to her. But the moment of her death marked a belated emancipation. A decade later, his cantata *Saint Nicolas* expressed Nicolas's emergence into adulthood in words which must have resounded through his own experience.

> My parents died.
> All too soon, I left the tranquil beauty of their home,
> and knew the wider world of man.

With the money left him by his mother, Britten bought a property in Snape, near Aldeburgh. It was the first time he had had his own home, and he set about converting an old windmill and the adjoining huts to suit his working pattern and his lifestyle. After emancipation came independence.

At this stage, Britten was being pursued (not very availingly, it seems) by the composer Lennox Berkeley, who was to share the Old Mill with him for a couple of years. But many of Britten's friends were becoming aware of his interest in adolescent boys. In his diary he commented on several who had caught his eye. In February 1936 he recorded having a conversation with a 'very nice little restaurant-boy' who had brought him his tea: 'Quel horreur!!', he added guiltily. 'But I swear there's no harm in it.'

There were others to whom he devoted a great deal of care and attention, none more so than Piers Dunkerley. He first befriended the boy in his final year at Britten's old prep school, South Lodge, and then kept in touch with him during his years at Bloxham public school. He was seven years older than Piers, but 'very fond' of him – 'thank heaven not sexually', he wrote, before adding: 'I am getting to such a condition that I am lost without some children (of either sex) near me'.

Piers's parents had separated when he was a small boy. His mother lived in London, and he boarded at both his schools.

Britten's friendships were often to arise with boys who had physically or emotionally absent fathers. He was conscious of playing a stepfather's role, and referred to Piers at one point as his foster-child, yet the short age gap (particularly when Britten looked so young for his years) did not lend credence to either description. He took Piers out in London – to see films by Charlie Chaplin and Walt Disney and to the stage version of 1066 *and All That*, which they both found 'riotously funny', and treated him to tea at the Strand Palace. The tea-party in the garden at Lowestoft had not been an isolated event: Piers was invited back to Kirkley Cliff Road on several occasions. After one visit, he wrote:

> Please thank your mother and Beth for their love and give
> them mine, also say that I am still being the old good
> mannered and <u>well groomed</u> Piers; the last adjective for
> your benefit.

Piers was emphatically good-looking, as is clear from the photographs Benjamin took of him larking around on the beach. (Ten years later, as an officer in the Royal Marines, it was clear that the looks had come to stay.) Benjamin knew that his feelings for Piers were potentially problematic, as was becoming clear in his diary. In January 1936 he wrote of his good fortune in having friends such as Frank Bridge and his wife, his old Lowestoft friend Basil Reeve, and 'young Piers Dunkerley – tell it not in Gath'. His diary used this biblical phrase in several different contexts to indicate a confidence, but when applied to his friendship for Piers it does seem to resonate with the Old Testament story of David's love for Jonathan, from which the quotation comes. A few days later he was writing of Piers: 'But what a boy to help! So splendid in brain & form – and delightful company.' He told John Pounder that he had had a long talk with Piers 'which was a great strain on me ("the normal functions" etc. etc.) You can't imagine how delightfully paternal I can be!' During further outings in the Easter holidays, the boy confided in him about sexual approaches he was receiving at Bloxham.* 'Bloxham seems a queer school', Britten wrote. 'It makes one sick that they can't leave a nice lad like Piers alone – but it is understandable – good heavens!'

The letters he was receiving at this time from Piers at school, 'very faithfully & sincerely & truly & lovingly', are touching and sweet. He was in tune with Benjamin's love of tennis and cricket, and admired his taste in flashy cars:

Very glad to hear about the new super tuned $3\frac{1}{2}$ litre, 30 horse power, 120 mph Lagonda and the description sounds marvellous; but you paid rather a fabulous price for it didn't you, I hope you are not broke. [. . .]

I hope you have been having a good time & the car is functioning well. How many times have you had her re-bored? [. . .]

All the best, with love, hugs & kisses, Piers M. Dunkerley.

That summer Britten's emotional quandary was deepening. 'Life is a pretty hefty struggle these days – sexually as well', he wrote. 'Decisions are so hard to make, & its difficult to look unprejudiced on apparently abnormal things.' In the holidays, he had Piers to stay for the night at his London flat, along with Beth Britten's future husband, Kit Welford. The sleeping arrangements were innocuous, but their description in Britten's diary is instructive. 'Kit & Piers both sleep here – Kit in the sitting room, & Piers shares my room – in my bed, & me on a camp bed'. He was almost teasing the reader (perhaps therefore himself) with each phrase, saving until last his self-exoneration. Yet would not the more conventional solution have been for Piers to sleep in the sitting room, and the two adults to share the bedroom – or, failing that, for the fifteen-year-old boy to take the camp bed? Benjamin was clearly an unusually accommodating host.

---

* His brother Tony had also been pursued by predatory masters at Bloxham, according to his widow Barbara.

As Piers progressed through Bloxham, the treats continued. In summer 1937 Britten took him to see the Marx Brothers in *A Day at the Races** and out to tea afterwards. 'He's a charming kid', he said: 'essentially normal and healthy – most refreshing'. But he was aware that Piers was no longer the lad of thirteen he had first met. He had noted with mock alarm in the spring that 'the boy has suddenly become extremely mature – having turned 16 – & more adult than adults themselves!'.

By this time, Britten had found a new thirteen-year-old, another 'charming kid', to take under his wing. On this occasion it was not someone who shared his own outlook and background, but a handsome boy from a straitened household in North London. He was called Harry Morris. Britten's sister Barbara had met Harry's mother through her WVS work, and Britten was determined to do his bit by raising the boy's sights and giving him opportunities that his family could not contemplate. Harry was a promising musician: he was having singing lessons from Dr George Aitken, who taught at the Guildhall, and he was a treble soloist in the choir of Hampstead Parish Church. He also played the violin and piano, and later took up the guitar and banjo. His mother was overjoyed that Britten was taking notice of her son, but his father – a hard, cold Army man – regarded music lessons as evidence of effeminacy.

Britten championed Harry's cause and in 1937 invited him to Crantock in Cornwall to join the Britten family holiday. But it is remarkable for being his one friendship with a boy that came to grief. Harry died in 2002, still distressed by the memory: as an old man, he had revisited Crantock, and the experience had made him feel ill.

Benjamin evidently delighted in laying on for Harry the same sort of treats as those he had given Piers Dunkerley, and in seeing his eyes light up with fresh experiences beyond his reach at home. This was what motivated him all his life in establishing friendships with boys. One afternoon he took Harry to the

---

* Britten saw this film three times in a fortnight.

cinema – or, more precisely, a news theatre. He noted in his diary: 'It is grand to treat a poor kid to these things – his first trip to Piccadilly! His face is a picture.'

Harry's first appearance in the diary had been on 15th May 1936, as a boy of thirteen 'who is very interested in music & has bought himself a violin & saved up for lessons etc. It is early to predict a genius, but he is very enthusiastic which is the root of all success – & a bright boy altogether.' In July he invited 'the little boy Barbara found' to tea, and recorded that 'he is getting on with his fiddle, & sings very nicely, & seems very intelligent. He is terribly keen on everything – especially gym at the moment – he shows me some of his especial tricks.' He was also impressed by his drawing ability ('a very good draughtsboy'), and tried to arrange a meeting with an architect, in the hope of finding him a job when he left school.

After his mother's death, his developing friendship with Harry was intertwined with a period of regular contact with Christopher Isherwood, who was nine years Britten's senior, and saw it as his mission to help him resolve his sexual dilemmas. In late June they dined together and went on talking until midnight. 'He gives me sound advice about many things', Britten noted in his diary, '& he being a grand person I shall possibly take it.' The next day Britten took Harry for a walk on Hampstead Heath, invited him back for tea and a chat. 'He is a splendid little boy & I hope I'll be able to do something for him.'

A week later, Isherwood made another attempt to bring Britten round. In the evening they sat 'for ages' in Regent's Park, and talked 'very pleasantly & then on to Oddeninos & Café Royal – get slightly drunk, & then at mid-night go to Jermyn St. & have a turkish Bath.' Isherwood clearly thought that direct experience of one of London's main rendezvous for homosexuals would be salutary. It came six months after Ronald Duncan had taken Britten to a Paris brothel, which he had fled in disgust at the female prostitutes. His reaction to the Turkish Baths was very different:

Very pleasant sensations – completely sensuous, but very healthy. It is extraordinary to find one's resistance to anything gradually weakening. The trouble was that we spent the night there – couldn't sleep a wink on the hard beds, in the perpetual restlessness of the surroundings.

Isherwood later said that both he and Auden had 'tried to bring him out, if he seemed to us to need it. We were extraordinarily interfering in this respect – as bossy as a pair of self-assured young psychiatrists.' He and a mutual friend had a conversation at this time, during which they asked themselves, 'Well, have we convinced Ben he's queer, or haven't we?'. Britten had clearly confided in him about Harry Morris, because Isherwood asked to meet the boy. A few days after the Jermyn Street adventure, Britten arranged it. 'Christopher Isherwood has tea with me & Harry Morris – who is a charming boy.'

Benjamin then invited Harry to join him and his siblings on holiday in Cornwall, and went to discuss it with Harry's parents. 'They are charming & terribly keen for him to come with me.' It was clearly a golden opportunity for the boy, who had probably never been on holiday before, and it became quite an expedition. In late July, 'young Harry comes round after tea to try on some clothes for Cornwall. Long walk with him on heath after – he is a grand kid*.' The train journey was set for 13th August.

In between, Britten saw Isherwood again: 'He is an awful dear, & I am terribly tempted always to make him into a father confessor'. He also went to the boys' school run by his brother Robert in North Wales, and clearly felt in his element. On the long train journey to Prestatyn, he struck up conversation with 'a nice lad' who had now left the school, and had a snack with him. When he reached Clive House, he recorded that 'they certainly have a charming set of boys here – & the three boarders – Brown, Preston & Musgrave – are delightful

---

* Britten used the same phrase a few days later to describe his nephew John, who was five.

kids. I walk to church with them & Robert.' He blotted his copybook when he took two of them for a long walk with the Britten family dog, Caesar: 'Lovely walk with splendid company – actually I keep them out too long, & we all get into a row on return.' On the fourth day of his visit came the end of the summer term, but he was still enjoying games with the boys: 'Young Brown is a splendid boy & we make great friends. He comes to see us off at station.' Before leaving, he had another long talk with his brother: 'We get on much better now', he noted, 'even tho' he is very much out of things, & considers me very "free"!!'.

Back in London, Britten tried to re-order his adult friendships. He spent an evening with a friend in advertising, Alan George, who was clearly keen on him.

> He takes me out to a good dinner at Spanish Restaurant,
> & then drives me all over London – down to E. India
> Docks (which are very beautiful & romantic) & then
> I go back to his flat until rather late.

'He brings me back here by 1.0', Britten noted, before adding enigmatically, 'I decide to end this little friendship'. It was earlier that same day that he had been keeping up his friendship with Piers Dunkerley by taking him to see the Marx Brothers.

The same week, in a moment of boredom, he smoked two cigarettes, the first since 'adolescent efforts at school'. He noted tersely that there were 'disastrous consequences in morning. Never again.' The boy Emil, on the cusp of adult experience, was uncomfortable over taking the plunge.

The Cornish holiday was fast approaching, and Britten was determined to give Harry Morris the time of his life. He arranged for the boy to stay the night at his London flat, in preparation for an early start for Cornwall in the morning, and looked after him with almost maternal concern.

> Harry has a wretched night – very homesick, & I have to
> stay with him a long time until he goes to sleep. However

in the morning, he's much more cheerful, & excited at the prospect of train journey to Cornwall.

He had arranged the excursion in style. They caught the Cornish Riviera from Paddington at half-past ten. 'It is exhilerating [*sic*] to see his face when he sees things for the first time. Perhaps the meal in the dining car is the most tremendous experience!' Six hours later, they arrived at Newquay, to be met with apparent apprehension by a headmasterly Robert and his wife, Marjorie.

They don't seem too pleased to see us – Harry is going to be a bit of a nuisance they think. But I suppose they never think of doing anyone a good turn.

But Britten wasted no time in plunging into his beloved sea: 'get a grand bathe & a surf at Crantock Bay before supper'.

The first part of the holiday went relatively well, though it is clear that his often tense relationship with his brother did not improve in the sea air. Indeed, there were two camps at Crantock: Robert, Marjorie and their son John were in one, and Benjamin, his sister Beth, her husband Kit – and Harry – in the other.

No quarrels, to any extent; certain antagonism as Robert will insist on asking his newly made & very intimate friends in – no one likes them. [. . .] Harry sleeps in the double room, Robert & family in the little N. one – Beth, Kit & I on verandar.

Once again, the boy had pride of place.

Harry seemed to be well over his homesickness. They took him to see some amateur dramatics: 'Harry is terribly struck by this his first visit to a "theatre". He is getting on very well with us. Very quiet – it is difficult for him having us all around all the time – but useful.' He remained with Beth in Cornwall, while Ben and Robert paid a flying visit to London. This ended in a row between the brothers at their other sister Barbara's flat, and the argument continued on the streets of Chelsea. Ben wrote in his diary:

It is a bit of a come-down to find them all wild with 'in loco parentis' wrath at my so-called conceit & bumptiousness – etc.etc. So we have (R & I) a first-rate bust up.

Robert said later that he and Barbara had agreed that they should take their younger brother 'down a peg or two', and while he and Ben were walking near the Tate Gallery, they 'argued very hotly, and got very angry with each other'. They parted company somewhere near the Houses of Parliament, 'I to a restaurant for a meal', said Ben, '& he to wander London.' They met up again at two o'clock in the morning to catch the train back to Cornwall. Robert took the comfortable seat ('I think I was rather a cad', he said), leaving Ben with the uncomfortable one. During the journey, they did make common cause in search of refreshment. The engine driver offered them a swig of his cold tea, and a ride on the engine to Newquay. To Ben's delight (this was the year after *Night Mail*), the fireman showed them how the boiler worked, and the driver got out his family photos: so intent were they all that the train shot through Quintrel Downs station. 'The driver said to the fireman, "Ought we to have stopped there?" So the fireman got out a timetable and looked it up. "Yes", he said, "we ought to have." So we solemnly stopped the train and backed all the way into the station to pick up the passengers.'

But this adventure did not heal the breach. When Beth came to Newquay to pick up her brothers, she found they were at 'either end of the train, and not on speaking terms, still'. That, she said, did not change for several days – which is confirmed by Ben's diary. 'Split is very marked we never join for anything – always Kit, Beth, Harry & me – & John, Marjorie & Robert. Personally I'm not distressed.' He reported that 'our section, K.B.H. me' went surfing in Treyarnon Bay.

Whether the boy felt uncomfortable in this family stand-off, or whether it had always been planned that way, Harry Morris left Cornwall early. He himself always maintained it was a sudden departure, for a quite different reason. In later life he told his wife Beryl and their son Tim that he had been alarmed by what he understood as a sexual approach from Britten in his bedroom. He said he screamed, and hit Britten with a chair. This brought Beth rushing into the room, who, he said, shouted at her brother. She and Ben left, and Beth locked the door. Harry got dressed, packed his bags, and sat waiting for the morning. Without speaking, Beth took him to the station, and dispatched him to London. When he reached home, he told his mother what had happened, but she told him off and refused to believe his story. He never told his father.

There is no reference to anything like this in Britten's diary. Indeed, the odd thing is that Harry just disappears from the holiday. He is mentioned during the visit to Treyarnon Bay on 25th August, and then on 31st August Britten records his own return to London overnight with Beth and Kit. The five days in between are blank, which is extremely unusual in the diary: Britten maintained a daily entry with almost religious devotion. In the previous eight and a half years he had missed only four days, three of them the previous week, and the fourth earlier in the year when he had crashed his car. Thereafter the blanks became more frequent (after his return to London, the diary was left virtually empty for a week) until it petered out altogether the following summer. The spell had somehow been broken. Whatever the reason for the five-day lacuna, it is certainly strange that, after devoting considerable space to the preparations for Harry's holiday and his arrival in Cornwall, Britten did not refer to the boy's departure.

Harry's account (as remembered by his widow and his son) is not itself proof of anything untoward: indeed, the account is more about a sense of threat than about an actual incident. It is possible (though unlikely) that, even after two weeks at Crantock, the boy misread the situation. There are also some major inconsistencies between the diary and Harry's account: he suggested that the episode, whatever it was, happened on the second day of the holiday, whereas the diary makes clear that Harry was in Cornwall for thirteen days at least. Perhaps the boy was disturbed by the continual arguments within the Britten family and absconded to London, armed with a story to explain his departure. But such a story did not help him escape his mother's censure, and the fact that Harry, as an old man, felt so uncomfortable when revisiting Crantock suggests that it was not invented.

Beth Britten refers to this holiday in her book. She does not mention Harry by name, but, as an example of her brother's efforts to help children, says that they took a boy from 'the east end of London' with them to Cornwall. Ben was apparently horrified on the first night when the boy took the pyjamas he had supplied and put them on over his underclothes.

If there had been a reason for Harry's alarm and lifelong distaste, it perhaps marked a unique moment in Britten's journey of self-discovery. The liberation he was experiencing in the wake of his parents' death, with the active encouragement of Isherwood and Auden, had given him both a knowledge of, and a taste for, 'the wider world of man'. But, early in his journey, he had bumped into a boundary fence, which reminded him of the moral framework of his upbringing. If there ever was a 'moment of madness' that so distressed Harry Morris, it was not to recur.

The strongest evidence that Britten, in his own mind, did not misbehave is that he maintained some contact with Harry in London afterwards, though he acknowledged that there had been a hiccup in Cornwall. In October 1937 the boy came to tea: 'I am surprised to find that after the slight over-dose of him in the summer, I am pleased to see him'. The following February he visited the Morris family to discuss Harry's future: 'architect or butcher – butcher wins'. He then took Harry off to see a film. That was the last time they met.

The friendship with Piers Dunkerley continued without interruption. In the summer of 1938 Ben invited him to stay in London, to 'hold his hand' in preparations for a concert (probably the first performance of the Piano Concerto). Piers, now seventeen, was clearly tickled by this idea, which he refers to in two separate letters: 'I <u>want</u> to come up and hold your paw – dirty or not'. 'By the way, if I'm to hold your hand, how are you going to tickle the ivories?' Ben had also sent Piers a photograph of himself standing proudly and assertively outside his new home in Snape.

> My dear Ben,
> [. . .] I have your sweet face on my desk, with the Mill in rear* and a boy, the School captain actually, recognised your beautiful fizz the other day; so we even find good taste at Bloxham!!! [. . .]
> With best love, Piers.

He invited the boy to stay at the Old Mill. Piers said he was 'simply dying' to see Ben's 'country seat', though he apologised in advance for his lack of horticultural skill. 'Although I wield quite a pretty spade, slow & sure is my motto, and then I rest for 25 minutes every half an hour.' But it is not clear whether Dunkerley ever went to Snape before the war. Britten's attention, for a while, now moved elsewhere.

---

* This was presumably the photograph used earlier in 1938 in *Radio Times*, reproduced as plate 7.

CHAPTER 5

Full marks for that boy!

Britten's independence was well-established by the summer of 1938. Eighteen months after the death of his mother, he had his own home in the country, a *pied-à-terre* in London when he needed it, and his own car to drive between the two. Musically, his *Variations on a Theme of Frank Bridge* had been well received on the international stage, his film and radio work had brought his name to prominence at home, and he had a Piano Concerto ready for performance that August at the Proms in Queen's Hall. Personally, he had a number of male admirers some of whom he was confident enough to discard, while others he kept at an affectionate arm's length. But that summer, at the age of twenty-four, he met a German youth with whom he was to have his first real romance. By the time Britten died in 1976, the name of Wulff Scherchen had been air-brushed out of history, partly through his own doing. None but Britten's oldest friends had ever heard of him, and his name was never mentioned. Yet in 1938–39 Scherchen was the most important person in Britten's life, and he was still at school. He, more than any other, was the figure who embodied Aschenbach's (and Britten's own) dilemma in *Death in Venice*: the enchantment he found in the beauty of boys.

They had met before. Shortly after leaving the Royal College of Music, Britten travelled to Italy on his first foreign trip, away from the bosom of his family in Lowestoft where his father was seriously ill. There it was that he briefly encountered Wulff Scherchen for the first time. Britten was twenty; Scherchen was, as it happened, thirteen.

It was the end of March 1934 when Britten set off to Florence with his old schoolfriend John Pounder, to attend the festival of the International Society for Contemporary Music, where his *Phantasy* Quartet was to be played at a chamber recital. They stayed at the Pension Balestri, and the hotel bill is meticulously preserved in the Britten archives. Another guest remembers Britten (who was otherwise 'shy and retiring') appropriating the 'elderly upright piano' in the hall of the hotel, just as he always had in Morling's music shop in Lowestoft, and imitating on the keyboard the sight and sound of the tall, heavily built Pounder nimbly tripping down the staircase.

The versatile and eccentric German conductor, Hermann Scherchen, was also staying in the *pensione* with his family. The day after conducting an orchestral concert of Honegger, Ravel and Bartók, which Britten attended, Scherchen munificently organised an excursion for the orchestra. Five buses took them to Siena. Britten tagged along, and his companion on the journey was not Pounder, but Scherchen's thirteen-year-old son, Wulff. At that stage the boy spoke little English, but it barely mattered: the rapport was instant. 'There was no language barrier', Wulff Scherchen recalls. 'This is the beautiful thing about friendship – languages don't matter, you make signs, you can nudge one another with your elbow . . . all sorts of things to overcome the language difficulty.'

Britten wrote in his diary:

> It pours with rain all day, so Siena is rather lost on us.
> Lunch given by the Mayor etc. – visits to Cathedral. Young
> Wulff Scherchen (son of Hermann) attaches himself to me,
> & I spend all the time with him.

In Britten's mind, it was usually the boy who took the initiative, though it is hard to believe there was no encouragement. Wulff Scherchen was almost the same age as Piers Dunkerley, who caught Benjamin's attention that same spring of 1934.

Scherchen remembers that Britten was the only member of the party who had brought a raincoat, for which he was teased as a typical English gentleman (though Mrs Britten would have admired his practical forethought). But he had the last laugh when the heavens opened – perhaps not the last, because he offered half his mackintosh to his new friend Wulff, who was wearing shorts and sandals. 'He opened it out, stuck his right arm into the right sleeve and got me to put my left arm in the left sleeve. The mac was big enough to accommodate us both fortunately. We thought that was hilariously funny but then we had to walk along with our middle legs together, and then the outer legs, doing a three-legged march which increased general hilarity. Oh, it was wonderful!' This brief escapade in the rain, and their refuge in the church of San Domenico, was not perhaps of Virgilian significance, but it did strike an emotional spark between the young teenager and the young composer – a jocular moment of lifelong meaning for both of them.

The following morning, Benjamin went for a short walk with Wulff – a mark of high favour in the Britten family canon. But at lunch he was summoned home to Suffolk because his father had died, and that – apparently – was that.

There is one memento of their Tuscan encounter. Wulff took a snap of Britten in the street. In his left hand was his newest score, *A Boy Was Born* – which fits Scherchen's memory of him. 'Look at his face in that photo – it's the face of a young boy, just come out of the egg, not of a grown-up young man. I didn't feel he was seven years older than me. I thought we were much closer in age than that. We were boys together.' This matched Christopher Isherwood's impression of Britten a couple of years later: he 'always seemed younger in appearance than he actually was, with his curly hair [. . .] very boyish in his demeanour'.

In 1934 the Scherchen family was temporarily based in Switzerland. Wulff and his mother, Gustel, had fled Berlin in a hurry twelve months before. A friendly neighbour who belonged to the SS had tipped them off that they were about to be detained by the new Nazi authorities. They took the train to Lugano, where they were reunited with Hermann, although he and Gustel had been divorced six years before. Hermann had subsequently been married and divorced a second time. Shortly after the 1934 visit to Florence and Siena, Gustel moved to

Cambridge (unbeknown to Britten) where a place was found for Wulff at The Perse School, thanks to the good offices of the renowned musicologist, Professor E.J. Dent. The rather self-conscious foreign boy was mortified on his first day to find that he was the only one wearing knickerbockers, and he took some while to acquire the taste of British schoolboy humour. In the South House dormitory after lights-out, he could not understand the ribaldry which accompanied the question: 'Why does an engine have a tender behind?', and was still nonplussed when told the answer: 'Because it passes so many telegraph poles'. His obvious ignorance delighted the rest of the dormitory so much that they let the game go on for some time before they took pity on him and tried to explain the joke, to even louder hoots of laughter. Eventually the penny dropped, and he was 'admitted to the club'. His English developed apace, and he became an avid student and writer of English poetry.

Wulff and his father went to the next ISCM Festival in Barcelona in 1936. So did Britten, whose Violin Suite was being performed there. They might have bumped into each other at the concert at which Wulff's father conducted the first performance of the Berg Violin Concerto, which made a deep impression on Britten. But Hermann Scherchen had told his unescorted son to stay at the hotel, so there was no opportunity for a chance meeting.

It was not until two years later that Hermann Scherchen let slip to Britten that his ex-wife and son were living in England. It prompted him to write to the boy who had so impressed him in Italy.

Dear Wulf [*sic*],
I do not know whether you will remember me or not –
but in 1934 – during the Festival of Modern Music in
Florence – we spent a long time together – especially
one day in Siena. I have been seeing your father a lot
in London this last week, & he suggested that I should
write to you.

I have now got a flat in London – but I live mostly in a windmill in Suffolk – not so very far from Cambridge. I should very much like to see you again. I suppose you can't get away from Cambridge during the term? If so I might come & fetch you in a car. Otherwise when do you next come to London? Are you going to Neuchatel [his father's base in Switzerland] for your holidays? If so I might meet you when you travel through London. Anyhow, do write to me, & I am sure we shall be able to arrange something.

Yours sincerely,
Benjamin Britten.

It is a letter that is both tentative and persistent. Britten laid the blame for it on Wulff's father, yet his detailed list of alternatives for a meeting shows that his interest was more than simply polite. In all likelihood, Wulff would be almost unrecognisable more than four years on from the day in Siena. Yet still he wrote.

His confidence was rewarded by return of post. Wulff had clearly embraced the English vernacular with an effervescence of expression, had a cheeky, anarchic sense of humour (which doubtless appealed to Britten), and, most important, was keen to meet up.

Dear ?,
Excuse the question-mark, but I am quite at a loss whether to address you 'Dear Sir', 'Benjamin', 'Britten', or just 'Hello, old chap, fancy writing to you after all that time!' I should be very much obliged to you, etc. . . if you would kindly mark your preference, etc. . . thanking you in anticipation, etc. etc.

Wasn't that day in Sienna a whole 'family' outing, with the whole orchestra and that wonderful saxophonist Rascher, who is by now professor in Sweden or somewhere? We two went tramping to the piazza something or other and explored the 'guildahalla'. Nein? I was in shorts and sandals (as I am now) and it started to rain. I got thoroughly wet, but it was worth it! – pleasant reminiscences of a glorious past! (Excuse my poetic strain).

At the moment, I am basking in the sun, only the sun doesn't appear to be there somehow. Curious fact, but there it is. It is very nice of you to ask me to come and see you sometimes (rather apt quotation from Mae West don't you think?) I should just love to come and have a look at your windmill. I have always wanted to do that, since reading Daudet's 'lettres de mon moulin'.

I am usually free on Saturday afternoons and Sundays and I hope you will be able to manage a week-end. [. . .]

Yours sincerely,

W. Scherchen

P.S. As an afterthought: what about 'Dearest', 'Darling Benjamin'. You have my full permission to make me eat my words – with a three course dinner preferably.

P.S.S. Shall we see you in Cambridge during the Festival? I include programme.

P.P.S.S. Best wishes from my mother.

Scherchen was delighted with his own cheek when he read this letter again after sixty-five years: 'It's a good way to start a letter off, isn't it? Full marks for that boy!' The first postscript and the reference to Mae West suggest a comfortable intimacy in their friendship four years earlier. Scherchen's laughter stopped for a moment as he re-encountered it: 'It's wonderful to be young and carefree . . . The best part of it is that that letter should have survived. I kept all his letters, I'm glad to say. But why should he have kept mine?'

Benjamin replied to 'My dear Wulf', and was almost importunate in suggesting dates for a visit by a lad he barely knew. It was arranged that he would come to stay at the Old Mill two weeks later. The mode of address, he said, was up to Wulff, 'although if you dared to call me anything more formal than "Benjamin" I should be very angry!' Characteristically, he added: 'Don't forget (a) bathing things – if you bathe (b) tennis things – if you play tennis'. It was to be a mark of special honour that the friendship with Wulff lasted as long as it did when he was not much good at either.

Their first weekend together at Snape in July 1938 set the seal on their encounter four years earlier. In the years since, Scherchen has often wondered what his mother was thinking of, letting him go off to spend the weekend with a man they had met only briefly four years before in Florence. Britten drove to Saxmundham to meet Wulff off the train, either of them apprehensive about recognising the other. As Wulff walked out of the station, Benjamin got out of the driver's seat, and it was clear to Wulff that he had not changed. 'He was standing the same way, he walked the same way . . . He was slim and straight and he walked like that too. He held himself well – a sportsman. He portrayed his personality in the way he walked, behaved and moved about. There was no hesitation, no awkwardness. We just said "Hello, Ben", "Hello, Wulff". What became our usual companionship was there straightaway.'

Wulff however had changed quite a bit. He was now eighteen – no longer a slightly gawky boy in spectacles but a rather beautiful young man, tall, lithe and blond. From his 1938 school photographs, Wulff seems a self-confident, assertive youth, with a touch of the hardness bred at secondary school. But the studio portraits Britten commissioned from his friend Enid Slater some months later reveal a softer, more vulnerable character – and in the informal snaps taken in the garden at the Old Mill he looks even more the boy, in sleeveless jersey and baggy trousers (see plates 8 and 10).

In his eighties, Scherchen is still a strikingly handsome man. He lives in Australia with his wife Pauline, and in 2003 they celebrated their diamond wedding. They now have four children, nine grandchildren and seven great-grandchildren to their name. Until the making of the television documentary that gave rise to this book, he had never spoken publicly about his intense and important friendship with Britten before the war.

That first weekend in July 1938, Ben proudly showed Wulff his new home, freshly renovated with his mother's legacy. It had been a working mill just a few years earlier: Britten had turned the mill chamber into his studio, and had raised the roof to accommodate a large bedroom on the upper floor, with a panoramic window looking across to the River Alde and the marshes, and east to the sea. In the middle of that vista were the maltings, which thirty years later Britten would convert into one of England's finest concert halls. On the ground floor, his grand piano was tucked in beside the spiral staircase leading to his bedroom. For Wulff it was 'an enchanted house, so unusual, and so welcoming'. As he crossed the threshold for the first time, he was required to add a piece to the large jigsaw just inside the front door. For him, it was to become a metaphor for the way in which he and Ben 'just seemed to fit together'.

There was the obligatory attempt to play tennis, which Scherchen now remembers as a fiasco. 'I'm no good – I only play for pleasure', he had told Ben, who replied: 'Never mind, bring your racquet'. When it was clear that Wulff did indeed have little ability on the court, Ben lapsed into a silent fury. 'He could have spat nails', Scherchen says. 'Here was the former junior tennis champion of Suffolk, and I didn't match up to his preconception of me – another champion at the same age.' After ten minutes Britten simmered down, and it was all forgotten – though when they walked on the beach later, they did not go for a bathe. 'I don't know why I brought my swimming things.' At one stage during their walk, Wulff stopped and admired the view. 'Ben turned and gave me a bearhug, a comradely hug, a confirmation of a shared pleasure.'

In the evening, Ben offered to play some Beethoven on the piano, without realising the effect it would have on his listener. Or perhaps he did. It was another moment that has stayed with Scherchen all his life. Indeed, when he visited the Old Mill in 2003 for the first time for sixty-five years, the memories streamed back. In his early eighties, Scherchen spontaneously, and gamely, sat down on the floor on the opposite side of the room, just as he had done that July evening in 1938. 'My back was against the wall, and as he played I drifted away. The music just over-whelmed me – the feeling that music arouses, the fact that Ben was playing for *me*, not for anyone else. This was a personal performance. I was taken out of myself, and I had an outpouring of emotions – the tears were streaming down my face, and I couldn't stop. I was blissfully happy. Ben stopped, terribly concerned, and found a handkerchief for me to dry my tears with. He said "Anything I can do? Are you all right?" and I said "I'm perfectly all right, I'm so happy I can't explain it to you." '

At that stage it was natural for Britten to choose Beethoven. Professionally he was in the thick of scoring his Piano Concerto, which was ten days from completion. By now he had discovered Mahler and Berg, but his youthful obsession with Beethoven – as experienced by Basil Reeve ten years before – had not begun to wane. He was also no doubt keen to play for Wulff the music that had meant most to him at Wulff's age – another way of holding on to his own boyhood. Wulff would not of course have known that Britten's inspiring but overbearing friend W.H. Auden had once recommended piano-playing as an aid to seduction. After Britten had received some rebuff, Auden had asked: 'Did you play the piano? Most important'. He went on to advise on 'future policy':

> What you did before with such success. A slight coldness.
> Quite friendly, but cold. And LOTS of music. Suggest a
> little temporary infidelity.

Britten was not very good at being cold to those he was drawn to: indeed he could barely contain his enthusiasm. But he could certainly lay on the music.

There was at least a touch of nonchalance in his letter to Wulff the following week:

> Well, old thing, I did enjoy having you for the weekend. It
> was grand to see that you hadn't altered from that kid in
> Florence & Siena (I hope you take that as a compliment!).

But he now began, 'My dearest Wulff', and there is no doubting the attraction he felt for the boy on the strength of a single visit. He seems to have bragged about him to his friends, to judge by a letter from the composer Lennox Berkeley only a few days after Wulff had gone home to Cambridge. Berkeley was wishing Britten well for the première of his Piano Concerto four weeks later, and added:

> I'm sure you're going to have a terrific success; and I hope that you will have a further success afterwards which I know you hope for. If music be indeed the food of love, I think you stand a very good chance.

If this refers to Wulff, Britten had either been discussing him with Berkeley the last time they met (which was two days before Wulff arrived), or they had been in touch by telephone since. Britten clearly told Auden during a weekend he spent at the Old Mill a fortnight after Wulff's visit. That explains the mischievous enquiry in a letter he was to receive from Auden straight after the Piano Concerto's first performance: 'And what about its effect on a certain person of importance?'

Britten did indeed press Wulff to listen to his concerto. The boy was away in Strasbourg with his father, but the première was broadcast as part of Henry Wood's Promenade Concert season, with Britten himself as the soloist. The concert at Queen's Hall was carried live on both BBC radio and the infant television service (in the case of the latter, without any pictures!). Ben told Wulff it was 'a thousand pities that you can't be there – at least I think it is!', but urged him to 'listen in hard' (and reminded him twice in subsequent postcards).

The effect was not quite the knock-out blow Britten had hoped for. Wulff did indeed tune in (as was possible that far south on the less crowded pre-war airwaves), but had the nerve to tell Ben that the finale sounded 'pompous'. In his reply, he let Wulff off uncharacteristically lightly:

I can assure you it is not, whatever else may be! Anyhow I'm glad to know that you recognised the work as mine & that quality about it which reminded you of the Mill. <u>That</u> certainly pleased me!

Wulff had so far been to the Old Mill for that one July weekend. He spent the rest of the summer holidays in Europe, much to Britten's frustration, with family and friends. Britten thought of travelling to Neuchâtel on the pretext of visiting Hermann Scherchen, but realised he could not get there until September. 'Then you won't be there', he wrote to Wulff, '& I don't think I shall go unless you are'. But Britten (as he always did, however busy he was) nurtured their embryonic relationship with a stream of postcards and letters, even the occasional international telephone call. Wulff reciprocated, but Britten was always more persistent and more artful: too many endearments would deter the boy, but so would too few. His light-hearted tone veiled a suppressed affection, designed to leave him wanting more. He kept pressing Wulff to return to Snape. The boy finally arrived just before school term began in September.

At the Mill, Wulff quickly adapted himself to Ben's composing routine. 'He'd suddenly say, "I've got to go and work. Have you got a book or can you amuse yourself for an hour or so?" – and he'd just disappear. An hour later he would come back and forget all about work and say "let's go for a walk".' They would explore the estuary of the River Alde, or go for a spin in Ben's Ford 8. He tried teaching Wulff to drive, without great success. Much the same went for his attempt to introduce Wulff to contemporary music: he briefly flared up when the boy objected to some Stravinsky on the wireless because it was giving him a headache. As Britten's culinary skills did not extend beyond the limited demands of breakfast, meals were usually eaten out with friends, or left for them by his housekeeper, Mrs Hearn. 'I think she took pity on us', Scherchen recalls. 'She was concerned about these two young men – well, boy and a young man – not eating properly.'

During term-time, they fortified each other with letters, often incoherently typed and ripe in schoolboy humour on both sides. 'I've got to stop now', Ben wrote, 'as some orchestra is just going to maule MY maulation of Rossinny about on the raydio. Pity you ar'nt hrerere to make your customary rude remarx!' Wulff had a penchant for spoonerisms: 'Bennox Lerkeley', 'Ceachbomber' and 'kouseheeper'. On the back of one of Wulff's missives, Ben played no fewer than eight games of noughts-and-crosses with himself – not the most rewarding pastime, but the boy Benjamin was alive and well.

He invited Wulff to Snape for a whole week. But instead it was he who paid three weekend visits to the Scherchens' home in Cambridge during October. He told Wulff he 'enjoyed being with you like hell'. By now he probably realised that Wulff's musical sensibility did not afford any particular insight. But they shared an enthusiasm for literature. After his first visit, Ben urged 'Wulff Liebchen' to write some 'serious' poetry.

> You have a great knowledge of language – you love our really great poets (Shelley & Keats etc.) – & I think you've got great observation. Why not try? There seems to be something at the back of that silly old head of yours – & it might help in getting it out.

He said he was writing Wulff some music (probably the incidental music for *On the Frontier*, a play by Auden and Isherwood): 'Damn it all – man – [. . .] do the decent thing & reciprocate with something!'

It was as though Britten had turned on a tap. A stream of poetry began to flow from Wulff's pen, which was to infuse the rest of their friendship. As soon as he had read Ben's letter, he sent him two poems he had already written about the Spanish Civil War, and conceived a new one that very day: '*Sturm und Drang* (Storm and Urge)', which he said was 'written for my greatest friend, Benjamin Britten'. After describing the violence of a storm, the final section ('*Drang*') expresses the tumult of his own emotions, and the 'strange unsatisfied desires' of his heart.

> But in my heart, what aching,
> What strife for clear decision.

Britten took this, as it was surely meant, personally. 'Sturm &
Drang I was very impressed (& flattered by!).' He analysed the
first part of the poem, but held back over the final section.
'I really feel that a bit too deeply to write about it. When we
next meet you must read it, & I'll tell you lots of things.' The
relationship was deepening.

Shortly after Ben's second visit in October, Wulff sent him
another poem. The language is more sensual, with its reference
to 'your soft body, supple at my touch'. It is unclear whom
it addresses, but his emotional tension is evident: 'my heart is
fully satisfied / although my mind is troubled'. He feels some
hesitation in giving full expression to his love, and some pressure
to go further than he wished.

> [. . .] Yet can our love not be fulfill'd,
> our attachment not be complete.
> yet always shall I keep the treasure of your love,
> the beauty of your affection,
> they shall be stirred within my heart–
> a memory of a beautiful attachment,
> of what might have been.

When Ben had left the third time, Wulff sent him a love-poem
entitled '*La maison déserte*'. It told of the emptiness of the
house after 'she is gone', no longer 'filled with light' as it had
been when 'she was here'. (Wulff later told Ben: 'all my works
are really dedicated to you, including such poems as "maison
déserte" and others, since you first gave me the stimulus to write
any decent kind of poetry at all'.) That same October day he
wrote a second poem, specifically dedicated 'in unbounded
affection' to 'Benjamin Britten, my best friend'. It began: 'Let
not the florid music cease' (a conscious reference to the Auden
poem which opens Britten's 1937 song-cycle *On This Island*)
and ended with a flourish of Keats – all in praise of the power

of music, an echo of that first evening at the Old Mill in July when he had been overcome by Ben playing Beethoven. But it again expressed his emotional quandary.

> [. . .] I love you, oh, beyond all comprehension.
> but should I not restrain and guide that love?
> for can I give you aught that you already not possess?
> your music calls and I become your slave
> yet linger I and dare not go, nor dare I stay.
> a friend, such as you are, is truly rare,
> but can I do honour to your friendship?
> for is't not you who has to give me help?
> how will you then find consolation and
> the recompense that is your due?
> therefore play on, play on and quench me with
>   harmonious sound,
> make me oblivious of all else, for in your oblivion
> music, everything's contained. [. . .]
> fled is that music: – do I wake or sleep?
> O! Benjamin.

Ben stayed with the Scherchens for a whole week in November, for the opening of *On the Frontier* at the Cambridge Arts Theatre. Britten conducted the tiny ensemble from the piano, with his schoolboy friend sitting next to him, 'proud as Punch' to be turning the pages of the score. Britten later gave him some of the manuscript sketches. What he particularly remembers from the first night is Britten's solo accompaniment of the National Anthem: 'he galloped through it at top speed, and had almost finished before the audience started to sing! There were actually one or two claps – in fact, it's a rollicking tune played that way'.* Perhaps Britten was reasserting his boy-ishness, in the shadow of his twenty-fifth birthday a few days

* Britten also used to play the National Anthem backwards, as he once did for the Mothers' Union, as remembered by a favourite schoolfriend, Francis Barton. On another occasion, he delighted a village party by playing the anthem as if on a wind-up gramophone that was running down.

later. Most young men relish this as a landmark of maturity, but for Britten it was an unwelcome harbinger of old age. He wrote to Wulff just before going out for his birthday tea (itself a reaffirmation of evanescent childhood): he was excited about starting on his Violin Concerto,

> but otherwise <u>very</u> depressed. The strain of becoming a quarter of a century is bearing hard upon me. It's a horrible thing to feel one's youth slipping o-so surely away from one & I had such a damn good youth too. I wish you were here to comfort me!

In his letters, Ben was torn between his deepening fondness for a boy of his own age, as it were, and a loftier paternal concern for an immature adolescent. Although Wulff says Ben never lectured him face to face, he did sometimes write with a wagging finger, as after some domestic flare-up in Cambridge:

> My dear Wulff,
> I'm hoping to hear in the morning that everything is O.K. with regard to the Catastrophy [*sic*] on Saturday. You are an old fool to have gone and upset things like that. I could see your poor mother was very sick about it [. . .] Life is much too short to go kicking up against authorities on such matters as those; save the epic rebellion for larger issues!! I'm not trying to be 'in loco parentis' or anything so daft as that, you're much too much of an individual to need that, nor am I trying to force useless 'experience' down your throat, I'm merely – God knows what I'm trying to do, and it is much too late to think. ONE thing I *do* know, and that I like coming over to see you but I don't want these silly fusses every time I come!!!

He relented only in the postscript:

> Sorry about this letter – was feeling very grim last night – but haven't got time to rewrite it. <u>Let</u> me know how things go.
> Much love – my dear. Benjamin.

Britten knew of course that Wulff had a totally absent father in Hermann Scherchen, and he relished the opportunity that gave him to provide comfort and advice. He was always meticulous in enquiring after Gustel, and passing on his love. Even so, it is surprising that she agreed to let Wulff spend Christmas and the New Year (more than a week) at Snape. Ben was reassuring when he first suggested the idea: his musical colleague Peter Pears would be there, as well as Barbara ('my elder sister – very nice'). In fact Pears was present only on Christmas Day itself, and Barbara left the following Friday, leaving Ben and Wulff alone at the Old Mill between 30th December and 2nd January. It was Wulff's longest visit there, and by far the most important.

CHAPTER 6

Lost to the worlds

Three weeks before Christmas there had been a significant change in the tone of Wulff's letters to Ben. His letter of 6th December began 'Darling Ben', the first time he had taken up his own suggestion in the postscript to his first letter back in June. Instead of his normally skittish, sometimes flirtatious pleasantries, he gave a stress-laden account of the exams he was sitting for a modern languages scholarship to Christ's College, Cambridge. He signed off: 'Wish me luck darling, all the best, Wulff', before adding a lengthy postscript about his proposed visit to Snape over Christmas.

> I shall need a rest. My nerves are getting frayed . . .
> Conclusion: send nerve-tonic, half a dozen doctors,
> or come at once. I wish you could. Well, it cannae be.
> Till Xmas dearest. All my love.

Then, as he crammed his final words into the only clear space left at the bottom of the page, the flippancy suddenly dissolved.

> Love, love, love. I'm going to go sentimental & cry if I
> continue this letter. Try & change Xmas to next Sunday.
> Oh my darling, I love you. Yours ever, Wulff. Love, love,
> love, love. (Give my love to Peter & Lennox*). Please send
> a post-card every day till end of week. I'm feeling absolutely
> desolate. Don't ever leave me darling. xxxx

Wulff added a final touch before posting the letter, to ensure that, as Ben opened it, he would find the word 'love' written inside each fold.

---

* Wulff had met Peter Pears in London, and Lennox Berkeley at Snape.

It is not clear what had prompted this emotional outburst. Perhaps it followed an unrecorded visit to Snape. Perhaps it was just the exams. Perhaps Ben had induced it by a more fulsome expression in his own letters:

> Now, my dear, cheer up – things are never so black as they seem – & though you feel you haven't got friends of your age (which anyhow I don't believe!) – it is better to have one <u>real</u> confidant than lots of mere acquaintances – & that, my dear, is what I hope I am to you. Remember I love you very, very much & anything I can do for you, I will. See?

But the tone of this is more paternal than romantic.

Scherchen today is startled by his own uninhibited language in that December letter. 'Just on the surface one would accept that as an intimate and passionate love letter. I don't really think that's quite what I had in mind. It was obviously very deeply felt, but I do think that the feeling has been . . . overdone. It was an effervescence. Yes, I'm gilding the lily – "let's go the whole hog here". I certainly was overwhelmed, wasn't I? By him personally, by the whole surrounding, the whole ambience. But I'm surprised at all this "darling, darling, love, love" stuff I must say, though everybody said "darling" in that circle to each other.'

The emotional dilemmas in Wulff's poetry had caught up with him. Christmas could not come too soon.

Christmas Day 1938 fell on a Sunday. In those days the festival did not interrupt the railway service, and Wulff (who had not been successful in his scholarship attempt) arrived in Suffolk by the first train from Cambridge. For much of that week, Britten was entertained by friends in the neighbourhood, and Scherchen remembers an unvarying diet of Christmas fare, which did not assist their digestion, even after tobogganing in the thick snow. He had with him some tipsy Christmas-card doggerel ('to be read aloud') for

> Benjamin, my darling,
> O to-night you look so charming . . .

It told of their first meeting in Florence, and then his arrival in England.

> there I came to know again
> little Benny, sprouting swain.
> with him then in love I fall,
> body, soul, and all and all.

There was one absent friend at the Old Mill party, Lennox Berkeley, ten years Britten's senior, who that year had been sharing the house with him intermittently. Back in July he had been the first to encourage Ben in his prospective entanglement. He had then met Wulff on several occasions during the autumn. After one of them, Ben had told Wulff: 'By the way, Lennox approves of you & hopes you'll come here again!!!!!'

But by Christmas he had become quite jealous, as the embers of his own two-year infatuation with Britten were rekindled. He wrote somewhat ruefully to the American composer Aaron Copland that Britten was 'very successful in all departments of his life and enjoying it all'. Berkeley spent the holiday in Gloucestershire and Paris, but looked across to East Anglia with envy.

On Christmas Eve, he poured his heart out to Ben:

Darling,
I must write because I can't think of anything but you, everything seems drab and uninteresting except you [. . .] It's a sort of illness which I suppose I shall recover from some day [. . .]

My love to Barbara and Peter, and to Wulff though I can't feel quite so well disposed towards him at the moment as I shd like to. It is hell isn't it – not his fault, poor child.

All my love Ben dear, L.

Wulff was aware of the tension that his relationship with Ben was causing, and had been brave and sensitive enough to express his concern to Berkeley, who was almost twice his age.

Berkeley said it was 'uncommonly nice' of him to think of it, but it was 'not your responsibility or even your concern'. He commiserated with him over his unsuccessful scholarship attempt and explained why he would not be joining them for Christmas. 'I don't think it would be any fun at all the three of us being here [at the Old Mill] together. It's a pity, because, strangely enough, I like you.'

In another letter (probably written between Christmas and New Year), Berkeley told Britten that it was

> almost impossible for me not to be haunted by the green-eyed monster when Wulff is with you, but I still keep saying to myself that you are happy and that it's only this mean and horrible jealousy that I can't quite get the better of that prevents me from being happy too [. . .] When I've pulled myself together a bit I feel an awful fool to have let myself fall in love so violently – I really ought to know better at my age [. . .]
>   Love to Wulff; and I hope that Vally* isn't pining on account of his uncle's absence. He's so fond of me (V not W).

Britten was almost brutal in the heartiness of his reply:

> My dear Lennox,
> A <u>very</u> happy New Year to you! I am sure you're feeling fine now that you're in Paris & with José & all those friends of yours [. . .] I hope you had a good Xmas. Ours was definitely good, in spite of the very thick snow.

He must have known Berkeley would flinch when he added, after making clear his other guests had gone: 'W. is with me for the week-end'. He signed off by telling him to 'cheer up'.

Berkeley had good reason for his jealousy. There was a growing intimacy at the Old Mill. On 2nd January, Wulff had

---

* To avoid confusion in this already complicated ménage, it should be explained that Vally was the cat.

no sooner returned to Cambridge than he was writing a letter of thanks to Ben, who by then was travelling to Brussels to perform his Piano Concerto.

> Dearest,
> Thank you again for everything & especially for last
> night. You mean more to me and matter more than
> anything else.

He also embarked on a new poem, 'A Madrigal', which he dedicated to Ben 'as part-payment of an unpayable gift: his friendship'. It was the product of their time alone together, as the heading makes clear: 'Conceived 30.XII.38 / 31.XII'.

> lost to the worlds,
> beyond all stars,
> alone, yet one,
> two beings lie.
>
> oblivion rules
> their minds, their hearts,
> while tranquil there,
> voluptuous, they love.
>
> away from hate,
> above all scorn,
> but in their love
> they know existence.
>
> time has no sense,
> music no charms,
> beauty is lost,
> in lover's frenzy.

Britten carried this poem with him for years afterwards, long after he and Wulff had parted company. The Mahlerian first line, at least, must have resonated with him.

Ben's friendship with Wulff was more than an East Anglian idyll. The teenager was enthralled to enter Britten's artistic circle

during a week they spent in London together.* He was star-struck
to meet Auden, one of his literary heroes, as well as Christopher
Isherwood and Stephen Spender. 'Although I was only on the
periphery, I was involved in it: it seduced me. I felt, "Ah! How
marvellous it is to be here, to be part of this, to see what's going
on, to *know* what's going on!" ' He feels now that this may
explain the 'effervescence' in his letters: he simply did not want the
enchanted moment ever to end. 'But yes, there was a strong personal feeling for Benjamin – no question about that. "Passionate"
I think is too strong a term but . . . yes . . . Ahh! I couldn't have
done without Ben, not at that time, no! He was the centre of my
being definitely, for a while . . . Once we were together, we were
very close.' Even when Britten was discussing business with
Auden, he would include Wulff by giving him a look or a grin
every now and then. 'In other words, he'd say "I'm still here!" '

Because of his stay at the Old Mill shortly after Wulff's first
visit, Auden had been in on the start of the relationship – not
that he showed Wulff (or Ben) any mercy. He wanted to see
Wulff for himself, so he arranged to meet them both for tea,
upstairs at the Café Royal in London. There they found him
nursing an enormous brandy balloon. He offered Wulff a drink,
and the boy in his confusion said he would have the same. So
Wulff anxiously sipped a double brandy with Auden mischie-
vously looking on. Suddenly Auden declared it was time to
leave. The boy gulped down his drink, staggered to his feet and
down the grand staircase, determined to deny Auden the satisfaction of seeing him stumble and of showing him up in front
of Ben. Scherchen puts this down to naughtiness rather than
malice, though he says 'there was a malicious glint in his eye: he
knew exactly what he was doing'. But the figure absent from the
story is Britten. His naturally protective manner seems to have
deserted him in Auden's domineering presence. Or perhaps he
reckoned no great harm would be done, and was fascinated to

* In his letter of 5.4.40, Wulff referred to 'that week in London with you when I
met Christopher [Isherwood] and Wystan [Auden]'.

witness the innocent on the brink of experience. Wulff in the Café Royal was, for a moment, Emil in the railway carriage.

When in London, Wulff stayed at 67 Hallam Street, at the back of Broadcasting House. Here Britten shared a flat with Peter Pears, the singer he had first met some two years before. Wulff was thrilled to observe them rehearsing. One particular song stands out in his memory: Schubert's *Erlkönig*, in which the wraith of the Erl-King tries to abduct a boy, first by enticing words and then by violence.

> *Ich liebe dich, mich reizt deine schöne Gestalt;*
> *Und bist du nicht willig, so brauch ich Gewalt.*
> (I love you, your beautiful body excites me,
> And if you're not willing, I shall use force.)

The boy is hurt as the Erl-King tries to seize him, and he finally dies in his father's arms. Schubert's intense, eerie depiction of Goethe's trialogue between boy, parent and abuser is an uncanny foretaste of that between Miles, his governess and Peter Quint in *The Turn of the Screw*, as conceived by Britten and his librettist Myfanwy Piper in 1953–54.* Both *Erlkönig* and *The Turn of the Screw* end similarly – with the death of the boy. Wulff turned the pages for Ben during these private Schubertiades, and was flattered when Pears asked him for advice on German pronunciation.†

Beyond the confines of the Hallam Street flat, Wulff was of course more visible than in Britten's East Anglian backwater. One of Pears's friends, Basil Douglas, later said that he did not know whether they were having an affair or not, but 'certainly he [Ben] was absolutely smitten with Wulfie'. Indeed, Britten

---

* In Henry James's original book, the ghosts are silent, so a trialogue does not arise.
† Everything we know about Britten suggests that the story of this ballad, as so memorably set by Schubert, would have commended itself to him. So it is surprising to find no record of Pears and Britten ever performing it in public. It is of course a challenge to bring it off: the singer is required to take four roles (including that of narrator), while the piano part is notoriously difficult. But the fact that Britten accompanied Ernest Urbach in the song in 1943 suggests that he at any rate was not daunted.

sensed some anxiety on the part of Gustel Scherchen. In a note
to Wulff (quite possibly after the Café Royal episode) he asked
him to assure his mother that 'London was not that wicked
place she may have supposed it was'. But the greater risk was
to Britten himself, and to his germinal reputation. Until 1967
homosexuality in any circumstances was illegal. Furthermore,
Wulff was only eighteen, which meant in those days that he was
a minor. If whispers of a liaison began to spread, Britten's career
could have been ruined just as it was starting. Yet only once, in
January 1939, did he betray any sign of alarm. After his visit to
Belgium, he wrote to Wulff: 'our little friendship seems to be
rumoured all over the continent'. (The litotes in the word 'little'
is particularly revealing.) This was what Auden, ever the stirrer,
had relayed to him, no doubt with some glee – and the loose
tongue of Hermann Scherchen (not Auden's, of course) was
apparently to blame. 'So be a little careful, my dear', Ben wrote,

> in what you say. I personally don't care what people say –
> but it might react badly on you – a foreigner in England.
> I should love to shout it to the skies – as you know. All my
> love my dearest – I'm dying to see you again. Let's make
> it soon. Peter sends his love & a kiss! – <u>Burn</u> this. All my
> love – my darling. B.

Although in those febrile pre-war days Britten was right to be
concerned about a German exile in England, he must have
known the risks he himself was running. For the first time (apart
from two postcards from Belgium) he signed off with 'B.' rather
than his normal 'Benjamin',* and his insistence that Wulff should
destroy the letter showed that he regarded it as potentially
incriminating. But Wulff treasured the correspondence too much

---

* He continued to do so over the next few weeks, apart from the occasional lapse
to 'Benjamin', the appellation he used in letters to nearly all his friends and
family. The published letters show that, exceptionally, he signed himself as 'Ben'
when writing to his publisher, Ralph Hawkes, the previous summer: he eventually
did the same in letters to Wulff, but not until June 1939, although Wulff had been
addressing him as 'Ben' since at least the previous September.

to carry out his instruction. 'I must admit that Ben filled my life at that period of time. I concentrated upon him very much. He certainly concentrated on me as well. So the letter-writing was a way of continuing the conversation we had, the being-together that we'd become accustomed to and enjoyed. The mutual attraction – the mutual understanding – was always there.'

Whatever the precise status of their relationship, the boy became attuned to Ben's all-male intellectual environment, which was not unusual in the 1930s and in any event replicated his daily experience at The Perse School. That January, Britten and Pears held a small party in their London flat, just before Auden and Isherwood emigrated to America. Wulff was curious about Isherwood's relationship with his boyfriend, Jackie Hewit, and he quizzed Ben about them beforehand. 'A propos of our telephone conversation', Ben wrote, 'if you really want to know – Jackie means to Christopher a little of what you mean to me – but only a little, mind you!'

The comparison in their relationships is reinforced in the account of the party written by William Coldstream, Britten's erstwhile collaborator at the GPO Film Unit. He numbered among the guests 'Christopher's new boy friend, a German boy friend of Benjamin's, and Hedli Anderson'. It is a rare verbal snapshot of how others regarded Ben and Wulff. When asked how Britten had introduced him to his friends, Scherchen says Ben made no point of explaining who he was: 'He just said "This is Wulff", or "You've heard me talk about Wulff"'. Coldstream drew his own conclusions.

The singer-actress Hedli Anderson had begun the evening on stage at the Trocadero in Piccadilly Circus, leading the chorus line. Wulff was 'entranced' by 'the long-legged beauty who immediately caught my attention' and was thrilled when Ben and Peter invited her back to their flat for the party, where the music continued almost without interruption.

Coldstream's account, which amplifies Scherchen's memories, gives a remarkable insight into the Britten–Auden milieu. Hedli Anderson sat on, rather than at, the piano as she sang some of

Britten's *Cabaret Songs* (written for her to words by Auden), and, to Wulff's delight, the Victorian music hall song *Up in a Balloon, Boys, Up in a Balloon!*. Coldstream added that

> Benjamin played with great gusto. He likes to play all the time without stopping. He likes doing what he does well all the time.

This valuable vignette records in passing that 'a singer who lives with Benjamin* was part host'. Coldstream clearly never caught Pears's name, because he later observed that 'Benjamin's singer friend' sang a new Britten setting (now lost) of a poem by one of the other guests, Stephen Spender: *Not to you I sighed. No, not a word.*

The evening was apparently 'slightly sticky', largely because two straight couples were present, whereas

> Benjamin likes to be with Wystan and Christopher, all boys together without disturbing foreign elements such as slightly hostile ladies or gentlemen hostile to the gay music.

Spender 'took great pains' to sit near Coldstream's wife, and 'occasionally touch her as a guarantee of stable affection when in the camp of the enemy'. But any stickiness seems to have been over Wulff's head. He teased Ben afterwards about his flatmate, unaware of course of how things would turn out in the long run. Indeed, Wulff's thank-you letter makes clear that Pears's presence cast no shadow over his dalliance with Ben.

> I'm beginning to fall in love with Peter in the way one falls in love with a friend and not a sex-maniac like you. I give you full liberty to let him know, and no doubt you'll keep it a dark secret. [. . .]
>
> Tell Peter he's a darling & tell Jackie I hope to see him again soon. 'Tell me the truth about love' & the Spender song have completely obsessed me since I returned.
>
> I love you, darling. Wulff.

---

* This evidently refers to their sharing the Hallam Street flat.

This produced a mock retort from Britten:

> I'm awfully glad, my dear, that you <u>like</u> Peter (refuse to use
> another verb!) – the more you like my friends, the better
> I'm pleased. Certainly there is a limit – but I'm rather sure
> of my ground – hope I'm not too confident!! But, I <u>dislike</u>
> being called a s.-m – even by <u>your</u> fairy lips. See? T'aint
> true – Oim a good boy, Oi am.

He added his own tease:

> I've been working very hard all day – feeling abit down
> now. Wish I had my spouse with me – ha! knew that'd
> make you angry!

Then he turned serious:

> Good-night, my darling – wish 'lost to the world' were
> going to be appropriate to-night & all other nights too [. . .]
> Hope work's going on all right – don't forget that Latin
> Trans. my boy. You've got to pull it off this time –
> otherwise I'll never look at you again – perhaps.
> All my love, my darling. B.

From anyone else, this mixture of the erotic and the paternal
would be disturbing. From Britten, it was entirely natural.

In these early months of 1939, Ben's relationship with Wulff
grew ever more intense, and its written expressions (despite
Britten's sign of nerves in January) ever more fervent. Scherchen
today is anxious to discourage people from leaping to conclusions
about it. As a happily married man with a large family, he still
glows with the memory of a remarkable and beautiful friendship.
'It was all so new, so unaccustomed, so exciting – everything that
was happening to me – and in the midst of it all, holding it all
together, was this lovable person. Ah, thank heavens I didn't miss
it! I was naïve, of course. This was my first experience of a close
relationship with somebody other than a member of the family.
It was overwhelming. Yes, I was seduced. On Ben's part, it may
have been intentional, but I let myself be seduced quite happily.'

Many of Britten's close friends, adult and boy, say he was not physically demonstrative. Scherchen's memory is different. 'Oh yes, hugs and kisses – any time! The hugs, of course, were easy to accept, but kisses', he adds defensively, 'were more difficult. It was pleasant enough, but this isn't quite what boys do!'

Whatever feelings he had for Ben (and, at the age of eighteen, they may well have been confused), Ben's for Wulff were not in doubt. His letters to Wulff became increasingly incautious, almost reckless. They were certainly more ardent than any others from his pen, save only his later *lettres du coeur* to Pears himself. On one occasion in late January his plans to visit Wulff in Cambridge were thwarted by bad weather, and the depth of his frustration and disappointment could be sensed in the abnormal incoherence of his prose. He makes it sound a truly Schubertian winter's journey, with himself as romantic hero pitted against every obstacle to reach, or rescue, his beloved.

> My darling Wulff,
> It was no good – we tried, & tried & tried. Every road was blocked with rushing torrents of water & it was quite terrifying – cars were getting stuck – our brakes wouldn't function (the drums got wet) – & then we got abit lost in the 'tiger' country of Suffolk. However, we wandered for more than two hours, to no purpose. [. . .] It was then too late for me to come to you [. . .]. I was so disappointed that I couldn't come yesterday – seemed as if the Fates were trying to keep us apart – <u>let</u> them go on <u>trying</u> – they are powerless about us! [. . .]
> I love you <u>v.v.v</u>. much.
> Benjamin.

In his reply, Wulff signed off with uncanny perception: 'Your eternal pursuer (or pursued?) Wulff'.

Amid the torrent of letters and visits, it is easy to forget that Wulff was still subject to the normal term-time routine. But it kept his taste for schoolboy humour alive, which doubtless amused Ben. In February, with his tongue in his cheek, he asked Ben whether Hedli Anderson had moved into the London flat.

> Beware! better to have a wolf at the door than hedli quite madli in bedli not wedli undressedli. So what? Satisfied with the medli? mind, it's deadli.

The letter came with the now inevitable new poem, entitled 'the barrier (*l'histoire d'un rêve*)', in which he described himself spurning his lover's advances, and apparently enjoying the effect of his denial.* It is signed 'c.d.r.' – initials Wulff said he was using to 'hush himself up'.† He also proposed substituting Ben's initials with the final letters of his names, so that B.B. would become N.N. 'just to hush up to whom all my bloody poherms are to'.

Ben was still visiting Wulff at his mother's house in Cambridge when he could.

> It'll be heaven to have you for a few days. May I stay till the Monday? I was so sorry to hear that you've not been sleeping. I hope it's better now – you know what the cure for that is..!!!

But there were signs in March that Wulff's mother was getting concerned, and, rather like Tadzio's mother in *Death in Venice*, she sought to interpose herself between her son and his pursuer.

Wulff was clearly feeling her constant presence a constraint. In mid-March, when Ben was contemplating yet another visit to Cambridge, Wulff sent him a signal that the coast might for once be clear.

> If you're coming next week, here's a tip! Mother may be going to Southampton, Wednesday night, Thursday. [. . .] I'd prefer it anyhow if you came on W & Th. [. . .]

---

* Ben wrote back: 'Barrier is a grand <u>Idea</u>.'
† These initials represented 'Cedar', an anagram of Radec, who had been a senior figure in the German Communist Party, as well as a friend of Scherchen's parents. Scherchen today cannot recall why he chose this particular *alias*.

Whether Gustel went to Southampton or not is not recorded. But the same letter reveals a direct maternal intervention. Ben had invited Wulff to stay with him over Easter in early April. '*Am* I looking forward to it?' Ben had written. 'With the new car* & all. We shall have to be in London about four days & after that here [the Old Mill] or somewhere.' But Wulff explained apologetically that, after he had told his mother about the plan, she had 'sprung the gladdening surprise' that instead she was taking him to Bognor Regis for Easter, and the arrangements could not be altered because the hotel rooms had been booked and paid for. She suggested that Britten could visit them in Bognor if he wished.

Britten took it like a man. He resourcefully discovered that he would probably be spending Easter in Sussex, and 'might drive over & see you – or you might be spared for one night to come & see me!' But Wulff was not spared, so Ben did indeed drive to Bognor for lunch on the Wednesday after Easter, 12th April 1939.

Their friendship was now nine months old. More than eighty contacts between them can be traced during that time, in terms of visits, meetings, letters and telephone calls – and there were doubtless more that were never recorded.† But the relationship was reaching a crossroads – even a crisis. That came shortly after Easter, when Britten announced he was travelling almost at once to North America with Peter Pears. Because they ended up staying there for three years, it was later (and for a long time) seen as a hasty decision to emigrate, of which he repented at leisure. But his letters suggest that, at the start, it was a short-term measure: Pears expected to return at the end of the summer, while Britten's plans were less precise. He wanted to

---

* Lennox Berkeley had given Britten the use of his AC sports car.
† One such was at the Old Mill one weekend in late March or April 1939. It is notable for a few feet of ciné film, taken on Trevor Harvey's camera, which show Ben and Wulff together – Ben driving the AC sports car (which he and Lennox Berkeley had driven down to Snape together for the first time on 11th March) and Wulff walking behind.

explore a possible Hollywood commission, and he felt disgruntled with the BBC and the British musical establishment, so a change of air was required. But, like Pears, he booked a return ticket.

The decision to cross the Atlantic came to besmirch both their names: they were believed to have run away from the threat of war in Europe. Years later, Pears gave this credence by suggesting they had wanted to avoid spending a long time in prison as conscientious objectors ('which didn't terribly appeal'). Britten may have been happy to let that canard run rather than reveal the more problematic reason: his relationship with Wulff had become too hot to handle. He did not have the heart (or the will) to break the bond where he stood. He could do it only by bodily removing himself from the scene.

He told one friend: 'I got heavily tied up in a certain direction, which is partly why I'm crossing the ocean!' Another, Enid Slater, who had taken the photographs of Wulff and acted as an occasional go-between, said many years later that 'one relationship' had become difficult before Britten went to America. 'I used to go and try and sort things out a bit', which she did on several occasions in the months to come.

Britten confided in Wulff about most things – even the approach from Hollywood, which he kept secret from many people. But he could not bring himself even to hint about going away, although he and Pears had taken the decision by mid-March – three weeks before Easter. For Wulff it was a blow in the solar plexus. He first heard about it when he visited Ben in London in mid-April, and found himself at what turned out to be one of the Britten–Pears farewell parties. So upset was he that Ben had to abandon the party and take him by taxi to the station, to make sure he got on the train to Cambridge. 'It came as a bombshell. At the party I was in tears – but that was chiefly because I'd had too much gin, and that's how the gin affected me! I sat in the corner by myself, slobbering away, and Ben took pity on me and said, "Get this kid out of here" '. Wulff was still crying when they got to Liverpool Street: 'I didn't know how I was going to cope with suddenly losing this intense relationship that had gone on for the best part of a year by then'. Even today he can't really explain why Britten left, because, he says, he never understood it himself at the time. 'He never said anything that satisfied me or that really explained why they were going, except I definitely got the impression that it was just a temporary measure. He was not emigrating.' When I suggested that the main reason was that their relationship had become too complicated, Scherchen replied: 'That really hadn't occurred to me before. It's part of it, perhaps'.

Pears may well have influenced Britten's decision. Scherchen today is generous about him, his kindness and consideration. But, in spring 1939, Wulff was in Peter's way. It was two years since he had met Ben in the aftermath of the death of Pears's close friend, Peter Burra, in an air accident. They had performed together frequently, they shared a flat in London, they were now firm friends – and Pears seemed to be falling in love with Britten. The problem for Peter – as it was for Lennox Berkeley – was that Ben had eyes only for Wulff. Financially, for a young and still inexperienced singer, a transatlantic move was a leap in the dark. But, on the emotional front, it was too good a chance to miss. Away from Wulff, away from London, away from Snape, Peter could perhaps win Ben round.

Scherchen says today that, at about this time, he had a problem of his own. He remembers an occasion when Ben had arranged to meet him in a bar in London. He says he arrived first: while waiting for Ben, he became aware that it was a haunt for homosexuals and became uncomfortable. It was then, he says, that he realised Ben wanted more from their relationship than he was prepared to give, and told him so. He believes this happened early in 1939, but there is no cooling-off in the correspondence to match – quite the reverse. After experiencing the world of Isherwood, Auden, Berkeley and Britten, let alone participating in the intimate correspondence with Ben, it is hard to believe there was much scope for Wulff to be shocked by a homosexual environment, but he was still eighteen and, by his own admission, naïve. As an impressionable youth, he was dazzled to be part of this milieu. 'I wanted it never to end', Scherchen says. 'So I didn't try to finish the relationship between us – that was the last thing I wanted to do.' But he says they did discuss it frankly: he told Ben he could not give him the commitment he was seeking, and Ben was 'very upset', but they reached an understanding.

Whatever the actual catalyst, it is clear that by the time Britten went abroad, he and Wulff had indeed made new resolutions. They would (*force majeure*) give each other up, but without rancour, without recriminations, and they would remain friends. Significantly, Scherchen says Pears brokered the deal. If that was the case, he was no doubt happy to do so.

One of the last contacts with Wulff before Britten left England had a sour note. On 21st April, the BBC broadcast an orchestral concert from Birmingham, which consisted entirely of Britten's music – including two brand-new settings of poems by Arthur Rimbaud which would later form part of his orchestral song-cycle, *Les Illuminations*. Britten had the nerve to presume the wounded Wulff would be loyal enough to be listening. He was not, as Britten discovered during a telephone call the next day. He erupted in fury and, as soon as he had put down the receiver, wrote to him with no more than a veneer of contrition.

Wulff darling –
I'm sorry I was such a pig on the 'phone tonight but I felt so damn sick that you hadn't taken the trouble to listen to my concert. You see – the first <u>complete</u> concert of one's music is a pretty good trial – & the fact that it was a great success makes one rather bucked – BUT the fact that you didn't hear it – especially as I was thinking about you so much during it (especially in the new Rimbaud songs) – is very gruelling. However one looks at it it is beastly. But I was writing this just to comfort you, but it doesn't seem to do it – perhaps it is a good thing I'm going away. Blast it. – Anyhow Lennox will have listened.

Goodbye my dear, Love to Gustel.

P.S. I do love you. P.T.O.

Sorry I've not got a 1d stamp – so you'll have to pay 2d for the doubtful pleasure of receiving this.

In this final thrust from Ben, which he did not even sign, his throwaway reference to Lennox Berkeley (at least he could count on the loyalty of *that* jilted lover), can only have been intended to hurt Wulff further. To cap it all, he made the schoolboy pay the postage. On 29th April he set sail for North America, while Wulff went back to school for the summer term and his Higher Certificate exams. Gustel Scherchen presumably breathed a sigh of relief. And Peter Pears turned the page to a new chapter.

CHAPTER 7

So young Apollo anguish'd

The partnership for almost forty years between Britten and Pears has become so legendary that it is hard to turn the clock back and imagine them before it began. But when they set off across the Atlantic in 1939, they were not a couple. One of Pears's former flatmates, Basil Douglas, knew they were both homosexual, but never thought of them as a pair. The freedom with which Britten discussed with Pears the ongoing emotional problems with Lennox Berkeley suggests he viewed Pears as a close confidant rather than as a rival for his affections. He wrote to Pears at this stage as 'my dear Pete' and signed off, 'much love, Benjamin' – run-of-the-mill greetings compared with those for Wulff. Wulff himself had never thought of them as potential lovers: 'It just seemed a perfectly normal working relationship. They were sharing this apartment, they were working together, it was a most convenient arrangement – they didn't have to go off to a studio to rehearse. Beyond that I didn't find it necessary to look. And neither Peter nor Ben ever gave me any need to look any further.'

The first thing that Britten did after leaving Southampton Water aboard the Cunard White Star liner SS *Ausonia* was to put Wulff's photograph (one of Enid Slater's portraits, presumably) on his cabin table. 'He carried me with him to the States', is how Scherchen puts it today. It was not a good omen for the success of Ben's resolve. The cabin steward was both nosey and rather perceptive: he was so struck by the photograph that he quizzed Britten about him. 'Is that your brother?', he asked disingenuously, adding (by way of excuse for his inquisitiveness): 'You're so alike!' This pleased Britten, even though it was manifestly untrue, and he proudly reported the exchange to the newly renounced Wulff, as he brooded on the transatlantic journey. This letter* was the first he wrote, ahead of any to his sisters, his publisher, or his housemate at Snape. He bemoaned the boredom of the ten-day voyage, prolonged because of icebergs and fog: 'eat, sleep, ping-pong, eat, walk decks, eat, eat, deck-tennis, eat, read, sleep – etc. ad infinitum'. But he did not tell Wulff what he confessed to Berkeley: 'as usual a small boy has attached himself – a nice kid of 14, but inclined to cling rather. But they're nice animals!!'

Before leaving England, he had asked Enid Slater to keep an eye on Wulff. Even as he was catching the boat train at Waterloo Station, he had urged his friend Trevor Harvey, who had met Wulff at Snape a month or so before, to 'let me have news of Wulff from you & do see something of him'.† During the voyage itself, as his letter makes clear, 'my darling Wulff' was still uppermost in his mind.

> What a fool one is to come away – the more I think of
> Snape & the visits to Cambridge & yours to Snape – the
> more I feel a fool to have left it all. [. . .] Goodnight
> darling – how I wish you were here.

There is one critical sentence in this letter which supports Scherchen's contention that he had told Britten he could not give him his total commitment. But Ben was already nursing a hope that their relationship was suspended rather than broken.

> I miss you pretty acutely, darling; it is a terrifying thought
> that I shan't see you for such ages. But I'm sure it's a good
> thing – *you will know your mind completely when I come*

---

* Ben's letter to Wulff took the form of a travel diary, rather as he was to write to several other young friends: to Roger Duncan sixteen years later, during his round-the-world trip (see pages 221–2); to John Newton in 1965 during his visit to India (see pages 272–3), and to Ronan Magill in 1970 while visiting Australia (see page 279).

† Harvey did indeed invite Scherchen 'to come & see him sometimes & help him over the hard and dreary times of Whitsun (bed being provided & even separate bedroom)', as Wulff facetiously reported to Ben on 19th May.

back [author's italics] – being a well-brought-up creature I
shall doubtless fall in with it. I adore the photos.

This suggests that Wulff had voiced his reservations very recently, possibly only days before Ben's departure. But Ben had
passed the initiative in their affair to Wulff, by saying he would
'fall in with' whatever he decided. It suggests that, in his heart,
Ben was committed to a full partnership, even if his head was
telling him to draw back, to give himself some breathing-space.
In the middle of the ocean, he was clearly not at all ready for
anyone else to displace the 'adored photos' from the frame on
his cabin-table.

Very soon, as Pears must have realised with some despond-
ency, absence was making Britten's heart grow fonder. A week
after arriving in Canada, he was already looking forward to his
return to England. He told Wulff he was planning to stay there
a month or so before going to New York to visit Auden and
Isherwood. 'We may spend the rest of the time in the States',
he wrote, making clear the trip was finite in his own mind.

> Much love, my darling, it's still horrible being away from
> you – & I'm looking forward terribly to seeing you again –
> it won't be long – luckily time goes very fast.

A week later, at a country hotel at 'a heavenly spot' in the hills
outside Montreal, Wulff's photograph was still on display.

> I'm thinking of you more than I would care to admit – the
> old physiognomy stares at me from my dressing table all
> the time!

He went on to draw a revealing distinction between his relationships with Peter and with Wulff:

> Peter is also working hard & getting much better at the old
> voice. We usually work it that when he wants to make
> noises I go out for a walk & he walks when I want to work
> – & so far it works well & we haven't fought at all. If it
> had been you, my dear, we should probably have scratched

each other's eyes & pulled each other's hair all out – but all
the same – well, you know what I feel about it!

There is a chance that we may go down to Mexico. But
no definite plans yet after the month we expect to stay here.
But for God's sake, my darling, do write. There – there's a
cri de coeur for you! [. . .]

And all my love, my darling, je t'aime trop! B.

But at first there was no word from Wulff. He was keeping
his distance, nursing his wounds and revising for his exams.
When he did get round to writing a letter, he forgot to post it.
At the time of Ben's departure from England, the Scherchens
had invited Lennox Berkeley to lunch in Cambridge: perhaps
one of Ben's friends would help ease the pain. But of course
Berkeley was upset as well, as he told Britten:

I longed to talk to Wulff about you and about how I was
feeling, but we were both too shy – and perhaps too proud,
anyhow we were rather hearty.

Stirred by the warmth of two letters from Ben, Wulff finally
posted him a letter a month after his departure, on his own
birthday, and then he sent three at once. He had clearly been
depressed, yet he had begun to mature emotionally.

I have lost something very important to me with your
departure. I seem somehow shut off from the rest of the
world, however pleasant the people in it may be. The
complete and sincere understanding that existed between us
seems to have disappeared, and with it the full appreciation
of life I had while with you. Life seems so silly, ridiculous,
empty, not worth while nowadays. But please do not
deduce from this that my views on life have suddenly
turned pessimistic and that I am merely sitting here,
moping. That would not be at all true, for I am leading a
fairly happy life in many ways. Yet somehow everything
seems emptier, appears to have lost its proper value, and my
outlook on things is different. You mean so much to me in

the many minute, small, and at first sight, unimportant ways. That's why not to speak to you, nor to see you anymore, becomes so difficult. You see, for all my resolutions I have not given you up.

Wulff's eagerness to resume contact led him to send this letter by the new transatlantic airmail service, even though he had little money. He ended it a touch forlorn:

I hope you aren't sending me anything for my birthday. [. . .] You know how I feel about you, and because of that, presents make no difference. I shall not love you any more because you give me presents, because I love you so much already. In fact, and to clinch the matter, I think presents are wholly unnecessary. But all the same I hope you've sent me one.

This letter touched Ben. He wrote to Enid Slater in early June, asking her to visit him: 'I've just had a very sweet letter – & nearly broken all my resolutions!' He replied to Wulff with an apology for the lack of a present:

Since I got your letter I've been travelling all the time [. . .] so I haven't been able to consider your birthday present – but I will. To think of you 19! God – you don't seem it to me but in some ways – I can't believe that there's six years in between us!'*

But, if Ben had missed his birthday, he was missing Wulff more. In the same letter, written on 9th June in Toronto, his self-denial was clearly breaking down:

* The last two sentences are instructive. At first, Ben seems to balk at the idea that his friend is as old as nineteen: he still thinks of him as younger. Perhaps the 1934 image of the thirteen-year-old is still in his mind. Then he seems to contradict himself by saying that he thinks Wulff is older than nineteen: 'I can't believe that there's six years in between us!' But maybe Ben is reflecting more on his own advancing years. He had been miserable about reaching the age of twenty-five the previous autumn, and we know from Imogen Holst's diary in February 1953 that he always thought of himself as thirteen. So perhaps that was the age at which both he and Wulff were stuck in his own mind.

It is awful how much you mean to me – I had terrific
resolutions when I left – & I renew these resolutions every
day (you know what these resolutions are!) – but I simply
can't help thinking of you & what you're doing, & I can't
bear it if your photo isn't grinning at me from the
mantelpiece! I love you more everyday – & seeing all these
people (& some very nice & attractive) can't put you out of
my head. So there! There's a declaration.

Yet it was precisely at this point – during the same brief visit to
Toronto – that Britten's friendship with Peter Pears became more
intimate. A few days later, they became lovers for the first time,
while staying in Grand Rapids, Michigan. For Pears at least, it
was a seminal moment which he frequently recalled later in
life.* He certainly seemed sufficiently sure of his position just
beforehand to write this peculiar note to Wulff:

Dear Wulffchen – How are you?
I am looking after Ben as well as he deserves, and am trying
hard to keep him from breaking out, but the Canadian girls
are terribly attractive!

It sounds both hearty and heartless – Pears must indeed have
found Wulff's ubiquitous portrait dispiriting. But perhaps Ben
had not confided in him in any detail about Wulff: despite the
resolutions, the pain of separation may have been still too raw.

Wulff himself was unaware of any change in Ben's relation-
ship with Peter. Ben gave him no clue. He preferred to tell Wulff:
'I still feel very much the same about you', before adding that
'Peter is being very nice & we're getting on well'. It was the
Ben–Wulff relationship that appeared to be picking up steam.
'Just got your letter', Wulff wrote in response to Ben's letter from
Toronto. 'Why did you ever have to go away, can't you see how
much I need you?? [. . .] All my love, Darling. My resolutions
seem to have crashed too.'

* The milestones in the evolving Britten–Pears relationship are discussed by
Donald Mitchell in *Letters from a Life*, Volume I, pp.20–23.

'Talk about resolutions!', Ben replied, adding that he always carried Wulff's poem 'A Madrigal' in his pocket. It was more than six months since that poem had been sparked by their New Year together in Snape, and a month since his sexual relationship with Pears had begun. But he kept on writing to his 'darling Wulff'.

> I feel worse & worse about being away from you – & think of you more than I'd care to admit. [. . .]
> I still feel very much the same about you. [. . .]
> I was delighted to get your letters. I had supposed that the '<u>resolution</u>' had come into force, & that you had crossed me off your life, so to speak [. . .] But I do miss you [. . .]
> You can't imagine how I want to see you.

It cannot have helped Ben when Auden told him that he was 'mad with happiness' because of his affair (the start of a lifelong partnership) with an eighteen-year-old New Yorker, Chester Kallman. Despite the zig-zag nature of a transatlantic correspondence with its unpredictable delays (or perhaps because of it), Ben and his one-time eighteen-year-old were recovering their intimacy. At the same time he was mentally extending his stay in North America. In mid-June, he told Wulff that Canada '<u>may</u> be the Country'. Three weeks later he implied that Pears would be returning to England in the autumn, while stressing that he himself had no such plans. This suggested that at that stage he did not see his relationship with Pears as permanent. He wanted to be in New York for some of the winter. 'Unless anything drastic occurs I may stay [in North America] till Xmas or even longer.' In September something drastic did occur, but with the opposite effect. After Hitler's invasion of Poland, Britten and Pears asked about returning home, but the British authorities advised them to stay where they were.

The start of the Second World War gave Ben's absorption with Wulff a fresh legitimacy. He became worried about how he and his mother were faring as German exiles in England. Wulff had taken his Higher Certificate exams at the end of July, just before leaving The Perse School, and had spent the first ten days of August at an air cadets' CCF camp near Selsey on the Sussex coast. He wrote to Ben four times in ten days – remarkably prolific for this erratic correspondent – and then again just before the outbreak of war. He reassured him that he and his mother had been 'all right so far', and were 'feeling calm and as confident as we can in the circumstances. [. . .] I merely wonder why Germany should have started the war, it seems so senseless.' Britten responded that his heart was set on getting them both out to America. 'I think of you <u>ever</u> so much', he wrote, making clear that Wulff's photograph still had pride of place at his new base in Amityville, on Long Island.

> The old photo looks good on the mantelpiece here – I think it's a grand one (I mean the one Enid took!) – but it makes me horribly home- & Wulff-sick!!

The letter ends: 'you know what I feel & always shall about you', its ardour apparently quickened by the onset of war. Pears is mentioned only in the postscript: 'Peter sends his love, & says he's looking after me – as he certainly is – like a mother hen! He's a darling – .' By damning Pears with faint affection, Ben again deliberately concealed from Wulff (and maybe from himself) that his fond friendship with Pears had been for some months in at least a higher gear. 'Of course I didn't know about it', says Scherchen. 'Nobody wrote to me from the States and said "Do you know what those two have got up to?" There was nothing that came across to suggest that there'd been any special development in their relationship.'

But the idea that something dramatic had changed in Grand Rapids has emerged only with hindsight, and only at the suggestion of Pears. He fostered the notion that their lovemaking that night sealed their relationship for the next thirty-seven years. But at the time, in Britten's mind, the night may have been more an experiment than a consummation of marriage, and his longing for Wulff throughout this period seems to confirm this.

That autumn there was no answer from Wulff. Britten's anxiety was alleviated by news from the faithful Enid Slater that she had seen the Scherchens in early October. She avoided drawing the censor's attention to potential enemy aliens (let alone to the delicacy of this particular relationship) by reporting that she had visited 'Cambridge', and referring to Wulff and Gustel as just 'he' and 'she'.

> I had been a little worried about them, as things might have been – & still might be – difficult.

But she had found Wulff busy making tongue-and-groove black-out frames for the windows, and rather pleased with his carpentry skills* – although he grumbled about not hearing from Ben. He could not find a job to augment the meagre family allowance from his father, and his mother was worried that, with nothing to do all day, he was getting depressed. But, Slater said, 'there's no need to worry yet'.

Britten was cheered to feel there was no rupture, although puzzled that none of his letters was getting through. He claimed to have written 'once or twice, at least, every week by airmail'. This letter to Slater in early November was phrased as elliptically as hers had been:

> Thank you more than I can say for going to Cambridge, it was the first news I'd got since the beginning of the war.

Then he made the telling confession:

> I'm afraid a lot of resolutions have gone up in thin air, especially, funnily enough, since the war.

He went on to say that, as far as 'other problems' were concerned (his dogged pursuit by Lennox Berkeley), his mind was firmly made up to reject him – thereby making clear that Wulff was still very much on his radar.

---

* News of his prowess must have spread, because at the end of October Boris Ord (Organist at King's College, Cambridge) asked him to build similar screens for the difficult semi-circular window of his music room – for a fee.

A month later, still without any direct word from Wulff, he could no longer restrain himself. To compel a response, he splashed out on a reply-paid telegram to the Scherchen household. The word 'desolate' related more to Wulff, presumably, than to Gustel:

DESOLATE THAT NO NEWS FROM YOU BOTH PLEASE CABLE DETAILS ALWAYS THINKING OF YOU LOVE BENJAMIN BRITTEN.

The answer came back within hours:

EVERYTHING WELL WROTE TUESDAY LOVE WULFF SCHERCHEN.

Britten was so relieved that he sat down the same day (8th December) to write him four dense pages of foolscap:

My darling Wulff,
So at last I've got some news of you! And it took some doing – 4 dollars on a reply-paid cable! But it was worth it – do you realise that it is three <u>clear</u> months since I heard anything of you at all. I admit I was getting pretty frantic. I can scarcely contain myself until your letter arrives [. . .]
I hoped that you wouldn't be molested by any stupid warmongering English patriots. I was abit scared that you might feel terribly sad about everything & go & do something crazy.

He mentioned that Auden had been visiting Amityville when the cable arrived, and 'was terribly glad for my sake', which gives a clue to Britten's excitable state of mind.

The screed of news about his experiences in New York, his family at home, troubles at the Mill with Berkeley and at Pears's London flat (their lodger, Jackie Hewit – Isherwood's feckless boyfriend – had defaulted, and robbed the gas meters) must have taken a good hour to write. It was a letter which bore out what he had told Enid Slater. The resolutions had indeed evaporated. 'With all my heart I want to see you again', he told Wulff. 'All my love, Dein – Benjamin.'

The intimacy was not confined to the letters. It also appeared in his music. In 1938 he had imagined his score for *On the Frontier* as being for Wulff in a rather unspecific way. In North America, Britten embarked on two projects that were much more pointed.

Soon after arriving in Canada, he was commissioned to write a work for piano and strings by the Canadian Broadcasting Corporation. It took him just a week in late July. It is a glittering piece, unlike anything else in Britten's output, and he was rather satisfied with it. The day he completed it, he wrote to Enid Slater:

> It is very bright & brilliant music – rather inspired by such sunshine as I've never seen before. But I'm pleased with it – may call it 'The Young Apollo', if that doesn't sound too lush! But it is lush!

The score of *Young Apollo* bears some unfinished lines from Keats at its head:

> Soon wild commotions shook him, and made flush
> All the immortal fairness of his limbs;
>   [. . .] so young Apollo anguish'd:
> His very hair, his golden tresses famed
> Kept undulation round his eager neck.
>   [. . .] At length
> Apollo shriek'd; – and lo! from all his limbs
> Celestial

Britten's programme note for the piece explained how Apollo, called to be the new god of beauty, 'foresees his destiny; and in one final convulsion throws off his mortal form. He stands before us – the new, dazzling Sun-god, quivering with radiant vitality.'

It no doubt helped to have Enid Slater's portrait of Wulff smiling at him as he worked. In a letter to Wulff, he left no doubt about the identity of his muse and the object of his yearning:

I am playing my 'Young Apollo' [. . .] – you know whom that's written about – founded on the last lines of Keats' Hyperion – my God, don't I <u>long</u> to see you again.

Enid Slater certainly made the connection. No sooner had she received Britten's letter about *Young Apollo* than she drove to Cambridge to see Wulff. It was hard for her to discover how Wulff was coping in Ben's absence, because his mother was always in the room. But everything else in her report could only have gilded the image in Britten's vision.

Wulff was beautifully brown & very well. [. . .] What a beautiful creature he is. I was struck again, only more so – he has somehow got more formed with his face – I wish someone good would do a bronze head of him, he is rather <u>unusually</u> lovely don't you think?

For Ben, the question was entirely rhetorical.

When Lennox Berkeley heard about the new piece, he knew exactly what (or, rather, who) was in his friend's mind.

I'm afraid I did laugh a bit over the title, but I admire your nerve in choosing it; it may give rise to a certain amount of ribald comment, but the music itself is the only thing that matters, and I'm sure that it's good.

Scherchen professes bewilderment then and now about the idea that he inspired *Young Apollo*. 'You wonder to yourself: "How does he see me? And why does he see me like that?" '

The 'unusually lovely' Wulff was not the sole inspiration for *Young Apollo*. Surprising as it seems, the seventeenth-century composer Dietrich Buxtehude may have been too. Britten had bumped into him that summer. 'He is absolutely astounding', he told Berkeley.

Since my discovery of Mahler I haven't been so excited over anything. I think he's so much better than Bach!!! He has a wonderful harmonic sense & a most extraordinary tonal feeling – he writes often in one key with no modulations for a whole piece, & the result is eminently successful. And his figuration is wonderfully inspired.*

To write a whole piece without any changes of key was just the sort of game which interested Britten,† and in the ten minutes of *Young Apollo* he never modulates away from A major. It is his *Death in Venice* key for youth and beauty, and there is certainly an almost visceral aural depiction of youthful perfection: whether it gave rise to the 'ribald comment' that Berkeley had forecast is not recorded – but then Berkeley had, as we now have, privileged information. Britten himself called the piece 'very Romantic': the piano solo is a torrent of scales, the epitome of childhood, and yet in combination with the string quartet and string orchestra the innocence teeters on the brink of sensuality. There is a compelling physical energy in the piano part, while the intervening string chords suggest the straining of sweaty sinews in the heat and sunlight. The lines of Keats are vividly realised in the music. The simple material is spaced in such a way that it creates what the composer Robert Saxton terms a 'halo-like resonance'. Its hypnotic repetition and its static nature have led some to call it the first piece of minimalist music.

Young Apollo was Britten's first commission, and his first completed concert work, since crossing the ocean. Musically it broke new ground, but he was undoubtedly looking over his shoulder at what he had left behind. It was not the only

---

* This letter must have been written on 8th September 1939 (not, as *Letters from a Life* suggests, on 1st January 1940). It was sent via Britten's sister Barbara, and written on the same ruffle-edged paper as he used for a letter to her. Berkeley replied, in a somewhat superior tone, on 24th September: 'I've got a book of organ pieces by Buxtehude and I like some of them immensely [. . .] I had never thought of comparing him with Bach, it's so utterly different.' Auden suggests in his *New Year Letter* that, on one of his visits to Amityville (as it happens, on 1st September, the day Poland was invaded), he and Britten had been playing Buxtehude.

† A decade later, during a discussion of the relative merits of Mozart and Haydn, Britten told Humphrey Maud that 'Mozart's greatness often lay in when he actually *didn't* change key, he didn't modulate'.

piece that Wulff motivated. Indeed July 1939 was quite a Wulff month. One of the Rimbaud poems Britten set in *Les Illuminations* is dedicated to 'K.H.W.S.' – his initials. 'Antique' was written just before *Young Apollo*, and in the same way the music harnesses a childlike simplicity to a sensuality which matches Rimbaud's words:*

> Graceful son of Pan!
> Around your brow crowned with flowerets and berries
> your eyes – precious globes – move slowly.
> Your fangs gleam,
> Your breast resembles a cithern, tinglings circulate in your
>   golden arms.
> Your heart beats in that belly where the double sex lies
>   dormant.
> Walk forth, by night, gently moving this thigh, that other
>   thigh and that left leg.

The dedication of this setting to Wulff is apparently offset by that of another song in the cycle to Pears: 'Being Beauteous' is headed, 'to P.N.L.P.' (Pears's initials). But in fact this movement had been composed some months earlier, in England, without any dedication at all, whereas Britten assigned 'Antique' to Wulff as he was writing it. Only at that point did he think of adding the Pears dedication. Perhaps he felt he owed Peter parity, at least. We also have it on Britten's own authority that when 'Being Beauteous' was first sung in Birmingham by the soprano Sophie Wyss, it was Wulff, not Peter, of whom Ben was thinking 'so much'. That was why he was so annoyed that Wulff had not been listening.

After the first complete performance of *Les Illuminations* in London, the conductor Trevor Harvey, who had met Wulff at Snape and had shared a flat with Pears, asked Britten in a

---

* Although 'Antique' is undated, the full score makes clear that *Les Illuminations* had an interim stage, when it consisted of four movements: 'Royauté', 'Antique', 'Being Beauteous' and 'Marine'. This suggests that 'Antique' was written shortly before or after 'Royauté', which is dated 'July 6th 1939'.

letter: 'Who, by the way, is K.H.W.S.? Wulff? Gracieux fils de Pan, indeed.' The wink and nudge are palpable – but not in the reference to Pears which follows: 'But Peter P being beauteous is a pleasant thought'. Harvey clearly reckoned Ben's real interest was still in Wulff. He had no idea that Pears and Britten were now lovers, and had not picked up any clue from the music.*

To complicate matters still further, the *Seven Sonnets of Michelangelo*, which date from 1940, were the first songs he wrote specifically for Pears, and the homoerotic nature of Michelangelo's poetry has been taken as an expression of the composer's love for his new partner. But one of Wulff Scherchen's most vivid memories is of Britten wrestling with Michelangelo's poetry two years earlier, during one of their weekends together at the Old Mill. 'He was trying to set the words of a sonnet, and he got completely stuck. I think for a start he was unable to render the Italian into English for his own purposes to get the real feeling of what was being said, and then inspiration didn't so much run out, it's just that he couldn't express what he wanted to say. He was really concerned – he was still full of it, and he just had to tell somebody – "I'm going to put this away, I'm going to forget about it". He'd come to a dead stop.' So perhaps it was Wulff who struck the original spark, even if it was Peter who kindled the flame.

Young Apollo was well received when Britten gave the first performance on Canadian radio in August 1939, exactly a week before war broke out. He told his sister Beth, 'It went well – but I wasn't feeling so happy about things that I could enjoy it as much as normally'. He was hoping for a performance in Britain. His London publisher Ralph Hawkes was enthusiastic. Initially the war brought nearly all public entertainments to a stop, so Britten told Hawkes in October he doubted England would 'have the privilege of hearing that masterpiece' until

---

* When Britten played a single movement to illustrate *Les Illuminations* in a BBC radio interview with Joseph Cooper in 1957, he chose 'Antique'.

concerts resumed. The erratic transatlantic mail in wartime meant that the score and orchestral parts did not in any case reach London until November. But that month Britten told Enid Slater (who had sent him a good luck cable for the Toronto broadcast): 'The performance went well, & I like the little thing'. So there was no sign of second thoughts.

Britten acknowledged it as an important work by giving it an opus number (16). He played it a second time at the end of December, for CBS in New York. It was carried by most of the radio stations on the Mutual Broadcasting System in the United States. Hawkes was impressed that Britten had achieved two networked performances, and thought the BBC were 'bound to do it soon'. But the British performance never materialised, perhaps the victim of an irrational but pervasive view that Britten's American works were 'unpatriotic'. Indeed, *Young Apollo* was never heard again during his lifetime. Britten suddenly withdrew the work and forbade its performance, though fortunately he did not (as other composers might have done) destroy the manuscript. It was hidden away, and opus 16 became a blank in the Britten catalogue. It had to wait almost forty years for its third performance, after his death.* Only then was it published. 'Fled was that music' indeed.

Britten never explained why he abandoned *Young Apollo* – he never spoke of it again. Although commentators presumed that he had been dissatisfied with it musically, there was no evidence of that at the time, and its unique treatment suggests there was a more personal motive. In April he had forsworn Wulff, in June he had given himself to Peter Pears, yet in July he still had Wulff's intimate poem in his breast pocket, in September he was still – by his own admission – 'Wulff-sick', and staring at his photograph on the mantelpiece. As if that were not enough, his almost ecstatic four-page letter to Wulff of 8th December wound up with a fusillade of affection and memories of their 'fateful' first meeting in Tuscany in 1934. In his

* Aldeburgh Festival, 21st June 1979.

Wulff-sickness, he saw the young man of nineteen as once again a thirteen-year-old boy.

> With all my heart I want to see you again – <u>where</u> is that photo of you (aged 13) I wanted so badly. I've just remembered – the Mayers [his hosts on Long Island] have a photo of that loge [*sic*] where you & I sheltered from the rain that fateful day in Sienna [*sic*]! It's called the Chiesa of S. Domenico or something. It brought back terrific memories!

He went on to relate that he had recently met one of the other veterans of that Tuscan idyll, the saxophonist Sigurd Rascher:

> We had a grand pow-wow – you remember him?* The Saxophonist with the Red Hair? [. . .] O – what memories – what heaven it all was when things were (more or less) peaceful.

Before signing off 'Dein – Benjamin', he wrote: '<u>Everso</u> much love, my darling', and then, as a perhaps guilty afterthought, 'Peter sends love also'. (Many years later, Britten used the same formulations when writing to Pears: he spoke of suffering from 'Petersickness' and signed himself 'Dein B.')

The letter Wulff had promised in his telegram finally reached Britten in the middle of December, with news of his existence since the start of the war. For some weeks he had been banned from travelling more than five miles from home, but the restriction had been lifted once he was deemed a 'friendly alien'. After gaining his Higher Certificate in German, French and English, he had joined Queen Mary College (which had been evacuated from London to Cambridge) to study (of all things) engineering. No wonder he claimed to have been 'shoved in' by his mother.

---

* Wulff had mentioned Rascher in his first letter to Britten in July 1938: 'Wasn't that day in Siena a whole "family" outing, with the whole orchestra and that wonderful saxophonist Rascher?'

You can rest assured that we are not suffering because we are Germans, on the contrary our real friends are nicer than before, since they know what we are suffering by virtue of our attachment to our own country, but not to its rulers.

The lengthy epistle took him almost two hours to write. He saved his emotion for the end.

Know that you are in my thoughts all day, even though I may not write. I still do not forget, indeed how could I? Absence has made my heart grow fonder and my love for you is stronger and greater than ever. Good-bye my love, au revoir.
    All my love, my darling, Wulff.

If Pears ever caught sight of their exchanges, he would surely have found them galling. He thought he had won Ben's heart, but part of it seemed beyond his reach. It was as if Keats's first reference to Apollo in 'Hyperion' were being played out in reality:

> A voice came sweeter, sweeter than all tune,
> And still it cried, 'Apollo! young Apollo!
> The morning-bright Apollo! young Apollo!'
> I fled, it follow'd me, and cried 'Apollo!'

Wulff's letter arrived at Christmas-time, just after the second performance of *Young Apollo*. Ben replied immediately. His letter has not survived, but in it he repeated his request for a copy of the picture of Wulff at the age of thirteen, and suggested he try his hand at writing prose. Then, straight after the New Year, he set off on a two-week trip to Chicago, where he was to play his Piano Concerto. He probably carried Wulff's December letter in his wallet, which would explain why it became heavily creased and worn. In Chicago, he sent him a postcard, which promised a further letter. But instead, without warning, his torrent of correspondence dried up. There was a sudden, and significant, silence.

As soon as Ben's Christmas letter reached him, Wulff wrote back at even greater length, covering four sheets of foolscap in his dense and minuscule handwriting. He was unusually forthcoming about his mother's handling of their naturalisation application, about his latest poetry, and about wartime rationing of food. He promised to get a copy of the photograph made. It is written in the facetious, juvenile tone that by now Ben knew so well, with its anarchic enjoyment of words and language. He chided Ben for the illegibility of some of his letter, caused by 'the placing of your strokes (referring to the nib of your pen – before your thoughts lure you astray)'. The limerick he included was typical:

> A Lesbian of Khartoum
> Once took a pansy to her room.
> When they got into bed
> They questioningly said:
> 'Now who does what, how, and to whom'?

I hope old bluepencils* enjoyed that as much as I did when I first heard it. You probably know it anyhow, naughty old man.

Suddenly, at the end of this screed, the tone switched. He peeled off the jocular façade and spoke touchingly from the heart, heedless of any censor.

> I've desperately tried not to make this a love letter, because the thought of another prying, as it were, into our hearts, is humiliating.
> But dearest know this: we have known each other for well over a year now and the greater part of that time has been spent in separation, yet the one person which was constantly in my thoughts and on my mind without fail was you. No one else occupied my heart, my mind or my body. Love Wulff.

Even today these words, from that handsome, rather lonely boy in Cambridge facing an uncertain future in a country at war

* A wartime nickname for the censor.

with his own homeland, prick the heart. His sentiments seemed bound to draw Ben into an immediate response. But the change to the past tense in the final three lines was unknowingly prophetic. There was no answer from Ben.

Wulff was not to know that, when his letter reached Amityville in mid-February, Britten was seriously ill, apparently with some sort of streptococcal infection. He had a raging fever – his temperature was said to have reached 107°F at one point. His nurse said that he talked and talked about his childhood and his schooldays. Even when the recovery began, it was slow. He wrote no letters at all for three weeks, and he was only just well enough to attend the première of his Violin Concerto in New York at the end of March. His convalescence gave him plenty of time to think – too much perhaps – and he was free of the normal pressures of composing and performing. But there was no word to Wulff.

By April Wulff was pleading for a letter, in dismay at the three-month silence.

We seem to be growing apart, out of each other's reach.
I feel that more keenly, as I have changed v.much since
I left school [. . .].
    The suspense of not knowing why you have not written
is the worst thing about it. If I at least knew that work had
been too pressing or even that you were ill, I could write
and not worry. As it is, my imagination runs wild in
devious vicious circles.

He sent Ben a new photograph of himself, taken for his identity card. But not even this spurred Ben to take up his pen, which was busy writing the *Sinfonia da Requiem*.

Six weeks later Wulff wrote again, reporting that he had been interned as an enemy alien, shortly before his twentieth birthday. He was initially taken to Bury St Edmunds, where among his guards was one of his former head prefects at The Perse School. He marvelled at the calibre of his fellow internees:

One begins to realise what Germany lost in driving them out. [. . .] They are nearly all of them excellent philosophers, and that beside their particular métier. We have some eminent astronomers, lawyers, humanitarians, mathematicians, and [. . .] nearly all speak or know several languages. [. . .]

In short the conglomeration of intellect is really astounding.

The internees had already begun to organise classes in literature, maths and astronomy in their camp. The downside was the patch of cemented floor on which, at the start of the internment, each of them had to sleep.

Quite a refreshing experience – especially when the cold starts slowly creeping up through your blanket, until it finally seems to grip your bowels in an icy hold.

Around this time, Ben did suggest to his sister Beth that, if she had no better use for the money his London publishers owed him, she might send it to Gustel Scherchen: she 'may need it to pay transportation fares if they want to send her or Wulff to Canada'. But not even the news of his internment provoked a direct response.

The war was certainly playing its capricious part in their relationship. Some letters were lost altogether in transit, others were interminably delayed. Britten later claimed that the letter about Wulff's internment took two months to reach him. But neither his month of illness, nor the pressures of his work, nor the vagaries of the mail, could explain the continuing silence from such an indefatigable correspondent as Ben. It was undoubtedly deliberate. The illness, in Auden's view, resulted from indecision over whether to stay in America for good. Britten himself said later on that the real cause had been 'mental perplexities'. Wulff may have been part of them. The emotional stresses of Ben's life were perhaps too great. It would not have been surprising if the long-suffering Pears told him to make up his mind between them, and get Wulff out of his system. Removing *Young Apollo* from circulation would be a start.

During his long convalescence, he made up for lost time in dealing with unanswered letters from friends and family. Wulff would normally have been top of the list – but not this time. The resolutions made half-heartedly the previous spring were reaffirmed with greater conviction. The determined self-assurance so evident in his music at last spilled across into his life. *Young Apollo* was banished, both musically and in person.

CHAPTER 8

Peter and the Wulff

Back in England, Enid Slater was unaware of Britten's change of heart, and, as instructed, was keeping an eye on Wulff by telephone and occasional visits to Cambridge. In February she suggested to Britten that she could help Wulff financially by arranging some translation work for him. When Britten responded, as he returned to health in April, he thanked her for 'being so sweet about it' but added tersely: 'Don't bother any more about Wulff'. Enid Slater was saddened by this, and noted that he sounded 'so much older & perhaps harder'. Some months later, there was a revealing slip of her pen, when she was telling Britten about the music she liked to listen to during the Blitz. 'I find Mozart and Bach best', she wrote, 'the kids' choice being Peter & the Wolf and yourself'. But she had absent-mindedly written the word 'Wolf' as 'Wulff': she then corrected it by rounding the *u* into an *o*, and crossing out the second *f*. Then, in embarrassment, she wrote '(sorry!)', with the superfluous explanation 'Prokofiev' in brackets.

Wulff's war, meanwhile, was taking a new turn. His engineering studies had been curtailed by his internment. He was moved from Bury St Edmunds to Liverpool, where he was frog-marched through the streets, 'urged on by brutish, bellowing sergeants', and thence to Huyton, where he awaited transfer in early July to either Canada or Australia, though the authorities told his mother nothing. Then came the news that, on 2nd July, the *Arandora Star* had been sunk off Ireland, with the loss of six hundred German and Italian internees and prisoners of war. In desperation, Gustel Scherchen contacted Britten by letter and telegram to enlist his support in finding out whether Wulff was among them. At last an anxious (and perhaps slightly guilty) Britten involved himself again. He cabled Gustel on 18th July to say that his hostess Elizabeth Mayer was trying to trace Wulff through the Red Cross. He told his sister Beth that he had worked out that Wulff should have left England for Canada 'on the day that the Andora Castle [*sic*] went down with hundreds of his kind – so I've been hopping around Red Cross Societies & making inquiries in official circles trying to trace him & to bring some comfort to his poor mother'.

Wulff had in fact had a narrow escape. By pure luck, he had missed embarkation on the *Arandora Star*, because the ship was already full, and had taken the next passage. He arrived at internment camp Q, four hundred miles north of Toronto, in late July, with a large number of his compatriots, but isolated from family and friends. Gustel discovered on 26th July that he was safe, and cabled Britten immediately with a possible address. He at last wrote to Wulff, but told Elizabeth Mayer that he would wait until he heard back before doing anything more. The letter never got through.

In August he received two letters from Wulff on the regulation twenty-four lines of prison notepaper, asking for chocolate and cigarettes to relieve the tedium of the camp. He said it was hard, on the wrong side of the barbed wire, not to be bitter 'when you have watched the rise of Nazism and gone into voluntary exile [. . .] you feel lost, hurt and disillusioned'. The same no doubt applied in the more personal context of their own friendship. Wulff pointed out that he had had no direct news from Ben since January, and appealed twice for a reply by return of post. He was suffering 'veritable agonies of suspense at the thought of being comparatively so close to you again, after the years of parting'. But he might as well have been sent to Australia. No visitors were allowed, though at least the mail from New York promised to be less problematic.

Eventually, on 3rd September 1940, Wulff received a response from Britten. 'At last we have traced you!' Britten wrote, with apologies for his long silence. 'Although I haven't written', he said, 'I have thought about you constantly'. The silence had evidently resulted from an act of will, rather than fading interest. But Britten's deliberate emotional detachment matched the discretion needed when writing to a prison camp internee: he wrote to 'My dear Wulff' rather than the 'darling Wulff' of his last letter before the long silence. He also wrote consolingly to Gustel, saying what a great relief it was to be in touch with him again.

> It is tragic for the dear boy, but we must, & he must, just regard it as a period of 'marking-time' (as it is for everybody else). I will get all books that he wants for the continuation of his studies & I will send him everything I possibly can to make the physical discomforts less, & I have such faith in him that I feel sure that he will pull through all right. It is the period <u>after</u> the war that will be most trying – but pray God there will be someone around who can help him – & I am sure there will!

But the implication was that he himself would not be that 'someone'.

The letter from Ben was the first contact Wulff had had with anyone on the right side of the barbed wire for eight weeks. In Liverpool the internees had been held in complete isolation, unaware of the battle for France and the evacuation from Dunkirk. Then they had had a rough ocean crossing, worried that the fate of the *Arandora Star* awaited them. Now he was a virtual prisoner in a strange country, and had only recently enjoyed his first change of clothing for two months. 'Don't think any more that I've forgotten you', Ben wrote. 'I can't say how relieved I am that you are in Canada [. . .]. You are certainly the right side of the Atlantic Ocean.'

Wulff was sustained in the internment camp by his thirst for poetry. He asked Ben for volumes of Keats, Auden and Housman, and for the Shakespeare sonnets, vindicating Britten's assessment of his literary muse the previous year:

'really pretty good taste, if slightly exaggerated enthusiasms'. He also requested an English dictionary, and wrote twenty poems in two months. Ben sent a parcel of books, and also some size 11 gumboots (to help Wulff 'squelch through inches of mud' to get to the tents at night). He also sent cash for toothpaste, pipe tobacco, chocolate and haircuts.

Nearly all the letters Wulff wrote at the start of his Canadian internment were to Ben, and towards the end he confessed that their 'enforced separation' had not dimmed his feelings, but had brought about 'a longing and craving' to see and hear him once more, 'and to be able to feel again that we at least understand each other and supplement each other'. He added, 'It is only here I am beginning to realize – painfully – what you once meant for me'.

Wulff was released in December 1940 after more than six months in detention, and sent back to England. He had been offered the chance to resume his engineering course, but insisted on volunteering for the Auxiliary Military Pioneer Corps, which had been set up to accommodate 'friendly aliens'. The correspondence with Ben became spasmodic, and as the months passed Wulff became uneasy that they were losing touch. He clearly knew they could never pick up where they had left off, but he said that, in trying to 'overlook the past', he had found it 'still terrifyingly alive'.

I sometimes long for your company, more than I can express in words, but not in terms of a marvellous past that is an ever-present memory, but rather on [the] footing of myself as a different person, more grown up, more secure, and stripped of a number of illusions.

You are probably the greatest influence I have ever experienced, and in all my subsequent relations with people, whether in love or friendship, your image was always present and never blotted out.

It was now July 1941, three years since his first weekend at the Old Mill. Amid news of bomb damage, and a growing desire to retaliate against his compatriots, his memories of Ben were still tender, as in his account of an afternoon with Trevor Harvey, listening to records.

I was beautifully recumbent on a delectable couch and exuded lazy enjoyment of life [. . .] with my boots off and my tunic unbuttoned, when without warning, Trevor put on part of your 'Variations' [*on a theme of Frank Bridge*]. The memories flooded back & their insistent surge overwhelmed me as he put your photo in my hand. Suffolk was incarnate in the room & outside through the window the sky languidly sending its clouds past the sun brought all the past in stark panorama.

Wulff's rather sensual expression continued as he told Ben of the manual work he was doing in the Army. The once willowy youth, already toughened by the exigencies of internment, now found himself wielding pick and shovel, laying telephone cables, erecting Nissen huts, building roads and railway lines.

It is hard but I delight in it & it is perfect revelry to feel one's body growing taut and wiry with muscular development. It is excellent to move like a healthy animal, watching the play of your sinews. I, of the lily-white complexion, am acquiring a most graceful tan and satisfying bronze of the skin. I am by now so full of zest & vitality. I even go out hay making or timbering on nearby farms in the evening.

As Ben read this letter, it would have been surprising if the old flame did not flicker again (as it was perhaps designed to). He responded to his 'dear old Wulff' in September 1941 by saying he was 'glad all the time which we spent together hasn't been completely effaced by the long time that I have been away'. The letter was, he said, typical of the Wulff he remembered so well and with such affection, 'yet plus a little something that all the trials & tribulations of the past few years have added, and maybe, just a little of what being 21 means?' He said he too had changed a great deal. 'I feel much, much older &, well perhaps wiser as well.' But he still craved Wulff's devotion:

> I have a feeling that you are still somewhat sympathetic to me. [. . .] Very little is ever censored in your letters [. . .] so you can feel quite free! [. . .] Much love my dear – I think of you more than I can say – wonder how you are, & what's occupying you! What I wouldn't give to see you again. . . .

Wulff replied almost immediately. He had, he said, grown up at a tremendous rate. 'I'm told I'm rather handsome – pleasing thought.' But he said he had not matured nearly as much. The rest of the letter reads almost like an epitaph:

> Your friendship I have never been able to forget & I am just beginning to realize it's the one thing I've been missing for a long long time. It is an aching void of longing for the most intimate acquaintanceship I have ever known. [. . .] Remember that when I lost you I lost half of myself, for you were my first friend & the hours we spent together were and are the happiest and best of my life. I still feel that we are bound by a tie that is so lasting & deep, nothing not even separation, and ours has been a long one, can depreciate its particular values. [. . .]
> Always & always Yours, Wulff.

When I read part of this passage to Scherchen recently, he thought for a moment I was quoting what Ben had written. He was taken aback to realise they were his own words. 'It's interesting to see how intense my feelings had in fact been at the time. Because of course the memory and the passage of the years mellow things and you no longer feel the same passions. . . It underlines everything, doesn't it? I'm sure it has left something in my character that is due to Ben – to his influence, to our closeness. If I'm at all a nice person, Ben had a lot to do with that, because he was essentially kind and good, and fostered that in me as well.'

About six weeks after Wulff's letter, Britten had a new fourteen-year-old friend, Bobby Rothman. Auden chided him at about this time for always making for himself 'a warm nest of love' and 'playing the lovable talented little boy', and that was what he had done when settling in New York State. He may have been three thousand miles away from England, but he found himself living in a county called Suffolk, and often visited the town of Southold on the coast. The English Southwold was halfway between his birthplace Lowestoft and his home at Snape: the Long Island town may have been missing a *w*, but the landscape was flat, and the sea was at hand.

When he and Pears went to stay almost indefinitely with the Mayer family in Amityville, Ben excitedly drew a map for Beth to show that they were sleeping just inside the Suffolk county line. Elizabeth Mayer, their dominating hostess, adored her boy Benjamin, and became for him a second mother less than three years after the death of his own. She never acknowledged Britten's homosexuality – indeed her family thought she lived in hope that Ben would marry her twenty-eight-year-old daughter, Beata. Ciné film shot by William Mayer shows Britten and Pears larking around with her in the garden, but Ben appears very much the kid being chased by a maturer Peter and Beata.

The Mayers introduced him to David Rothman, who owned a music and hardware store seventy miles away in Southold, on the north-eastern tip of Long Island. There he met Albert Einstein, who was on vacation nearby, and also Rothman's son Bobby, who was eleven at the time. But, significantly, it was not until he was thirteen or fourteen, and darkly handsome, that Bobby impressed himself on Ben. They met only half a dozen times, but Britten was soon saying that he wanted to give up composing and work in the shop, perhaps so that he could be close to Bobby. One photograph showed them apparently arm-in-arm (though they were not), and Britten in his late twenties looked much younger than that. Another, taken the last time they met, had Ben carrying Bobby on his shoulders, holding him up 'like a sack of coals': this was Britten's favourite, and he kept it on his piano for years afterwards (see plate 11).

Britten drew great comfort from the Rothman household, not least because Bobby's father David helped to bolster his confidence when he had composer's block. But he confounded the Rothmans' image of a composer. Bobby remembers them all going for a walk on the shore of Long Island Sound and watching the seagulls flying and crying above the fish traps. David made the mistake of suggesting it might give Britten some inspiration for his music – not the sort of remark which would be welcome to many composers, and certainly not to one as prickly as Britten. When David's back was turned, Ben looked at Bobby 'and this I remember very well: he said, "You know, those sea-gulls don't give me any inspiration. It all just comes to me up here – I really don't need the seagulls for it!" ' Back at the house, Bobby was astonished and impressed to find him writing music at a desk in his bedroom, just as if he were writing a letter. 'It took me by surprise, because downstairs there was a piano, and at that time I thought you composed by tickling the ivories, until you came up with something soothing that suited your needs at the moment, and then you filled in the manuscript. When I asked him how come he didn't use a piano, he said no, he doesn't need the piano, he hears every note he writes down right in his head. That's the way he does it.'

On another occasion, Bobby took Britten bowling, and was reprimanded, as he recalls, by his father: ' "How could you think of asking a man of that stature, with his interests and abilities, to spend time bowling?" ' Little did Rothman senior realise that the competitive sportsman in Britten loved the experience, and time spent with a boy who was indulging his favourite pastime was never time wasted. 'In fact', Bobby says, 'I think he probably had a better time than I did!'

David Rothman filmed a family picnic with Britten on a sunny but not particularly warm day at Orient Beach State Park in November 1941. His ciné film captures Britten the 'boy' remarkably well – playing with a stray dog, joshing with 'the grand kid' Bobby and experimenting gingerly with toasted marshmallows. Bobby comes in and out of the picture in his blue checked shirt, and there is a noticeable physical closeness between them. Britten wrote two thank-you letters which refer to the picnic: 'I don't think I have ever eaten so much in my life!' He also wrote to Bobby's younger sister Joan, singling out for special mention 'that "rapscallion" brother of yours'.

Bobby points out that he saw Ben for no more than ten days in total across a three-year period, and he was completely unaware that Britten had any sort of crush on him. He was neither a father figure, nor a brother figure. 'It was just a certain fondness, a certain kindness. Nothing took place that I would have been upset about if anyone else was watching. There was at one time a tender hug, and that was about it.' This refers to the occasion when they shared a twin bedroom in the Rothman home. They sat up talking, and then 'as the hour got later and it was time to turn out the light, he said, "Would you mind terribly, Bobby" (and those were the words he used) "if I were to give you a little hug and a kiss before we turn out the light?" And I said, "No, give me a hug". And he got out of the bed and came across to the other bed I was in, and gently put his arm around my shoulders and gave me a friendly kiss on the cheek, and said goodnight.' Bobby says he felt neither uncomfortable nor embarrassed. 'That's the way it was', he adds with a chuckle. 'It was a different world then.'

Shortly after his return to England in 1942, Britten arranged a Somerset folksong *The trees they grow so high* and dedicated it to Bobby. He promised to send him a copy. But perhaps he pulled back at the last minute. Thirty years later, during Britten's final illness, David Rothman wrote to say he had just found out about the dedication. Britten replied: 'Please give my greetings to all of you, and special ones perhaps to Bobby. I never told him about that dedication, I think I felt too shy, but the poem of the particular folk song used to remind me so much of him.' The song tells the sad story of a girl's doomed love for a much younger boy. The second verse was probably the one that brought Bobby to mind:

> Oh, father, dearest father,
> You've done to me great wrong.
> You've tied me to a boy
> When you know he is too young.
> Oh, daughter, dearest daughter,
> If you wait a little while,
> A lady you shall be
> While he's growing.

It suggests that, when Beata Mayer said Britten had been in love with Bobby, she was not far wrong. Rothman today regards this with somewhat embarrassed amusement. But his memories of Ben are entirely benign. Although their meetings were few, Britten kept the friendship warm, as he did so often, by his prolific and attractive letters, addressed to 'my dear old Bobby'. At one point, Bobby cut the airmail label off Ben's envelope, and used it for his reply: he asked Ben to do the same, and it became a game between them to see how many times the single label could cross the Atlantic. 'He entered into the spirit of things with me. I liked that.' He gave the boy an idea of his priorities for a happy life.

> Well, what kind of a summer have you had, old thing? Lots of bathing & sailing, I suppose. Gosh – how jealous that makes me feel. Do you know, even in this small country, I have only seen the sea twice, & haven't bathed once! That's a poor summer for you. I've played tennis, maybe three times, but pretty bad stuff, as it was always raining, & anyhow the balls were so lousy – tennis balls are things you can't get for love or money.

He asked Bobby for photos of himself bathing or sailing, and he assured the boy he had not forgotten him. 'How could I when I have a large photo of you staring at me all the time when I'm working!'

During 1941 Britten's disillusion with America had grown in proportion to his homesickness for England. But it had taken months to secure a passage home. He and Pears eventually found berths on a Swedish freighter and left in mid-March 1942, although it took them a whole month to limp across the Atlantic – a nerve-wracking wartime journey that gave birth to *A Ceremony of Carols*. Just before the voyage, Britten told Christopher Isherwood he was keen to see his family '& Wulff' again. He had sent him a Christmas present, but had had no response. Back in England, it was hard to track Wulff down in the Army, and Britten knew his mother had moved from her old Cambridge address. So it took him more than a month to make contact.

During that time, Wulff wrote to Ben in America on 1st May, unaware that he had returned home. It was a letter that Britten never read – indeed it only came to light in 1982. It gave a foretaste of what was to come. Wulff was listless. He wrote to 'My dear Benjamin' to apologise for not having written for so long.

> I suppose it is due to some extent that we lead completely different lives at the moment & that thus our interests & the circumstances that affect us are completely different.

He complained about the noisy routine of Army life and the restrictions on letter-writing imposed by wartime censorship.

> Oh, hang it, I really don't know what to write about any more – all the things I really want to describe – the beauty of this countryside, I fear wouldn't be passed by the censor, & there seems little else worth saying.

He knew the letter would disappoint Ben, and he signed off, 'With my best wishes, Wulff'. In Amityville, Elizabeth Mayer opened the letter and read it. She told Britten, 'There is really nothing much to the letter, strangely unpersonal (as he himself admits) being completely ~~wrapped~~ taken up and absorbed by his present life', and never sent it on.

By the middle of May Britten had tracked down Gustel Scherchen and asked her to forward a letter to her son. The passion of two or three years before had abated, but it was still a letter of real tenderness, calculated to remind Wulff of their idyll before the war.

My dear old Wulff,
Believe it or not, & it seems almost too good to be true, but I am now sitting at my desk at the Mill with a large picture of you sulking at me, [. . .] writing you this note! [. . .]
   I am of course very keen to see you, my dear. Tell me when you're in town next, or can manage to get there. [. . .]
   I gather from your mother that you're behaving yourself – don't be cross, it wasn't always true!!
   Much love, Yours, Benjamin.

The photograph was back on Britten's desk, presumably beside Bobby Rothman's. Perhaps, as in so many romances interrupted by the war, he still nursed dreams of a resumption. They arranged to meet in London within a fortnight, on 1st June 1942.

It was a disaster. Wulff had turned twenty-two two days before, but not even that lightened the mood. By a strange chance, they were observed by a street photographer. The resulting snap captured more than their likenesses: it summed up a relationship that was over. Ben's brow was furrowed, and a severe-looking Wulff, in uniform, was self-evidently no longer the soft youth Britten had left behind in 1939. His wartime experiences had put paid to that.

Britten was mortified. That evening he poured out his disappointment and frustration in a furious note to Pears – perhaps the tetchiest he ever wrote him. Since their return from America, they had perforce been living separately, which created its own strains. When in London, Britten was billeted with his sister Barbara in Chelsea, while Pears was staying with his parents in Barnes. Britten's anger was prompted by Pears's failure to telephone him at the time he had promised, which meant they had missed each other. Ben tossed off his reproach in pencil, and put it in the post. 'God – you blighter', it began. 'No wonder I'm cross. Why the hell can't you organise your times abit – why the hell don't you do what you say [. . .].' Then he revealed that his emotional turmoil was 'mostly because I've had such an <u>awful</u> time with Wulff. Poor dear, he's had such a hell of a time – but it's accentuated the old hard, vindictive side of him; the old conventional communist, materialist side; the boasting, garrulous side too – so that he's completely unbearable.' In the midst of his fury, there was a pang from the past. His young Apollo had returned: 'I must admit it, he was looking very pretty – & in retrospect, well – perhaps he is . . . but that's only because I'm so cross with you, you old so & so. Boohoo.'

What is fascinating is that the *dénouement* had caught him unawares.

> Seriously – poor old KHWS, he's the first real bad shock
> I've had since I got back – I've just grown completely away
> from him. He rather wanted to come back to-night, I think,
> but I choqued (choaked?) him off – but, damn it all,
> perhaps he'd be better than . . . here I go again – blast you,
> why can't you be in when I want you.

After meeting Wulff, he had taken himself off to the cinema to see *How Green Was My Valley*. It was 'a <u>lousy</u> picture' (the word 'lousy' was underlined three times) but it was, he said, easier than talking to Wulff.

Ben was upset by Wulff and upset by Peter, and he was quite ready, in a half-joking way, to play one off against the other. Pears barely mentioned Wulff in his reply.

> I'm sorry about Wulff – it's a great pity, but I imagine he
> needs very strong & beneficent influences all the time.

Wulff, one should remember, had been unaware – perhaps until that meeting – that Britten and Pears were now a couple. Ben may not have appreciated the shock this would cause.

A few days later he wrote to Elizabeth Mayer about the meeting, in calmer terms:

> He was rather altered, I am afraid. The ghastly time he has had, has made him rather vindictive, and hard. However, in time, he may soften, because underneath he is an awfully sweet boy. Perhaps if he could find the right girl whom he could marry – but his dictatorial manner, I should think, would put most girls off.

Both to Pears and to Mayer, Britten used the same word, 'vindictive'. It sounded as if Wulff had berated him.

He did see Wulff again in late September. Britten had just returned to London from Snape, where he had been entertaining his old favourite Piers Dunkerley, who was almost the same age as Wulff, and also in uniform. Britten reported to Elizabeth Mayer shortly afterwards:

> [. . .] my real friends are so sweet – even young Piers Dunkerley (you remember!), who is having such a stinking time in convoy work, spends as much time as possible with me. We were in Snape together a week ago!

As Wulff had risen in Ben's affections before the war, Piers had faded. Now the reverse was happening. 'We never got further than just saying, "Hello, how nice to see you again" ', Scherchen recalls. They went to Boosey & Hawkes' shop in Regent Street, where Britten gave a miniature score of *Les Illuminations* to his model for '*gracieux fils de Pan*'. Inside the front cover he wrote: 'For Wulff of course – Benjamin B. September 1942, i.e. 3 years too late*'. Scherchen poignantly adds: 'I don't think he even said "with love" '.

It was their last close encounter. Britten told Pears that Wulff was 'impossible' and that he agreed with his sister Barbara that he 'shouldn't see him much'. The international success of *Peter*

---

* He had completed the work in October 1939.

Grimes beckoned, and his relationship with Pears was now permanent. He had recently told him:

Thank you for one of the most heavenly week-ends of my life – no, the most heavenly. I couldn't have believed that one could have felt so completely at ease, & at one with a person, as I feel with you. [. . .] I just wanted to thank you for being you & for coming into my life when you did – but why didn't you come ten years earlier – that's my only complaint!

Within a few weeks, Wulff proved Britten wrong. He did indeed find 'the right girl', Pauline Woolford from Yorkshire, a radar operator with the WAAF*. Wulff had by then left the Pioneer Corps, and was serving in a bomb disposal unit within the Royal Engineers. As this could have involved him in active service, he was required, as all German-born servicemen were, to change his name, to protect him in the event of capture by the Nazis. This change of identity coincided neatly with his engagement to Pauline, so he adopted her surname, married her in October 1943 (despite her family's initial hostility to a bride-groom from Berlin), and put his German upbringing and his friendship with Britten behind him.

For Benjamin Britten, the unique love affair with Wulff was, for the rest of his life, a closed and secret chapter. For Wulff Scherchen, now John Woolford, it was not just a chapter that had closed, but the whole book.

---

* At the outbreak of war, Pauline Woolford had joined the Army, despite being under age, but had then been invalided out after an accident. She first met Wulff briefly in June 1941 while serving in the ATS, but they did not meet again until December 1942, by which time she had re-enlisted.

CHAPTER 9

The happy dirty driving boys

One of the hallmarks of Britten's sound world is the boy treble voice. He used it as naturally and as idiomatically as he did the oboe, the harp or the viola. For some, his reliance on its distinctive timbre has been uncomfortable, because they felt it denoted an unhealthy preoccupation in the composer's mind, even though the same people will happily melt at the sound (and sight) of trebles in surplice and cassock singing carols at Christmas.

Britten took the trebles out of their rarefied habitat of the chancel, which they normally shared only with altos, tenors and basses and the church organ, and put them in almost every other musical context he knew – on the stage and the symphony concert platform, in recital rooms, school halls and the cinema. In part, he disliked the breathy 'cathedral hoot' which was so prevalent in his youth. But he also knew that, both for him and for his audience, boys' voices conveyed resonances (of innocence, purity and vulnerability) that were invaluable to his musical and dramatic purpose. It was therefore essential that the treble colour should be available to him every time he took up his composing palette, not just on the rare occasions when he was writing for the Church. He could harness it to create a disembodied purity and timeless innocence in the *War Requiem*, a (rather tame) seductiveness in *The Prodigal Son*, an unsettling other-worldliness in *A Midsummer Night's Dream*, and an earthy cockiness in the *Spring Symphony*. According to his godson, the composer Michael Berkeley, the sound of boys' voices was 'the key to a door for him. It opened a door to his emotional landscape.'

He did write several canticle settings for Anglican Mattins (two versions of the *Jubilate*, and two of the *Te Deum*, scored for church choir and organ), as well as some anthems. But his real interest in the sound was directed outside the confines of church services, and this went right back to the start of his composing career. He specified that his first published work, *Three Two-Part Songs*, was for 'boys' or women's voices' and piano. Close on its heels came his first major choral work (and one of his early masterpieces), *A Boy Was Born*, a set of unaccompanied choral variations for men's, women's and boys' voices. Although this has sometimes been performed in churches, its scoring is unecclesiastical: the boys are used in contrast with women singing the soprano and alto lines, which distorts the balance of a normal church choir and gives the whole work a distinctive and unusual sonority.

Britten used boys' voices in almost thirty of his major works, including twelve for the stage. It is an astonishing total. Sometimes he specified children, rather than boys, as in his opera for children, *Noye's Fludde*, and in *Voices for Today*, his United Nations anthem. *Children's Crusade* is described as 'a ballad for children's voices and orchestra', but in the accompanying notes Britten makes clear that he has boys' voices in mind. Indeed that was his normal assumption. In *Friday Afternoons*, the collection of mostly unison songs he wrote after the example of George Dyson, the dedication to his headmaster-brother makes clear at whom they were aimed: 'To R.H.M. Britten and the boys of Clive House, Prestatyn'. He asked his brother what he should call the work. Robert said he had no idea. 'Ben then said, "Well, when do you do your singing?" So I said: "Friday afternoons". "Right", he said, "we'll call it that".'

One score refers to 'young people' – his last completed work, *Welcome Ode*, written for the prospective visit to Suffolk by the Queen on her Silver Jubilee. Although he was motivated by children's voices in general, his bias (according to the opera producer Colin Graham) was towards the individual timbre of boys' voices, and the strength and purity that they evoked – a combination that was the basis for his music and his life.

He would probably have had little sympathy for the current trend in cathedral choirs to accord girls equal honour with boys. It is no accident that, in *The Little Sweep*, he always cast the eldest girl (Juliet, who is fourteen) as an adult soprano,* despite saying it was 'essential' that real children should play the children's parts. The other two girls' roles (and the girl soloists in *Noye's Fludde*) were usually given to teenaged girls, whereas the three boys in *The Little Sweep* had to have unbroken voices, and not be 'scared of using their chest voices'. In the case of the two children in *The Turn of the Screw*, he was prepared to chance his arm with the twelve-year-old treble David Hemmings in the starring role of Miles. He auditioned some forty girls for the part of Miles's sister Flora in December 1953, but none of them came up to his exacting mark. By the time he came to write the opera the following year he conceived Flora as an adult role, and was fortunate to have the diminutive Olive Dyer to sing it. He had never before given such a big operatic part as Miles to a child, and as a practical opera composer he no doubt felt that a second child performer would have been too great a risk. Many modern productions do now cast a young girl as Flora, as Britten originally imagined, but she often has to struggle to be heard, since the scoring presumes an adult voice. For Britten, the immature voice of a girl did not carry the timbre or the strength he wanted, so he inverted the ages of the children from those in Henry James's original story, to make Flora into Miles's elder sister. This gave Olive Dyer as Flora a better chance of fooling the audience, as indeed she did on the first night in Venice.†

Britten never actually specified a girls' choir, although one of the choirs in the official première of his 1948 cantata *Saint Nicolas* consisted of girls. He said that they would have to be 'relegated to the galleries (where anyhow all girls should be in Church), because they are obviously the most efficient, & their breathy voices are obviously most suited to the wind noises &

---

* Anne Sharp in the first performance, April Cantelo in Britten's 1955 recording.
† Basil Coleman remembers that members of the audience came backstage afterwards, asking to see 'the children'.

so forth'. They were indeed placed in the Lancing College chapel gallery, and required to represent the storm and tempest. Britten's music assistant Rosamund Strode points out how effective the breathy quality was for the lightning hisses, 'which is quite different from the sound he got anywhere else'.

One of the most substantial of his works for boys, and certainly his most popular, is *A Ceremony of Carols*, which he wrote while tossing on the Atlantic waves on his way home in the middle of the war. This setting of medieval lyrics, loosely attached to Christmas, is usually performed in church, where the processional and recessional plainsong framing the work is heard to best effect. But once again Britten finds a peculiar, seductive and unchurchy sonority, because the sole accompanying instrument is the harp. It gives a glittering, sometimes brittle, character to the music.

Strangely the first performance, in December 1942, was not in church, and there was not a boy in sight. It was sung by the women of the Fleet Street Choir in the library of Norwich Castle.* It took another ten years for Britten to feel that any performance had achieved the work's full potential, and that was by a foreign choir. At the 1952 Aldeburgh Festival, the Copenhagen Boys' Choir 'sang (but not necessarily behaved!) like angels. They sang my Ceremony of Carols as I never thought it could be sung.' He was so impressed that he recorded it with them the following year.

His *Missa Brevis* of 1959 is, on the face of it, a more orthodox piece for the Church. It was written for his friend George Malcolm and the boys of his choir at Westminster Cathedral. Scored for three-part boys' choir and organ, it was first performed liturgically at the Roman Catholic cathedral's High Mass. Nearly fifty years later it remains a jewel in any treble's crown: there are few works of comparable quality or complexity for choirboys to sing on their own. Yet it is not simply an

---

* When published, the work was designated for treble voices. But Britten's earliest sketches were intended for women sopranos and altos.

exquisite piece of church music: it managed to smuggle into the chancel much of Britten's secular experience. The opening note in the Kyrie is a loud top F sharp, with the unchurchy marking, 'passionate'; the Gloria is written in 7/8, alleviated only by a few bars in 5/8; there are lots of dance rhythms – indeed there is an underlying physicality, especially in the *staccato* passages of the Agnus Dei. The Benedictus is bi-tonal, whereas the Sanctus unfolds with a twelve-note row, and has a drone virtually the whole way through. This opening was sketched out in Britten's schoolboy's diary for 1959 under the section for 'sports fixtures and results', and indeed Britten plays games with his singers along the way, which makes it fun to perform. But it is difficult to bring off, because it needs real precision, focus and attack. Most boys' choirs of the time would have failed, but George Malcolm specialised in the raw, edgy sound that Britten appreciated, and that made it possible.

With this choir, it was once again the physicality that made the difference. Britten was looking for the energy with which boys shout at each other on the football field, and wanted to apply that to singing. It was no wonder that Westminster Cathedral Choir won favour: George Malcolm always boasted that he found his best singers 'fighting it out in the playground'. The Wandsworth Boys' Choir attracted Britten for the same reason, though in this case there was no religious foundation at its heart, just the uncombed vigour of boys from rundown housing estates in south London, attending their local comprehensive school. It was Russell Burgess's remarkable achievement to turn such apparently unpromising raw material into a choir much sought after for concerts and recordings, until its untimely demise in 1985 because of reorganisation by the local education authority. In the late 1960s and early 1970s, it caught the imagination of Britain's premier composer. Critics winced at its rough, often coarse quality. That was just what Britten liked.

Burgess got his boys to make a *ragazzi* sound, with the hard edges of the Italian streets. The tenor Adrian Thompson, one of

Wandsworth's alumni, says it meant 'chesting up much higher than you would normally do, up to the A or even the B above middle C. You pushed all the sound forward – a sort of Nellie Melba effect, up as high as you could get until it broke. It wasn't always very attractive, but it was exciting and ear-catching. As a singing teacher myself now, it is something I would totally disagree with. But I think Britten liked it because it expressed ordinary boyish tones, rather than the way they'd been told to behave or to sing. It was more immediate – though it often meant we went terribly sharp, which was always encouraged so that we cut through the texture.' Russell Burgess told Britten how much his choir was enjoying learning *Saint Nicolas*: 'we now have over 150 trebles and they can all manage top B with ear-splitting clarity' – and that was intended as a commendation.

Britten's *Spring Symphony* might have been written express-ly for them, though in fact it dates from 1949, some seventeen years before the Wandsworth connection began. When he was only twenty, he had written a little song *May*, which suggested that he associated 'the month of Maying' with boys' voices.* The exuberance of the final movement of the *Spring Symphony* demonstrates that. In 'London, to thee I do present the merry month of May' (his setting of a passage from Beaumont and Fletcher's play *The Knight of the Burning Pestle*), he has the orchestra and mixed chorus swirling their arpeggios at full tilt round the maypole, until at the climax the boys' choir bursts out with the thirteenth-century song *Sumer is i-cumen in*, over the top of the general revelry. It is a heart-stopping moment of sheer genius. To help the boys cut through the tumult, Britten scored the four horns to reinforce the carol tune, triple *forte* and with the rare marking *cuivré*, which indicates that a ringing, brassy sound is to be forced from the instrument. Even so, many

---

* Although the first performance in 1942 was given by the soprano Meriel St Clair, the composition draft describes it as 'part song for boys'. (In fact it is written in unison throughout.)

conductors have to rein in their other players and singers, to let the boys be heard. But not, says Thompson, in his days with the Wandsworth Boys' Choir. 'We could even drown the horns out* – I think that's what Britten loved: we weren't part of the texture, we sat on top of it.'

This earthy, unsophisticated sound also enhanced one of the symphony's earlier movements, 'The Driving Boy'. It starts with the boys singing George Peele's words 'Whenas the rye reach to the chin', to the accompaniment of wind band and tambourine. The poet conjures up dreams of summer, with 'strawberries swimming in the cream, and schoolboys playing in the stream', and then reports his true love saying saucily she could not possibly remain chaste till then. Britten brilliantly interposes part of another poem, by John Clare, to suggest that it's the driving boy (with his team of oxen) who has won her heart. Clare's poem, 'May', is almost 500 lines long, but Britten's eye lit on the eight lines about the boy that suited his purpose. The soprano soloist depicts the boy cracking his whip, cocking his hat, turning his eye, singing and whistling, 'a happy happy dirty driving boy' – to the same exhilarating rising scale as the boys sang to illustrate the girl's itching desire. The driving boy is indeed a 'Jack the lad', a cock-of-the-walk, very much the rural version of a Wandsworth boy – still just innocent perhaps (with fingers crossed behind his back), but certainly on the brink of experience. Primmer, more accurate singing by church choirboys just does not work here. When Britten also required the boys to whistle the tune in unison, and to end with a wolf whistle, the Wandsworth lads were in their element. That was something Britten himself enjoyed, because (although this is not widely known) he was second to none in the knack of whistling. A friend of mine was astonished to see him

* Long before the Wandsworth boys sang the piece, Britten taxed the conductor Herbert Bardgett for letting the horns' reinforcement drown the boys in a performance in Leeds in October 1950. 'If the percussion is reduced', he wrote, '& the brass a bit too, I'm sure the wee boys won't have trouble in dominating the scene as they should!'

hail a taxi in Sydney in April 1970 by putting two fingers in his mouth and effecting the shrillest whistle he had ever heard. Wulff Scherchen remembers the same thing in London before the war. 'It was a very fierce whistle – I was quite ashamed of it. He made such a racket in the middle of a London street – and a taxi did appear too. I just thought it was wrong of him, as a composer of some standing, to behave like a schoolboy!'

Roger Duncan's sister Briony was transfixed by Britten's ability to hum one tune and whistle another at the same time. He may have learnt at least part of the trick from Enid Slater's young daughter Bridget: she liked to double-whistle. 'I can remember being stopped in mid-whistle by Ben before breakfast one morning and being asked to repeat what I had just done. I did my double-whistle again and he tried to copy it.' She was rather pleased to see how hard he found it, but thanks to the tuition of a ten-year-old girl he mastered it.

Another 'Jack the lad' had caught his attention in the 1930s and was featured in one of his earliest partsongs, a setting of Robert Graves's poem *Lift Boy*. It is a delightfully deft miniature for four-part choir and piano, which is unmistakably by Britten, even though he was only nineteen when he wrote it. It remains little known despite being rewarding to hear and to sing – though it is far from easy. Marked *allegro giocoso* (fast and jokey), it tells the story of a nonchalant youth ('with nothing in my pockets but a jack-knife and a button') who operates the lift. In irritation with one of his passengers, a fire-and-brimstone preacher who prophesies that 'not a soul shall be saved', he proves him right by cutting the cords of the lift (or so we think). The piece is powered throughout by vigorous *staccato* quavers and falling sevenths in the piano (and then in the voices) which come into their own as the lift plunges down the shaft: we hear it in accelerating free-fall, disappearing into oblivion. But the piece ends in uproarious laughter – wittily realised in sung form by Britten, a musical variation of the sneeze he concocted round the Slaters' kitchen table.

Britten sought out his child performers whenever he could. In 1964 he went to Vienna for a performance of the *War Requiem* and was particularly impressed by the singing of the Vienna Boys' Choir. He went backstage afterwards to congratulate them, and was invited to one of their rehearsals. 'They sang extremely nicely to me, and at the end (I thought there was a catch somewhere!) they said, "Now we'd like you to write an opera for us". And I said, "Oh yes?" ' The boys explained that on their tours, over and over again, they performed little operas like the boy Mozart's *Bastien und Bastienne*, accompanied on the piano. Britten reckoned they would like something 'a bit tougher', so he agreed to the request. 'And one little boy at the back put up his hand and said, "But need I be a little girl every time, please?" And so in this case', Britten explained before the première, 'I've written an opera without any little girls for them. And I think they ought to do it quite splendidly.'

Britten asked his producer Colin Graham to expand an old English nautical ballad *The Golden Vanity* into a short opera libretto. He then took the old tune of the same name, which had been collected and published by Lucy Broadwood in the 1890s, and built what he called his 'vaudeville' around it. It should, he said, be given in costume, but without scenery, and with only a handful of essential props.

This little opera, for five treble soloists, boys' choir (complete with drums) and piano has echoes of Britten's grand maritime opera *Billy Budd*. There are even one or two musical allusions to it in the score. The battle between the *Golden Vanity* and the Turkish pirate ship recalls the cannon-fire from the *Indomitable* at the start of the second act of *Budd*, and the cabin-boy in *The Golden Vanity* is clearly modelled on the young able seaman after whom the big opera is named. Both are handsome and brave, and both are betrayed by their captain, as a result of which they die. *Billy Budd* is notable for being an all-male opera (this was criticised at the time), and Britten kept his Viennese promise in *The Golden Vanity* by not casting any of the boys in a girl's wig – though the Captain's daughter is an important off-stage presence, as the prize promised to the cabin-boy for sinking the pirate ship, and the cause of his subsequent betrayal.

The music, Britten thought, was quite challenging for the Vienna choir. The words were in English, and, as a stage performance, the twenty-minute piece had to be committed to memory. 'It is a bit earthy and English', Britten said. 'I prefer this toughness. It is quite elaborate technically, more than I would write for Suffolk schoolchildren for instance.' The Vienna boys were undaunted, as Colin Graham discovered when he spent three weeks there, rehearsing them. 'They'd learnt it very well. Those boys were all such good musicians, they'd had such good musical training, that they didn't have any problems with it at all. They enjoyed it, because it was all about pirates and ships, not about little girls and love affairs.'

It was first performed at the 1967 Aldeburgh Festival in the brand-new concert hall at the Snape Maltings, which had been opened by the Queen the previous day. The Vienna Boys' Choir then set off round Europe on their long summer tour, ending up at the Royal Festival Hall two months later, when they gave the piece again. Graham says there was a marked change in vocal quality: 'the boys were quite clearly so tired at the end of their tour that Ben accused the director of exploiting them, not giving them enough free time, and over-working them. He said that, if he'd known this was the way the boys were treated, he would never have written the opera – whereupon the director of the Vienna Boys' Choir [Anton Neyder] said, "OK, we'll never do it again", and they never have.'

The Golden Vanity had a second parent, eight years older than *Billy Budd*. This was another ballad for all-male amateur voices and piano, another tale of betrayal and death, and it remains one of Britten's most perfect, and least-known, miniatures. Although it was not written for children, there is a naïve, childlike delight to it, very much in the manner of *Lift Boy*, and Britten's gamesmanship is never far away. His setting of the anonymous *Ballad of Little Musgrave and Lady Barnard* was written in 1943 for an old friend held captive near the German town of Eichstätt. Britten contrived to get it to him in the prisoner-of-war camp Oflag VIIb, to furnish the musicians there with something fresh to perform.

The piece thrived on its limited resources: amateur tenors, baritones and basses, with a substantial and atmospheric part for piano. This was not a large canvas on which to paint, and Britten self-deprecatingly said he was 'quickly scribbling a short choral work', but in fact he lavished care on this rounded eight-minute score, which is full of colour and intriguing detail. There was a touch of Lady Chatterley in the tale: the beautiful, but unhappily married, Lady Barnard falls for a philanderer, Little Musgrave, and arranges a nocturnal assignation. She is betrayed by her page-boy, and Lord Barnard surprises the lovers in bed. In his fury, he kills them both, but is then overcome with remorse at the loss of 'the fairest lady that ever wore woman's weed [clothing]'.

The opening bars on the piano establish Britten's sound world immediately, with a huge space in the chords (three notes across almost five octaves). The notes come from two asymmetrical phrases (one of three notes, the other of four, whose repetition produces constantly shifting harmonies) and an E flat pedal. The result is a rocking, disturbing lullaby, with no clear rhythm, against which the basses' melody starts the ballad. It remains in unison until Lady Barnard declares her love for Little Musgrave, when the voices suddenly flower into harmony. But these second-inversion triads have a lower third added in place of the fifth (rather like the piano arpeggios that open his later Canticle, *Abraham and Isaac*): there is something sensuous about the major chord when it lacks the muscle of the fifth interval. The second section, which portrays the treachery of the page-boy, is fast, *staccato* and physically vital as he races off to tell his master. Britten then has piano and voices imitating the hunting horn, as Barnard pursues his quarry. The scene switches to the lovers in bed: Musgrave (is he Little in stature or years?) thinks he hears Barnard coming, but Lady Barnard (who clearly does not know her husband very well) says it is only a shepherd-boy, and tells him not to worry.

But it is indeed Lord Barnard. By putting the voices in hushed unison *staccato*, Britten manages to convey milord on tiptoe approaching the bed, where the unsuspecting lovers are entwined beneath the covers. With the offbeat accents in the piano, and then the unexpected syncopations in the ever-softer *staccato* voices, he almost trips up in the dark – the suspense is so taut. He lifts up the coverlet, then the sheet. . . . There is silence. Then the choir takes a deep breath, as if gasping in astonishment at the naked lovebirds, and sounds the fanfare of the cuckold's challenge:

> Arise, arise, thou little Musgrave!
>> And put thy clothes on.
> It shall ne'er be said in my country
>> I've killed a naked man.

A sword-fight follows, with the same furious arpeggios that denoted Barnard's ride through the night. After the duel, and the death of the two lovers (Britten omits the description of the vengeful way in which Barnard – some shepherd-boy! – murders his wife), the work is crowned by a moving funeral march in C minor, which Lord Barnard's remorse transfigures into E flat major, which is where the ballad began.

> 'A grave, a grave', Lord Barnard cried,
>> 'To put these lovers in!
> But lay my lady on the upper hand,
>> For she comes of the nobler kin.'

Our sympathies lie with the adulterers until the end, when the music's hostility to the husband relents, because of his self-inflicted tragedy. As the agent of destruction, the boy – the traitorous, 'little, tiny page' – is for once the villain of the piece.

The original ballad is almost cinematic in its structure – perhaps one of the reasons it drew the one-time film composer. The dialogue switches between characters without guidance, as if cutting between shots in a film sequence, and the frequent changes of scene are sharply delineated by Britten. It is indeed clever – but the result is both profound and affecting.

The Ballad of Little Musgrave and Lady Barnard was often performed by the older Wandsworth boys, once their voices had broken. Britten's enthusiasm for the rough edges of the Wandsworth treble sound resulted, in 1969, in a work written specially for them, *Children's Crusade*. They already had in their repertoire *A Ceremony of Carols*, *The Golden Vanity*, *Missa Brevis* and *Rejoice in the Lamb*. Now they and their choirmaster Russell Burgess could look forward to another piece full of good tunes, clever rhythms and artful wit. So they thought.

Adrian Thompson remembers the alarm when the huge scores from Faber Music were delivered. 'It was all handwritten and lots of it – very difficult to decipher. I think Russell Burgess was shocked at how difficult it was.' Burgess knew the work was intended to mark the fiftieth anniversary of the Save the Children Fund, and that Britten had wanted to set Bertolt Brecht's poem about a group of displaced orphans wandering through Poland at the start of the second world war. So he knew the story could be depressing. 'But, musically, he thought: "What the hell have we got here?" And I think he panicked a bit to start with, which he passed on to us. So we rather panicked that we'd never be able to do it.'

The work is unique in Britten's output for being written for children's voices (including seven soloists and a four-part choir) and percussion orchestra. Although he did not say so, the assumption was that all the percussion players would be children, with the possible exception of the two pianists. He added a chamber organ, which mostly accompanies the singers, and helps them maintain their pitch. In the percussion orchestra, he distinguished between the six virtuoso soloists and the simpler parts in the rest of the ensemble, which was divided into three types of percussion: tuned (such as xylophone and tubular bells), rhythmic (drums and tambourine), and clashed or ringing (such as gong, cymbals or cowbells). The result was that the score was visually very unusual for Britten: Burgess was probably daunted by the lack of staves and by the quantity of unpitched notes, although Britten's use of the chamber organ was a practical way to help the choir navigate its way through the score.

When the Wandsworth singers and players assembled for the first time, the huge opening crash which represents the shells and bombs of war was unlike anything they had ever heard. 'To me, at the age of fourteen,' says Thompson, 'it sounded as if somebody with a huge tray of teacups and pots and pans had just chucked it all down a flight of concrete stairs! It was an incredible sound – just overpowering – and you thought, "My God, what is this?" '

The choir had already been struggling. 'We spent months and months in rehearsals before school, during the breaks, during the lunch break, after school finished in the evenings, just trying to get it right. It was a very difficult time for boys of our sort – we weren't specifically musicians but just happened to be there because it was the local comp[rehensive school] – so it was quite a challenge. We often used to be in tears at the end of the rehearsal because we just couldn't get the intervals right. We'd try to pitch the notes in a dissonant chord, and then Russell Burgess would bash them out on the piano, and we'd be way out, and think "Oh please, are we ever going to get this right?" '

The suffering of the children in the story was at least partly reflected in the suffering of the children in rehearsal. It was a strange, and uncharacteristic, outcome of Britten's piece, supposedly written to honour his favourite choir. What would the director of the Vienna Boys' Choir have said, if he had known? But Britten had experienced this frustration and exhaustion himself, at the same age. His composition lessons with his revered teacher Frank Bridge were, he said, 'mammoth. I remember one that started at half past ten, and at tea-time Mrs Bridge came in and said, "Really, Frank, you must give the boy a break." Often I used to end these marathons in tears; not that he was beastly to me, but the concentrated strain was too much for me.' Only later did he come to recognise that Bridge's strictness stemmed from his professionalism.

Adrian Thompson recalls that, when Britten started coming to the occasional *Crusade* rehearsal (which he did fairly early on), he was 'never ever critical – certainly not to us boys. He was always totally encouraging and gentle, trying to get us to do our best. But I'm sure he must have known we found it difficult.' The boys latched on to one or two colourful moments in the otherwise monochrome story – such as the drummer boy, and the dog (represented rather unsatisfactorily by a scraper) – though neither offered much light relief. Eventually they left the pain threshold behind them, and began to appreciate the piece. 'I think he knew us better than we knew ourselves, in that we rose to the challenge. If we got the notes or the rhythms wrong, he never said "That's wrong, you must do it like this, do it like that". I think he was interested – in that piece more than any – in the atmosphere it created, and it certainly created a lot of fear!'

After one of his early visits to Wandsworth, Britten reported that the rehearsal was 'rather exciting, and the children had considerable fun in extending their various bits'. He had in mind the percussion players to whom he had given some freedom to improvise, and to decide the length of their sections. But he did not refer to the boys who had to pitch the notes for themselves – the choir: the musical return for all their hard work is not high. He did later admit that *Children's Crusade* was 'a very grisly piece'.

The première was held during the Save the Children Fund thanksgiving service at St Paul's Cathedral in May 1969. The boys found (perhaps to their relief) that the cathedral's reverberant acoustic concealed 'a multitude of sins', as Thompson remembers. It was only the following month, when they returned to the piece for an Aldeburgh Festival performance prior to recording it, that they realised how many wrong notes they had sung at the première. 'We had to go back quite a long way and build it up again.' But by then they had lost their fear of the piece, and were beginning to enjoy exploring its dark colours. Britten was normally highly sensitive to the circumstances of a first performance. So it was strange and surprisingly unyielding of him to prescribe a percussion orchestra for the notorious expanse beneath the dome. Perhaps he had not done his homework: Rosamund Strode remembers him being 'very downcast by the colossal extent of the echo'. That alone ensured that the all-important words of the ballad were engulfed. Britten did say that he hoped 'the splendid sound that these boys make may defeat the rather curious acoustics of St Paul's, which is a little bit resonant as you know'. After the first performance, some of the boys' parents who were present 'were completely overcome, and overwhelmed by the strength of the music, and we all of a sudden realised, "Gosh, this is a great piece".' Britten himself railed against the 'assinine [sic] pomposity of the established church', but was pleased with the boys' 'tremendous impression of passion and sincerity' in their 'singing & hitting'. Rosamund Strode points out how difficult it was to prevent the more intimate passages of pathos being lost: 'I prefer not to think too much about that performance. It sort of went by!'

Britten could at least count on the BBC's sound engineers to come to his aid in the live broadcast, so that perhaps the work could flourish beyond St Paul's. But in the thirty years or more since, it has never established itself in the repertoire,* partly because the instruments it requires (from tam-tam to sleighbells) are beyond the resources of most schools, and expensive to hire. The work's technical difficulty is not mitigated by the subject matter, which is almost unrelievedly grim. It is remarkable how many of his own unwritten rules of composition Britten seemed to break in this piece. It was insensitive to its intended location,

---

* Perhaps the 2003 recording by Christ Church Cathedral, Oxford (in many ways superior to Britten's original) will make up for the years of neglect (Lammas Records LAMM 146D).

it was logistically beyond the reach of most schoolchildren, its theme and musical language were bleak, without any moment of redemption or transfiguration. The story (apparently a true one) is not really about the corruption of innocence: the innocence has been destroyed before the start. It is no wonder that, in a BBC *Omnibus* documentary,* which filmed him recording the work later in 1969, he seemed troubled and weighed down. There was no sign of the enjoyment and good humour which children normally provoked in him.

The reason for all this perhaps lay in a passionate horror of the trauma of war as it affected its most helpless victims. Britten's commitment to that subject overrode his normal felicity in writing for children. He was honouring a charity which worked at the sharpest end of cruelty to the young, and he was perhaps wary of producing a piece which was too cosy. Indeed, *Children's Crusade* has added force because the 'grisly' story of the suffering of children is told by children themselves. Before all the characters perish (even the dog starves to death), the children find themselves having to behave as adults, just as they had in his favourite film *Emil and the Detectives* – only this time their behaviour is not in shining contrast with adult failings, but a mirror-image of them.

Britten was one of the most skilled composers of his century in writing violent music, as he had powerfully demonstrated in *War Requiem*, most notably in the penultimate scene. There his evocation of the tumult of trench warfare can have the audience gripping its seats, until released by Wilfred Owen's extraordinary poem, 'Strange Meeting'. In *Children's Crusade*, he abandoned traditional instrumentation in favour of the varied percussion which he had used to such effect in two of the Church Parables. The result is perhaps the fiercest music he ever wrote. But the emotional pay-off is harder to apprehend.

When filming the work for television, I was surprised to find his own initial impressions of 1969 vindicated by today's

* *The Wandsworth Sound* 5.4.70.

children. There was no doubt the percussion players of the Oxford Youth Percussion Ensemble were having enormous fun, in particular two small boys playing the xylophone with intense concentration. One of them, Jake Morter, who was ten, said how much he liked the piece because it was loud. 'My favourite bit is the beginning, because you can bang the instrument, and you can hardly hear anything else but the bang.' The nine-year-old cowbell-player Alistair Duff agreed: 'I like the big clashing bits. You can whack it and then whatever you do for the next like second, it doesn't really matter.' Leila Unia, who was eleven, also enjoyed the bangs and crashes, and she understood what they represented. 'It tells you it's the beginning of the second world war: the crashes express all the gunshots and the firing and people being killed.' She appreciated the poignancy of bereft children wandering around Poland on their own after the death of their parents. But the darkness of the plot hardly bothered the boys. 'It's about these children who crusade around Poland. They take a dog, to eat it, and at the end the dog starves and doesn't recover: it's really funny.' So perhaps Britten understood better than most of us how to handle a subject which simultaneously contained horror for adults and macabre amusement for children.

The Wandsworth boys went to Aldeburgh just before the opening of the 1969 Festival to rehearse the *Crusade* at the Maltings. Britten knew how to alleviate the tension and stress of those rehearsals: he gave them a party at his home. On a sunny day in early June, they invaded the Red House. 'I just remember total chaos', says his agent Sue Phipps. 'Boys were in every corner of everywhere. But he was quite unworried by it and just seemed to enjoy allowing them complete freedom.' One of them was Adrian Thompson. 'We had a wonderful time playing on the tennis court, in the swimming pool, running in and out of the library, through the house in all directions, all around the garden. I do remember I was thrown in the pool – I think the others decided I would make the largest splash. I remember Ben standing on the side in gales of laughter. He was altogether very relaxed – chatting to us and watching the mayhem happening all around him. There was no "I'm Benjamin Britten and you are a lot of scruffy south London children". He was very much one of the boys – totally in his element. You could see it in his face, in his body language.' The same spirit infused Britten's invitation to the choir five years later to begin the rehabilitation of his American operetta *Paul Bunyan*. He asked them to sing the three ballad interludes with 'any guitars, banjos etc that you can muster (!) [. . .] What it needs is good old Wandsworth fun.'*

Many of the boys Britten had befriended over the years had been public school boys like himself. There had been one or two exceptions, like Harry Morris or 'Nipper', but even so the Wandsworth boys were unusual. Thompson believes that he was attracted by their lack of culture and sophistication, which allowed them to bring something more earthy and genuine to his music. 'You couldn't get away from the fact that he was from an upper middle class background, had been to public school and was surrounded by those sorts of people. He had very correct, clipped, beautifully-spoken English. It was a jolt to our ears to hear somebody speaking like that.† But he seemed to be very much at home with us and with all the boys calling him Ben. I'm sure that, if any adults whom he didn't know very well had gone up to him and called him Ben, he would have frosted them out. But with the kids that was fine.'

When the Red House party was over, the *Crusade* rehearsals resumed – one of the last gatherings in the Maltings before the concert hall was destroyed by fire a few days later. The performance itself was held in Blythburgh Church instead. 'He wouldn't

---

* The result, on 10th June 1974, was the first public performance of any part of *Paul Bunyan* since the original production at Columbia University in 1941.
† Even allowing for the changes in the inflexion of spoken English in recent decades, Britten's rather plummy speaking voice pulls many lovers of his music up short. His siblings (interviewed in Tony Palmer's film *A Time There Was*) did not speak in the same way, and his childhood friend Basil Reeve is certain that the plummy vowels were not present when he knew him. Perhaps they were acquired under the pre-war influence of Auden.

have got the results from us had he been rather distant and frosty. He gave us freedom to express ourselves, and we just sang our hearts out all day long for him because we felt that he loved us in that way. We wanted to give the best that we could back.'

CHAPTER 10

His undying friends

The idea that Britten's relationships with boys were based on reciprocal, innocent love was far removed from the censorious judgement of his one-time friend and intimate colleague Eric Crozier. In an often waspish memorandum about Britten written in 1966 he said the composer seemed compelled to 'corrupt' boys.

Crozier was his contemporary, and had begun working with him just after Britten's return from America in the middle of the war. He produced both *Peter Grimes* and *The Rape of Lucretia*, and wrote the libretto of Britten's next opera *Albert Herring*. The texts of the cantata *Saint Nicolas* and the children's opera *The Little Sweep* were also his, as well as the optional spoken commentary for *The Young Person's Guide to the Orchestra*. He collaborated with E.M. Forster in adapting Herman Melville's story into the libretto for *Billy Budd*. For several years he counted himself 'indispensable' to Britten. But then, to his dismay, his star waned, as the composer decided to broaden his circle of musical collaborators, and Crozier regarded himself as one of Britten's many 'corpses'.

Crozier's bitterness turned to gall when Imogen Holst published her book about Britten in 1966, which failed to mention Crozier's name in connection with any of the libretti or with the foundation of the Aldeburgh Festival. Not surprisingly, he took this to mean that his collaboration with Britten was not just forgotten but wiped from the record, and within a few weeks he dipped his pen in the gall to write the 14,000-word memorandum – a private document, but designed for posterity. Its sour character is evident from the extraordinary way he blamed Britten for his physical appearance:

I have been puzzled and astonished to see how much he has altered and how ugly he has become. [. . .] His neck is thicker, his features coarser, and when his face is in repose his expression seems to be largely compounded of arrogance, impatience and hostility.

Crozier (who was not himself homosexual) saw Britten's homosexuality as his Achilles' heel: it cramped his musical and dramatic range, and affected his personality. He was particularly disparaging about his attitude to children. Although Britten 'loved and respected and admired Pears to the point of idolatry', Crozier wrote, 'he was not always satisfied by their "marriage" '. After alleging that Britten had apparently once told him that he had been 'raped' by a master at school (this claim was neither repeated to others nor substantiated), Crozier went on to say: 'having been corrupted as a boy, he seemed to be under a compulsion to corrupt other small boys'. He found it significant that, when he wrote to Britten suggesting Racine's *Phèdre* (the tragic character of Greek mythology, Phaedra, who fell in love with her stepson Hippolytus) as an operatic subject, the composer replied enthusiastically, but said that, from his pen, the opera would have to be called 'Hippolytus'.*

Crozier conceded he had never himself seen any sign of Britten corrupting small boys, but he still used the word 'corruption'.

I know nothing about his methods of corruption by direct observation, but always and inevitably there was one particular young boy, or several at a time, whom he worshipped and who filled his thoughts. A friend of mine had two teen-aged sons, whom Britten made much of: both, after visits to his house, refused to go there again and they

---

* Nine years after this memorandum (which of course Britten never read), the composer did indeed set the story as a dramatic cantata for mezzo-soprano and orchestra. His chosen title was *Phaedra*.

would have nothing more to do with him. The same thing happened in the case of her nephews.*

With the pejorative context anonymously established, Crozier went on:

The technique seems to have been to flatter the boy with gifts, to play games with him, and sometimes to visit his school: to invite him down for a holiday and gradually captivate him by a display of admiration and affection, and thus make him a devoted acolyte. Or, in the case of a poor boy, it began with paying his fees at school or choir-school.

All these things undeniably happened (except perhaps paying for a choir-school education, of which Britten was not a notable fan). But Crozier's language was consistently peevish, despite his avowal that he had no wish to denigrate Britten: 'At a later stage, either the boy would be seized with revulsion and break off the friendship, or he would be dropped for some new victim'.

The most eloquent evidence against Crozier's view is the boys themselves. They all experienced Britten's 'technique' (although Crozier does not mention the warm, caring letters that Britten never stopped writing). They all enjoyed his generosity (in both time and money) and his encouragement. They remain to this day 'his undying friends', and cherish their fond memories without reproach.

After Britten returned from America in 1942, one of his first boy companions was Humphrey Maud, the eldest child of his friends John and Jean Maud. He remembers Britten staying with his parents during the war and playing through the first drafts of *Peter Grimes* on their piano. Humphrey felt involved from the start, even though he was only nine or ten, and 'it was nice to be treated as one of the group'. He remembers a 'riotous' picnic on the lawn at Glyndebourne after the war, when he and his sisters

---

* At first blush, Crozier may seem to refer to the two sons and two nephews in the Gathorne-Hardy family, dedicatees of *The Little Sweep*. But there was no interruption in their friendship with Britten.

played ducks and drakes on the lake, with Ben the most ardent competitor for the greatest number of ricochets by his pebbles. After the success of *Peter Grimes*, Britten dedicated his *Young Person's Guide to the Orchestra* to Humphrey and his three sisters 'for their edification and entertainment'. The parents were touched that the dedication included their eldest daughter Pamela, who had died in 1941. After Humphrey graduated to Eton at the age of thirteen, the friendship with Ben became closer and a paradigm for many of his later associations with teenaged boys. The ordeal of starting at a new school naturally excited his sympathy, and he made plans to see Humphrey before he took the plunge: 'poor kid – I'm sorry for him, what a nightmare new places are'. Maud today believes Britten was equivalent to the ideal godfather. 'He had exactly the same sustained interest in one's development, not just day by day but over the years. It was a very profound friendship based on interest, fondness and affection, such as a godfather has for a favourite godchild. And that encompasses the feeling I had towards him.'

Unlike many of Britten's young friends, Humphrey came from a stable family background. His mother welcomed the latitude that her son's burgeoning friendship with Britten gave him. On the family's first visit to Britten's new home on the Aldeburgh seafront, Humphrey and Ben disappeared after supper. 'He and I went off to a different room, it may have been upstairs or something, and got into a long talk, and everyone else was downstairs. When we came back my mother said, "Oh, where have you been?", and Ben said, "We've been having a nice chat". To her great credit, she replied, "Well, I think it's high time that Humphrey flew the coop. Very good for him to have someone outside the family circle to talk to." '

After that, Humphrey began paying regular visits to Aldeburgh during school holidays to stay with Ben. His parents saw these invitations to Crag House as 'a huge treat' for Humphrey, and regarded him as very lucky. The visits increased his musical maturity and broadened his experience: it was Britten who gave him his first taste of sailing, for instance, on the Norfolk Broads.

In the morning Humphrey would employ himself while Ben worked. In the afternoon they went birdwatching together, they went for drives around Suffolk, they played tennis. John and Jean Maud had absolute trust in Britten's integrity as a friend 'who would not abuse the friendship in any improper way'. After one visit, Humphrey wrote to thank him 'very, very much for having me for such a wonderful stay. I enjoyed every minute of it, especially the sail to Oulton Broad. I also enjoyed the tennis, and I am sure I have benefited from it.' On another occasion he said, 'I'm sure that I'm better off for our heart-to-heart', and signed off 'with firkins of love, Humphrey'.

Ben often fulfilled his role as the young person's guide by discussing music on equal terms with Humphrey. The boy was a talented cellist, and was to play with the National Youth Orchestra between the ages of fifteen and eighteen. On every visit to Crag House, Humphrey brought his cello with him: somehow, with Britten there, his playing sounded much better than it ever had before. He asked Britten who his most important influences were as an opera composer, 'and he replied, "Mozart and Verdi" – absolutely straight off like that'. He explained why he did not much care for Dvořák or Brahms. When Humphrey was excited about Beethoven, Ben demurred but added: 'Don't let that put you off. At your age, my home was full of busts of Beethoven, and I couldn't get enough of him!' Humphrey told Ben he imagined him writing 'superb operas, sensational cantatas, stupendous oratorios, and the odd ear-splitting Presto for cello and piano'.

Maud remembers the friendship with undiluted fondness. Britten, in his words, always carried 'a sense of fun and sunshine' with him. 'There was a bit of his character which never grew up, which was perhaps why he was so congenial to young boys. He clearly enjoyed my company, I enjoyed his, and we talked about everything under the sun. In that sense it was a very intimate, no-holds-barred, relationship. But there was absolutely no physical implication or connotation whatsoever in this. Nor, I think, did my parents feel that there was any risk of that.' When reminded that his mother had described Humphrey as having been 'a very fetching boy' at that age, Maud laughs and says: 'Perhaps it wasn't an adverse factor!'

Despite having been at boys' boarding-schools since the age of six, Humphrey's understanding of homosexuality at that stage was 'very shallow'. He remembers observing the relationship between the two men during his visits, the frequent bad tempers at breakfast, and their sometimes acerbic reaction to hostile criticism. Humphrey asked his parents why Britten was not married, and why Pears was also a bachelor. His father replied that they were, in a sense, married to each other, and the boy accepted that without further enquiry.

A year or two later, however, his parents became uncomfortable. Without Humphrey knowing, his father intervened to tone down the friendship. This was not the mild remonstrance of Tadzio's mother in *Death in Venice*. Sir John Maud was much more direct.

He invited Britten to call on him at his Curzon Street office (he was Permanent Secretary at the Ministry of Education) and took the bull by the horns. It must have been an awkward interview between two old friends. Britten was mortified when John Maud declared that Humphrey should no longer spend part of his holidays with him in Suffolk: 'He said that that particular aspect of our friendship should cease. And Ben was very upset by this. I think he couldn't understand how a friendship which had begun perhaps seven years before should suddenly be found objectionable. But the fact was that, from that particular point, I ceased to go off on school holidays to Aldeburgh.' Humphrey Maud believes his father had not lost his trust in Britten, but had been warned by a mutual friend (Nancy Astor's stepson Bobbie Shaw, who was himself homosexual) that it was unwise for the boy to be associated with the Britten–Pears circle. John Maud perhaps felt that, in his exalted position in the civil service, he could not afford the risk of scandal. 'I certainly don't think that he was ever afraid that I might be the victim of my friendship with Britten. I think it was a precautionary measure: just in case others might think ill of it, it would be as well that it should be seen to stop.' Humphrey Maud reveres the memory of his father, but at the same time believes his intervention was wrong. 'I think Ben was offended by my father's action, particularly by being asked to go and see him in his office. If he'd had doubts about the friendship, perhaps Britten might have thought, "Well, this is something that we can talk about, you know, over a glass of something". But to make it such a formal act was I think one of the things that most upset Ben.'

Humphrey was not told what had passed between Britten and his father until many years later, and he was unaware that the friendship had been scaled down because just as his visits to Suffolk ended, he began his heavy holiday commitments for the National Youth Orchestra. In his thirties he played through the Shostakovich Cello Sonata with Britten at the Maud family home in Oxford – evidence that, however prickly Britten could often be about real or imagined slights, in this case he maintained the friendship with Humphrey and his family, who were still occasional guests at the Red House in Aldeburgh.

The first child to appear in a Britten opera was Leonard Thompson as the Apprentice in *Peter Grimes*. But his role was entirely mute except for a high-pitched scream as he fell from Grimes's cliff-top hut to his death. In early drafts of the libretto, there were 'quite a lot' of words written for the boy, but Britten and his librettist Montagu Slater had great trouble finding the right boy to sing them. Slater's wife Enid became 'fed up' with their complaints. 'I lost my temper and said: "For God's sake, make the boy a dumb role". And they said, "If we make him dumb, he needn't sing, need he?" But it only happened because I lost my temper. [. . .] I apologised afterwards, but Ben said, "It's one of the best ideas you have ever had".'

It was not until 1947 that he gave his first operatic singing parts to children in *Albert Herring*. But the two girls Emmie and Cis were in fact sung by adult sopranos: the only real child was the boy Harry – or, to give him his full name, Harold Wood. This was a typically schoolboyish in-joke between Britten and

Crozier, which Britten thought was 'terribly funny': Harold Wood was the Essex village where they often stopped for a pub lunch en route between Aldeburgh and London. When the newly formed English Opera Group gave the first performance of *Herring* at Glyndebourne in June, the role of Harry was created by a thirteen-year-old boy, David Spenser.

Spenser had been recommended to Britten by Crozier's partner, the singer Nancy Evans. He had already played several speaking roles on stage and on radio when he told his mother that he was having a singing audition with someone called Mr Britten. 'She went berserk. "Benjamin Britten?" she said. "Ah yes, you must sing Brahms' Lullaby".' His attention during the audition was drawn less by the shy young composer than by a plateful of huge cream buns on the table. He sang the Lullaby 'with eyes still on the cream cakes. Afterwards it was extraordinary. There was a lovely kind of feeling there, and I was allowed to devour some of the buns.' It was an unconscious parallel with the opera itself. In the singing-lesson scene, the three children supposed to be rehearsing a festive song to hail Albert as the May King are far more interested in the sausage rolls, jelly and trifle lined up on the table. It is no accident that this is one of the funniest scenes in the opera, in which Britten's insight into the child's mind, combined with his acute sense of timing, avoids any risk of tweeness.

Spenser remembers the rehearsal period for *Herring* as a very happy time. 'He treated me with a lot of humour, which made it easy for me, because every time I opened my mouth to sing he would give me a look of utter astonishment which made us both laugh. His eyebrows would go up, up, up, and there was a quiver of a smile on his face, as if he was surprised I'd even attempted the last phrase.' From the start Britten was not a figure of authority or a father figure. The relationship was easier than that – 'more like a school friend that you really could trust. The other people in the production I'd been brought up to call "Miss Ritchie", "Miss Cross", "Miss Wood", and all men over twelve were "Sir". So Frederick Ashton was "Sir",

Peter Pears was "Sir" (until he told me, "please call me Peter", but I was never happy with that). Ben, from the word go, was "Ben". I had no difficulty with that whatsoever, and it was because, without patronising you, he was on the same level you were at – it was quite natural to him.'

Until he learnt the part of Harry, David had had no liking for modern music. But every night he used to loiter in the wings to hear Sid and Nancy's love duet, which moved him to tears. He loved *The Rape of Lucretia* too, which alternated with *Herring* during the EOG's European tour in July, and wrote to a friend in great surprise: 'I've found a modern composer that I really like'. He remembers with amusement one of the Glyndebourne performances, when he bumped into Ben during the supper interval. 'With a twinkle in his eye he said, "You know, David, very often you improve my music, but tonight I thought I knew better".'

As was becoming the custom with all the boys he befriended, Ben invited David to stay at his home. He drove the boy up to Suffolk as soon as the tour was over, just in time to help him move into Crag House. 'It was pure holiday and I think I must have been the first guest because the house wasn't ready for anyone else, and so it was a lovely adventure.' While Britten was composing at his first-floor desk overlooking the sea, he invited David to sit by him, and gave him a book of paintings by Hieronymus Bosch to keep him occupied. 'I found the paintings fascinating, but at the same time I was aware of this pencil going very, very fast and I couldn't resist saying to him, "Ben, you're doing that awfully quickly", and he said, "Yes, it's easier than writing letters!"'

They swam in the sea twice a day, after breakfast and before tea, and 'it was lovely because he would point out things on the shore from where we were swimming – particularly the Suffolk faces. He loved the characters of the fishermen.' They would go for long walks in the afternoon, and he would draw the boy's attention to particular birds and flowers. 'He loved the country around Aldeburgh, and when we were alone together he talked about it as I never heard him talk to other people, because he was passing on something that he loved and treasured.' On one walk, on David's first day there, they spent the best part of an hour near a dog's drinking trough, waiting to see if a dog would come to it. Spenser puts it down to a sweetness in Britten that was to do with 'a private world that we had. We were walking along the shore once, when he stopped and said, "You know, there are villages that have been drowned by the sea, and on certain nights you can hear the bells". Every time we went for a walk after that, we listened for the bells – and I often do that now. It has remained with me – a feeling that, if you can hear the bells from the sea, then something magical will happen.'

Spenser remembers discussing the atomic bombs dropped on Japan two years earlier, which had upset him deeply. 'Ben never said, "Yes, how dreadful", he never used the word pacifist, but he somehow took what I was saying and my own troubled mind into his cupped hands, as it were, and just held them for a little. It was quite healing, and he always had this kind of sweetness of approach.'

Every night, after dinner, Ben would play the grand piano for David for an hour, just as he had for Wulff Scherchen almost ten years earlier. 'I used to lie on the sofa like some Egyptian pharaoh, and was very excited listening to him, because he brought emotion to his playing – not romantic emotion, but a real something as though the piano was speaking. My favourite composers were Chopin and Brahms, and I would ask for them over and over again – the Chopin preludes, the sonatas, the polonaises, and Brahms's variations. He played them all without any complaint – it was totally for me. I'm sure he wanted to give this small visitor the pleasure he wanted.' One night he asked David if he could play something different. 'I listened for a little while, and he said, "You don't like it?" and I replied, "Well, it's very tinkly". He said to me, "One day you will realise that Mozart was the greatest composer that ever lived, and Brahms was the worst".'

For David Spenser, the time at Crag House was an extraordinary idyll. His parents had split up when he was only five; his father lived in Ceylon, so he had never really known adult male

155

company at home. 'Ben was a lovely listener, a soother. That was really the core of our relationship. I was not terribly happy at home, I was not having a good time. At thirteen I was doing all the cooking, all the sweeping, all the polishing, everything in the house, so staying with him in Aldeburgh was an unbelievable rest, and a relief from home. He was one of the few people in the world, at that time, that I could talk to. He could be very tender, as somebody that you can trust and who receives your trust is.'

At night David slept in one side of Ben's double bed. He says it did not strike him as strange, because Ben explained it was the only available bed in the house straight after the move. He nonetheless told his mother about it in a letter soon after his arrival. Rather surprisingly, she never asked any questions. 'There was no hanky-panky or I would have certainly told my mother. It was a very big bed, and I just went to sleep. The next time I came to visit, not long after, I had the spare room, which by then was ready.'

Looking back, Spenser feels that the friendship with Britten was of no greater significance than several others in his life, but it was very important to him at the time. In a thank-you letter after his first visit to Aldeburgh (a letter overseen by his mother), he wrote to 'my dear dear sir'* to tell him: 'I can't tell you how much I loved being with you, and what a happy time I have had during the time I spent with you. I don't think I have ever been happier in my life.' He went on to say that Ben had never been out of his thoughts, and he had been missing him all the time since his return home. 'It must be lovely', he added, 'to be with the ones you love all the time, but I am beginning to think one has to be dead to be able to do that'.

He had clearly confided in Ben about the difficult relationship with his mother at home, to judge by Britten's letter to Pears (who as so often was away performing).

Little David went off yesterday morning – rather sadly, poor little thing. His home life is hell, but I think his existence

---

* Evidently Spenser's upbringing reasserted itself when he was back at home.

has been made a little brighter by being treated properly for a few days. Barbara* was sweet to him, & he poured his heart out to me – rather self-consciously, but the old feelings were genuine, I'm sure.

Spenser says Ben never directly stated any fondness for him. 'I never took it for granted that he was especially fond of me and I never expected our friendship to go on. Occasionally he would put his arm around me when we were walking or when he was pointing something out, but I never felt it to be extra-affectionate. I do remember that at certain times when I was a little upset, he would not exactly cuddle but rather like a good friend at school would put his arm around and just hold one and steady one. But I wouldn't say he was an extraordinarily physical person to me.'

At the age of thirteen, he was fully aware of homosexuality, particularly with his stage experience. He recognised Frederick Ashton was homosexual, because he was 'slightly camp', but never made the connection with Britten and Pears. He says he would have recognised a sexual advance for what it was, not least because he was propositioned by a stranger on a London bus at around this time. But there was no hint of any advance from Britten.

He was aware, however, of concerns within the English Opera Group during the European and British tours of *Albert Herring*. Margaret (or Mabel) Ritchie, who sang the part of Harry's schoolmistress, Miss Wordsworth, extended her tutelage off-stage. She was a Christian Scientist and Spenser believes she felt responsible for his Christian welfare. 'I think she began to worry that there was something there. Often people with good intentions can stir up a lot of mud – and she spread it around, I think.' Anne Wood, who managed the EOG, was also concerned, and took rather hilarious preventative action: 'I made it my business to interfere, going in and out of rooms.

---

* Britten's housekeeper, Barbara Parker. Spenser remembers that she made 'the most lovely apple pies' and smiled all the time.

I just prayed we would get through with it, but I often wondered whether we would.' She was worried about Ben's fondness for David, 'partly from Peter's point of view'. She believed there were 'cracks' in Britten's relationship with Pears, 'and that seemed so important it was a pity'. When the tours were over, Mabel Ritchie asked Eric Crozier to use his influence with Britten 'to stop him using small boys in his operas. She felt it was a moral duty to try and protect these small creatures from a danger that she foresaw.' Perhaps it was she who planted the notion of corruption in Crozier's mind. She took the surprising step of writing to David to ask him whether he had been to stay with Britten. His response showed an interesting protectiveness towards the man by the boy. 'I said no, even though of course I had. I lied, because something told me I shouldn't go down that lane at all. But in a letter to my mother I was very worried that I'd lied.'

David Spenser sang the role of Harry only during the summer and autumn of 1947. The following year, it was taken over by Alan Thompson, brother of the first boy apprentice in *Peter Grimes*. But Spenser stayed in regular touch with Britten until he was sixteen. At one point, when they had been talking about poetry, Ben encouraged David to send him some of his own. The boy compiled a collection entitled 'Golden Thoughts', which he sent 'to Benjamin Britten, with love from David'. He said he had written the poems between the ages of thirteen and fifteen and that they were dedicated to his family and friends, and to those he 'dearly loves'. Wulff Scherchen was not the only one to be poetically emboldened by Britten. One of David's poems, entitled 'A Tender Remembrance', chimed in with the awareness of nature that Britten had fostered.

> When the apple blossom clusters on the trees,
> When daffodils and narcissi carpet the grass,
> And peeping violets and primroses
> Try to hide themselves away,
> I am reminded of you.

A tea party at the family home in Lowestoft for pupils of Britten's old school, ith Lodge, 1934. Piers Dunkerley is second from the right.

3ritten aged 22 with his mother and sister Barbara, 1936.
3en as entertainer at Shingle Street, at the mouth of the River Alde.

4 The pursuit of Grundeis (Fritz Rasp) in *Emil und die Detektive* (1931), 'the mo perfect & satisfying film I have ever seen'.

5 Harry Morris, a Hampstead chorister: 'a grand kid'.
6 Piers Dunkerley, 1934: 'what a boy to help!'.

The proud owner of the Old Mill, Snape, 1938.
Wulff Scherchen at the Old Mill.

Wulff Scherchen with Britten at Snape, 1938/9.

10 Enid Slater's portrait of Britten's young Apollo, Wulff Scherchen.
11 Bobby Rothman being held 'like a sack of coals', 1941/2.

12 The wartime reunion of Wulff Scherchen and Britten, snapped by a London street photographer, 1942.

Jean Maud and her children in 1943, the dedicatees of *The Young Person's Guide to the Orchestra*.

Humphrey Maud at Eton, 1952.

David Spenser, the first Harry in *Albert Herring*, 1947.

Robin Long ('Nipper') helps Britten steer Billy Burrell's boat, 1951.

17 Paul Rogerson, 'a really dear good boy', early 1950s.
18 'About to take off like a rocket': Britten's devastating serve.

19 (David) 'Hemmings the Menace sings opera in Venice': before the première o
The Turn of the Screw, 1954.

Reunion with Roger Duncan in Devon after Britten's Far East tour, 1956.
Robert Saxton, c.1964: 'you must tune your violin properly'.
Ronan Magill, 'Tyger': 'a dedicated and passionate young man'.

Britten 'shared' Roger with his father, Ronald Duncan.

24 Final rehearsals for the children's opera *Noye's Fludde*, 1958.

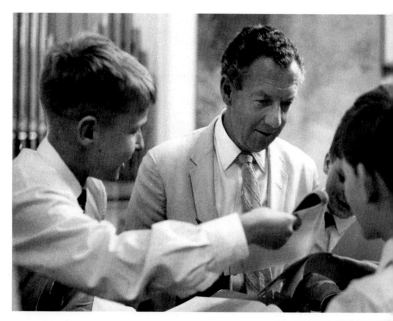

25 Preparing the *War Requiem* in Ottobeuren Basilica, West Germany, with choristers of Coventry Cathedral, 1964.

When the little spring breezes ruffled your hair
And the skies were reflected in your eyes,
When the sun turned your hair to gold
And your fingers were intwined round mine
May I banish from my mind your eyes, your touch?
Oh no! Those sweet memories shall ever be mine.

The 'sweetness' that Spenser so vividly remembers emerged only when they were alone, not when a third person was present – not even if it was Pears. Many of the other young companions testify to his volatility in the company of adults. Humphrey Maud recalls bad-tempered breakfasts and other petulant moments. Arthur Oldham reported 'quite bitchy' fights between Britten and Pears, with face-slapping. According to David Hemmings, there were 'furious rows', and Britten could sometimes be 'snappy – but get him on the right day, and he was just charming'. Bridget Kitley, the daughter of Enid and Montagu Slater, said she and her sisters were 'impressed by his unpredictability and irritability' when he came to stay during the war, so they were always 'careful to be good girls'. She recalls one of Britten's moods at his flat in St John's Wood. Pears was in the kitchen 'serenely making cauliflower cheese' while Britten worked off his temper by playing Haydn on the piano. The young girl was 'terrified of his sudden black moods' and on this occasion crawled under the piano, where she found the vibrations of his 'thunderous' playing 'dangerously delicious'.

Jonathan Gathorne-Hardy has written that Ben was 'not an altogether easy companion'. There were 'awkwardnesses, sudden fleeting tensions, silences', and Pears was a 'more relaxed and obviously charming' character. He was one of the seven children to whom Britten 'affectionately' dedicated *The Little Sweep* in 1949, whose names he and Eric Crozier took for the child characters in the opera. Britten was most concerned that the Jonny in the opera should be spelt without an *h*, just like the real Jonny, and made a late change in the proofs of the score to ensure that.

Gathorne-Hardy has elaborated his experience of Britten's empathy with children: 'facetious, boys together [the same phrase used by both Wulff Scherchen and William Coldstream], Ben – teasing, ironic, jokey, slightly flirtatious – the older, just'. Jonny was fourteen when he first got to know Ben and was 'at once aware I attracted him'. He admits a suspicion that he 'could not help flirting slightly' because he knew Ben enjoyed it. This may explain the holiday postcard he says he sent Britten, boasting that he was 'brown all over, even my bottom',* and his letter from school about his embarrassment at mistakenly asking for chocolate in a tobacconist's, and then realising that he had 'all my fly button[s] undone'. He has related an encounter at Crag House when he was eighteen: they had each had a bath after playing tennis, and were standing in their towels. Ben put his arms round him – a moment Jonny had anticipated, because he remembers announcing somewhat operatically, 'No, Ben, it is not to be'. Gathorne-Hardy says he never felt threatened by Britten, who behaved with gentleness and delicacy.

The name of Paul Rogerson has never previously surfaced in the Britten literature. Yet he was also a close (but chaster) companion in the early 1950s, also in his later teens. His friendship with Ben followed the Aldeburgh paradigm, but its outcome was unique, on account of the boy's strong Roman Catholic faith.

Paul came from an intensely musical family. His father, Haydn Rogerson, was for many years principal cello in Barbirolli's Hallé Orchestra, and his mother, Mamie, was an accomplished pianist. His uncle, Tommy Matthews, had given the British première of Britten's Violin Concerto in 1941 and led the London Philharmonic Orchestra and then the Covent Garden orchestra. To cap it all, Paul's godfather was Pablo Casals.

He stayed at Crag House for the first time in April 1952, when he was sixteen. Britten wrote afterwards to Paul's mother:

---

* Although Britten was meticulous in keeping his correspondence, there is no record of this postcard in the Britten–Pears library.

It was lovely having Paul here. He is a really dear good boy.
I am sorry that it was rather complicated by Peter [Pears]
not being well, so that I had to pack him off so soon; it
would have been nice to have had him here much longer.
But we all agree that it would have been difficult to have
had a nicer or more considerate guest. Do let him come
back again some time.

As was her practice, she had sent Paul with a present for his
host. Britten was typically prompt in his thanks, which conjure
up the image of a pied piper among the fishing boats on the
Aldeburgh seashore.

Thank you for the scrumtious (however you spell it!) package
of chocolates. It was most generous of you, & I feel guilty
because it'll probably have used up all of your rations* for
months to come! Anyhow if you could have seen a crowd
of children tucking into them on the beach yesterday
afternoon you'd have felt rewarded. They certainly are
delicious.

Paul's mother was a staunch Roman Catholic, and on this first
visit, Britten introduced the boy to the local Catholic priest,
Father Jolly, who had a yacht and took him out sailing. He also
relished going out to sea with Ben in Billy Burrell's fishing boat,
as Humphrey Maud and 'Nipper' had done before him.

Paul played the cello – 'badly', he says, 'but Ben was always
encouraging' – and Britten accompanied him on the piano for
longer stints than politeness required. They would go out for
drives, and watch and listen to birds, or rub brasses in the large
parish churches of East Anglia. Ben told him that he had only
recently started visiting these churches (although his eyes had
been originally opened to the 'magnificence of English ecclesi-
astical architecture' by Frank Bridge when, as teacher and pupil,
they had explored the South Downs in Sussex twenty years

* Wartime rationing of confectionery remained in force until February 1953.

before). Paul gave him a book about stained glass, which Ben started reading at once: a few months later, Britten thoughtfully sent him a transparency of the rose window at Chartres Cathedral, knowing that its glass would appeal to him.

Hold it up & imagine about 800 windows just like it all round & you'll have some idea of what that glorious cathedral is like!

When visiting Notre-Dame in Paris, he told Paul: 'I thought of you'.

Britten followed up Paul's April visit to Aldeburgh by taking him out of school in Derbyshire to see Pears performing at the Royal Opera House. He was his customary diligent self in writing to the boy at school and immersing himself in the preoccupations of a sixteen-year-old schoolboy.

My dear old Paul,

Here is the book I got you & then stupidly forgot to give you at Covent Garden. It is the one you started reading here & then didn't finish, because I sent you to bed each day too tired to read! [. . .]

I've been down here for a day or so, & it is really wonderful; but I won't tell you that the sea is very blue & that I'm going fishing with Billy this afternoon – because that would make you jealous.

I hope the term has started well, & that you're going to enjoy yourself. Don't forget to practice your tennis hard, & don't forget your cricket, because there might be a chance of playing here this summer . . . [. . .]

The enclosed apparently mouldy bits of chocolate arn't really mouldy. They just arrived in a parcel from South Africa, & must have had a rough passage.

Don't forget to write & tell me what you are doing – a nice long chatty newsy letter – sometime when you've got loads of spare time which I'm sure you've often got . . .!

With lots of love, Ben.

Letters flew to and fro – almost once a week. Paul asked for a photograph of Ben for the partition of his dormitory cubicle. When he gave news of a school debate on the new apartheid policy in South Africa, Ben responded with keen interest.

I was glad that the debate on Appartied [*sic*] was so serious; it is something we all must think seriously about these days, whether we agree or not. I was naturally pleased with the result!

After riding with childish glee on the miniature railway at the Tivoli Gardens in Copenhagen, he wrote to Paul that it was 'the most wonderful Funfair-Festival Gardens in the world'. But if Paul was slow to write, Ben took time to chide him:

Oy! – What's happened to you? Have you forgotten Crag House & its happy inmates? [. . .] it would be nice to have a sign of life of you [. . .] if there is any life in you. Love (doubtfull) from Ben.

Catherine Lawson, one of the English Opera Group mezzo-sopranos and a friend of the Rogersons, warned his mother about letting him spend time with Britten. But the advice passed right over her head: she hero-worshipped Ben, and would not hear anything against him. 'She didn't even acknowledge his homosexuality.' Rogerson says he was 'rather a pretty boy', but he knew Britten admired his parents and his uncle, so was completely trusting: indeed he felt that Ben was 'almost like a Jesuit priest – wonderfully good and kind, and spiritual too'.

From the age of twelve, Paul had cycled each morning of his school holidays from Hampstead to Mayfair in time for the 7 a.m. Mass at the Jesuit church in Farm Street, where he served as an altar boy. It was part of a bargain he had struck with Father Joe Christie: the boy would serve at Mass if the priest would convert his father to the faith.* After attending his Jesuit school (Mount St Mary's), Paul was destined to join the Jesuits as a

---

* Both sides of the bargain were kept. Haydn Rogerson admired Father Joe's sermons and later became a Roman Catholic.

novice. He was planning to leave school before entering the sixth form and to earn his living for a year. Perhaps with his own experience in mind, Ben was alarmed at his idea of leaving school early, and as usual was ready with career advice.

We will certainly talk about your future when you come to Aldeburgh – but don't be too impatient, 16 is no <u>great</u> age! [. . .] We get back at the end of August – could you come to Aldeburgh then? I'll write later to fix definite dates – letters, by the way, are forwarded from Aldeburgh (Hint!)

But Britten's extended European tour meant that Paul's decision could not wait. He was already working in Fleet Street by the time Britten returned home to an effusive welcome.

My dear old Paul,
When Peter & I staggered into the house at 8.30 this morning, having driven nearly 1000 miles in 2 days I find the hall <u>filled</u> with packages from you! You naughty boy – spending all your hard-earned pennies on me, & such a lot of those pennies too . . .

The Suffolk book I didn't know (& I thought I knew all the books on Suffolk too) but it looks very good to me & full of interesting things. Of course I love the glorious book of stained-glass.* It is a really beautiful book, with perfect reproductions of many windows which I have been revelling in recently. I am particularly fond of it because it comes with your first earnings – ! So you have left school & are a man of the world? I long to see you & to know the reasons, although I can guess some of them. When can you come here? [. . .] But don't bother to answer this – I will ring you up one of these evenings, for the pleasure of hearing your voice, & find out when you can come. [. . .] This is only to send my love & to thank you for the <u>lovely</u> books . . . you naughty boy!!
　　Yours ever
　　Ben

* This was evidently the second such volume he had received from Paul Rogerson.

During the autumn the correspondence continued, fortified by the occasional meeting. In November Britten told Imogen Holst that Paul had stayed the weekend with him 'to cheer him up'. He went on to say that 'he'd been very loving and it had been good to have him because he was so good and so beautiful'. In December Ben sent him a propelling pencil for his birthday, which he promised to have engraved. He urged him to bring his 'bathing suit' on his next visit to Suffolk 'because we may be swimming' – even in the middle of winter this notion was never tongue-in-cheek for Britten. 'Such a series of high tides', he continued with uncanny prescience, 'really rather scarifying – Over the top in many places, & even once or twice into the river! I'm afraid the sea will get us yet!'

Two months later, it did. In the notorious East Anglian floods at the end of January 1953, the ground floor of Crag House, which was only a few feet from the beach, was invaded by seawater. Paul was already expected for the following weekend. 'Everything is filthy & soaking', Britten told him, 'but we are much luckier than so many others in the town. You must come & cheer us up –' Paul arrived as planned and joined in the mopping up, much to the delight of Britten's music assistant: 'Found Paul there, which was <u>excellent</u> because I'd just been wishing he could be there to help'.

Much of Britten's friendship with Paul Rogerson overlapped with the composition of his Coronation opera *Gloriana*. He gave Paul (who was now seventeen) a ringside seat at the Royal Opera House gala on 8th June 1953, when *Gloriana* was given its first performance in the presence of the Queen, and arranged for a friend of his to accompany him. Paul was in seat C18 of the orchestra stalls, and Ben lent him an evening dress suit for the occasion. 'I look forward to seeing you in your tails!' he said.

Unusually, Britten's friendship with Paul Rogerson came to an emotional full stop. In July he was 'very depressed' to learn that Paul was set on joining the Jesuits, which he said meant '15 years away from everyone'. There was then a tear-stained weekend in Aldeburgh in August 1953, shortly before Paul was to enter the community at Harlaxton Manor in Lincolnshire as a novice. Britten had been looking forward to Paul's visit: he told Billy Burrell that the boy 'was coming the "day after tomorrow, for a long weekend, till Monday or Tuesday" '. Imogen Holst records a wonderfully vivid picture of the Britten–Pears household after his arrival. Britten had presumably spent the morning composing, and the rest of the day was devoted to his guest.

> Peter came round to my studio and said would I go out brass rubbing with them. [. . .] I went round at 12 & found them just going to have a bathe – Ben, Peter, Paul, Mary* and a v. nice schoolboy called Richard [Kihl]. Then we packed into the car with lots of food & drink and materials for brass rubbing, and went to Pettistree†: picknicked in a lovely field with a stream and immense trees. The brasses in the church were on the wall which was too difficult to begin on, so we went to Orford‡ where there were about 15 beauties on the floor: – it was very exciting trying to do the rubbings. Ben <u>straight away</u> did his very much better than anyone else! He was lovely to everyone and it was a good day.

Even when brass-rubbing, Britten's competitive urge never slackened. On the Sunday he sprained his ankle playing tennis (with Paul, presumably), and, when Imogen Holst came calling after breakfast on the Monday morning, she found him in a morose mood. He was sitting in the garden with his ankle 'bandaged & propped up'. He was 'obviously in pain & feeling wretched', and remarked to her: 'This is a judgment, isn't it!' – though it is not clear whether the judgment was about his zeal on the tennis court, or on the hopes he had pinned on

---

* The artist Mary Potter, who then owned the Red House.
† A Suffolk village north of Woodbridge.
‡ A Suffolk village south of Aldeburgh.

Paul's last day with them. The boy had gone out for a final trip in Father Jolly's boat, 'and Ben had meant to go with them. He minded not being able to swim in that heavenly sunshine.'

When she returned just before lunch, she found Britten in more reflective mood. He said 'he could never remember that he was older than some of the very mature young men who seemed so much more assured than he was'. He seemed to be revisiting the pre-war days when he had always been the boy in the sophisticated company of Auden and Isherwood. He went on to talk about Paul, 'and how he'd asked him about the 15 years [his commitment to the Jesuits] the night before'. He told her how he hated the word 'Jesuit', and how appalled he was that Paul could not take any possessions with him (even the silver propelling pencil was forfeit). She noted that both Britten and Pears were in a bad mood.

Her journal (often unintentionally comic) sets the scene outside Britten's house on the Aldeburgh seafront early the following morning. She had come to say goodbye to Paul as he left to catch the train, ready to take up the monastic life.

> Got to Miss Hudson's [the housekeeper's] door at 9 but
> Peter leaned through the hatch & said he was catching the
> 10.30 after all. He asked me in but I said I'd come back at
> 10 and wave to him. At 10 I waited outside the front door:
> Paul came out to fetch me in. All three were in tears, Ben
> being the calmest and most matter-of-fact. He hobbled to
> the front door to see them off and I waved from the
> middle of the road till the car had turned the corner. [. . .]
> I tried to walk off without looking back at Ben, which
> was agony.

This fragile farewell was unique in all Britten's juvenile friendships. Paul Rogerson was never dropped, nor did he outgrow the relationship, but he removed himself from the scene. Britten admired the strength of his religious conviction and commitment, although he was apprehensive about the effects on the boy of isolation and sacrifice. Three weeks later, on the eve of his actual departure for Lincolnshire, Ben wrote him an extraordinary letter. There is little of the hearty jocularity with which Britten so often diffused his affection: the depth of feeling is unconcealed.

My dearest Paul,

As your mother may have hinted to you I am afraid I shall not be able to get to London to-morrow to see you off to Harlaxton. In many ways I should have loved to have been there, in spite of the fact that I'm not at all good at 'farewells', but I'm hard at work again and, as usual <u>very behindhand</u>! So although I shan't be there, my thoughts will be, and not only at the station, but on the journey, & in your first days – and in the many months to come! In fact, my dear, my thoughts are with you more often than you would imagine. You have meant a great deal to me these last two years, a great comfort, & a great pleasure. And, although I shan't see you much for the next few years – I won't trouble you by making frequent calls at the Manor – the clear memory of our many times together will be also a great comfort & pleasure.

I am sure that you are clear in your mind about what you are doing. I know you will be always true to the real 'Paul'. Always know that whatever you do, and however, there is a great deal of love awaiting you in your

    devoted

    Ben

When Rogerson read this recently – for the first time in many years – he was moved to tears.

Britten gathered scraps of news about Paul from his mother*: 'They are very precious', he told her. 'Every sign of a high tide we think of him, & of his stirling [*sic*] work clearing up the

---

* As soon as Paul reached the Jesuits, he went into retreat for twenty-eight days. At the end of it, the Father Minister told him twenty-eight letters from his mother had arrived. 'This will have to stop', he said.

house after the Great Flood!' He talked of dropping in at Harlaxton to visit him (Rogerson says he would have been turned away). Two years later, when Paul was taking his vows, Ben wrote to him to say that he was thinking of him and praying for his happiness. The new Jesuit was to be allowed home for an afternoon's release, and Ben said he would do 'everything in my power to get to London for this opportunity, you may be sure, because I long to see you – with a great deal of love'.

Rogerson left the Jesuits after six years. He was 'in quite a bad way', and Britten went to see him in London. He invited him to stay for a fortnight in Aldeburgh, where he earned his keep by some heavy digging in the Red House garden. He stayed again in 1964, just before he married (but not again thereafter), and then settled in Sussex to begin thirty-five years' work in the management of the Chichester Festival Theatre and to bring up his family.

Seven months before his disappearance into the religious life, Britten had confided in Imogen Holst about his feelings for Paul. She reported in her invaluable journal that he had told her:

> 'Do you know, Paul & I fell in love with each other, if that is how you can describe it, a whole year before we met.' It was at a concert when Peter was singing the Serenade,* and they [Ben and Paul] just looked at each other. Then a year later Paul went to the 1st night of Budd† & they met & Paul said 'Do you remember going to that concert?'

This record of Britten discussing his friendship with a boy in emotive terms without any apparent awkwardness (at that *Serenade* performance, Paul had been fifteen years old) is fascinating for the way he assumed that their exchanged glance at a

---

* This was probably the concert in Sheffield on 2nd February 1951, when Britten's *Serenade* for tenor, horn and strings was performed by Peter Pears and Dennis Brain, with Paul Kletzki conducting. It took place only ten miles or so from Paul's school in Derbyshire.

† *Billy Budd* opened at the Royal Opera House, Covent Garden, on 1st December 1951.

concert betokened love at first sight. Much of their correspondence was conducted in terms that were relatively mild for Britten – he often signed himself as 'Ben B.', and on one occasion reproved Paul for writing to him as 'Mr Britten'. But the relationship, in Ben's eyes, amounted to falling in love.

The account also suggests the ease of his relationship with Imogen Holst, who had an almost schoolgirlish infatuation with him. Another entry in her journal rejoiced in Britten 'looking so beautiful that my heart turned over so that it was thumping when he embraced me, but I explained that I'd run down the hill too fast'. Perhaps her devotion was such that Britten felt complete safety in confiding in her.

All through these friendships of the 1940s and 1950s, he kept in intermittent contact with his oldest young friend, Piers Dunkerley. That too was unique – for the abruptness of its end. By the time Britten returned from America in 1942, Dunkerley was serving in the Royal Marines. After experience on the Murmansk and Malta convoys, he was seriously wounded shortly after the Normandy landings, and was for a while reported missing, but eventually he surfaced in a German prisoner-of-war camp. After the war, he served in Malta and Hongkong, but on home leave he always contacted Britten, and their friendship continued in fits and starts for fourteen more years, characterised by a gentle sweetness on both sides. When Piers was due to visit Aldeburgh in March 1951, after serving abroad for some time, Ben wrote:

You will be so grand now that I dare say I will not recognise you; but when I meet you on Saxmundham station I will look for the person with the most stripes which I am certain will be you.

Yours ever, Ben.

Looking forward to seeing you alot – bring squash things, so I can beat you – !

Dunkerley was bowled over by the first night of *Billy Budd* in

December that year. 'I have *never* been taken out of myself so completely for nearly four hours, or finished up in such a muck sweat.' He told Britten that going home had been an anticlimax, and 'although it could not be, I can't say how much I wanted to hop into your Rolls and come home to Aldeburgh'. The way he regarded Aldeburgh as home bespoke an easy tenderness, which the years of military service had not ironed out. 'Don't be surprised when I write to ask myself up to beat you in the squash court', he added.

He spent Christmas 1954 in Aldeburgh, perhaps discussing what Britten had mentioned after a previous meeting as 'the several big problems which seemed to face you'. In 1958 he left the Marines, but found civilian life difficult. For a while he worked for the coal merchants Charrington's, but he did not make a success of it, and lost his job after a few months. In spring 1959, he suddenly became engaged. Although this attractive man had had a string of girlfriends, he had never brought any of them home to meet his family, so his engagement to a Bournemouth doctor, Jill Home, came as a shock. His sister-in-law Barbara felt that, after years when the Services had catered for his every need, he was mentally at sea. 'He had never even had to wash his own socks', she says, 'and he realised he needed someone to look after him'. When it came to choosing a best man for the wedding in August, he turned to Britten, rather than to any of his contemporaries. To his consternation, Ben turned him down. Piers was 'furious – well certainly very upset and hurt', according to Barbara, and sent him this entreaty:

My dear Ben,
Thank you so much for your letter. I quite see that you may well be too busy for the duties of Best Man, but we shall both be <u>very</u> disappointed if you can not come at all. I only intend to get married once, and you <u>must</u> be there – I insist – and bring Peter. No excuses – it will be a good party; a short (10 min) service as Jill is RC and I'm a heathen, in St Mary Cadogan, Chelsea, and afterwards at the Basil

St Hotel, Knightsbridge, from which you may duck away at any time you have to. <u>Do come</u>. 15 August. [. . .]

Longing to see you sometime.

Much love as always, you dear old thing. Piers.

Britten was happy enough to be present at family weddings. He attended that of his close friend Marion Stein to the Earl of Harewood in September 1949, for which he wrote an anthem. But he had a problem when it came to the marriages of his boy favourites. The pressure of work was often a convenient excuse. For varying reasons, he did not attend Roger Duncan's wedding, or Paul Rogerson's, or Humphrey Stone's, or Humphrey Maud's. 'I think that perhaps Ben didn't *want* Piers to get married', concludes Barbara Dunkerley.

But the wedding was not to be. Shortly beforehand, Piers Dunkerley committed suicide, after an argument with his fiancée. Jill adored him, and in an emotional letter to his brother she wrote that she wished she had been more tolerant of his 'ridiculous jealousy'.

There is no reference to the tragedy in any of Britten's copious letters, even though Piers had been a dear friend of his for twenty-five years. The one exception was his letter to Piers's mother, which was short and formal, devoid of emotion or tenderness. Many friends and relations sent flowers to the funeral, caught by the poignancy of the tragedy, but Britten was not one of them. Just as in the case of Wulff Scherchen, it was almost as if their friendship had never been. Perhaps Britten felt responsible in some way for the tragedy. Perhaps his devotion to Piers as a boy belonged to his secret life, which he could not bring himself to acknowledge. The one time he opened up a little was in Australia many years later. In a discursive and revealing conversation in the outback with the artist Sidney Nolan, he talked of the tragedy of a friend of his who had killed himself just before his wedding: he seems to have been referring to Dunkerley. A clue to the anguish Britten felt lies in the dedication of the *War Requiem* in 1962 to four British soldiers who were friends of his. The implication was that they had all died in the Second World War, and indeed three of them had. But the fourth, Piers Dunkerley, had died fourteen years after it ended. Britten clearly felt that he was just as much one of its victims.

Barbara Dunkerley says that she was always 'in awe of Piers', because, like his brother Tony whom she had married, 'he was so good-looking'. He was 'great fun – the life and soul of the party'. But she thinks he was not so good at handling 'the serious stuff of life' – he never talked about that. She and Tony were impressed by how much time he spent with Britten. 'It didn't worry us', she says, although her husband was upset when Piers missed the christening of their son Jamie, his own godson. 'When we said to Piers, "Come for Christmas", or "Come to one of the children's christenings", there was always something that he was doing somewhere else with Ben and Peter Pears. He always seemed to be there.'

CHAPTER 11

Go play, boy, play

For a composer who worked in film and whose career began only shortly before the launch of BBC Television, there is frustratingly little film of Britten in rehearsal. There are complete performances, but only a few tantalising snippets of him in preparation – in the *Spring Symphony*, his overture *The Building of the House*, and *Children's Crusade*. There is also a rather more substantial film about the recording of *The Burning Fiery Furnace*.* Only the Canadians went to the trouble of filming a complete orchestral rehearsal (followed by a performance) of his *Nocturne*, which is a fascinating document.† It demonstrates his urgency and efficiency on the podium, and his determination not to settle for second best.

But the most revealing recording of Britten in rehearsal was made without his knowledge. Decca's producer John Culshaw took his life in his hands when he kept the audio tape running throughout the recording sessions for the *War Requiem*. This preserved some of Britten's rehearsal between takes and his comments to orchestra, choir and soloists. Culshaw gave the recording to the composer as a birthday present. Britten was appalled that it had been made behind his back, but posterity is forever in Culshaw's debt.‡

The first thing that strikes the listener is the fiery, almost percussive sound ('pssst!') that intersperses Britten's instructions

---

* *Workshop*, BBC Television 1967: documentary by John Culshaw.
† This little-known programme was filmed by the CBC in April 1962, when Britten was conducting the Vancouver Chamber Orchestra.
‡ These rehearsal excerpts have now been issued commercially, alongside the reissue of the original recording of the *War Requiem* (Decca 414383–2 DH2).

to his performers. It is the noise of Britten turning the pages of his full score, but he does it so fiercely and with such energy that it sounds as if he is tearing it up. The second thing is the tremor in his voice, a sign of the intensity – almost feverishness – that overcame him in performance. He says quietly to the violins, 'It needs *pianissimo* playing . . .' before adding, with great urgency, '. . . but *playing*'. He tells the chorus, 'Can you go back to *piano*? But it must be *clear*!' How much one would give to hear Beethoven, say, or Mahler rehearsing his own music: now we have the technology, it is still surprisingly rare. Culshaw may have caused great offence by what he did, but it is invaluable evidence about Britten as both man and musician.

This recording also demonstrates the way he treated the boys of Highgate School Choir in the sessions. There was no indulgence: he expected high standards and a professional attitude. Early on, he became testy when they were chattering among themselves instead of listening to him. At another point, he tried to get them to show more enthusiasm, instead of sounding rather 'early-morningy'. When they were finding it hard to hold their line in the Sanctus, he said: 'Boys! You've got to concentrate like fun on getting the note from the organ and not changing it when we come in with our music. It's *supposed* to be different. Don't make it sound nice – it's horrid, it's modern music!' In the final bars of the work, he wanted an 'ethereal' sound from the boys: 'Imagine yourselves, chaps, in heaven!'

The physicality and nervous energy evident in this surreptitious recording are two hallmarks of the way he made and wrote music. They stemmed from a deep-seated competitiveness and sportiness directly connected with his own boyhood. Unusually for a musician, Britten had not shied away from sport at school, and he remained a physical man, who kept fit and active until the onset of his final illness. Sue Phipps, who became his agent in the 1960s, particularly noted the 'very boyish' way he moved around, 'with his great long legs'. This sportiness was an essential, and perhaps underestimated, element in his character, and the key to much of his work. It was another way he kept his childhood – particularly his schoolboyhood – alive through his adult years. 'He was what the French would call *sportif*', says Colin Graham. 'He was besotted by youth, and he tried to maintain it in himself in his own life, until the day he died. He wanted to keep the physical side of his youth going.'

The producer Basil Coleman played a game of croquet with him – his first – and made the mistake of winning. 'Ha! That was a great moment. Ben didn't like losing. He had to win – which was a curious other side of him altogether.' David Hemmings found much the same. Ben slaughtered him at tennis, but on the croquet lawn the honours were more even. Sometimes he would pair up with Mary Potter's husband, Stephen, against Britten and Pears. 'I was actually rather a good croquet player, and Ben was slightly pissed off about this. He didn't like being beaten. Stephen and I used to say, "Ah, we've got you this time!" – well, we got them every time, actually.'

The competitiveness was there even at the most humdrum moments. Imogen Holst recorded one evening with him when he had insisted she finish off the bottle of claret they had been drinking.

> We fought over the last glass: I thought I'd won because I poured mine into his glass when he was in the kitchen, but as soon as I turned aside he poured it back into mine. I said: 'Do you *always* have to win?' and he said 'Well, I get very cross if I don't.'

As a small girl, Bridget Slater was once playing 'sevens' against the side wall of the family home, unaware that Britten was watching. 'When I got to the bit where the player has to bounce the ball off the wall and clap before it is caught, Ben came forward and asked if he could do it. His way was to clap after the ball hit the wall instead of simultaneously as I had been doing. He was clapping, as it were, on an off-beat.' Once again, Britten was enjoying physical activity, relating it to music, while asserting his competitiveness in going one better than the child with whom he was playing. The change of rhythm fascinated her, and she is convinced, quite reasonably, that the scene in *Albert Herring* where the children bounce a ball against a door, singing 'Bounce me high, bounce me low', derives from that moment.

Of all the ball games, Britten was really happiest with a racquet in his hand. He loved to take on Humphrey Stone at table tennis ('and *not* lose', remarks another ping-pong martyr, John Hahessy), he played squash with Piers Dunkerley and Roger Duncan, but his abiding passion was tennis. While he was living at Crag House, he would often visit Mary Potter at the Red House to play a few sets on her grass court in the garden. It must have been one of the main attractions for him when they swapped houses in 1957. Tennis had been his best game at Gresham's. David Layton remembers that he always won: 'Most people hit the ball hard straight back over the net until they win. But he didn't. He'd slice it and put it in the corner. He was cunning.' He tried to repay Frank Bridge for his musical tutelage by 'helping him with his tennis, which was wild and unconventional; I considered mine rather good and stylish'.

Britten offered his services as a coach to his young charges. The advice has stayed with Humphrey Maud ever since: 'Get your first serve in, hit it with a flat face, and then, if you have a second serve, cut it with a fiendish spin'. Humphrey Stone remembers long rallies, which ended with Ben running up to the net. He prodded Roger Duncan quasi-paternally about practising – his tennis backhand just as much as his tenor recorder. He held high hopes of sixteen-year-old Piers Dunkerley. 'Bit of tennis with Piers in morning – he's frightfully erratic, but may be good I think'.

Sue Phipps says Britten had a most unusual serve. 'He lifted one leg right up as he did it, as if he was about to take off like a rocket. The games with Mary Potter were devastating. She couldn't move all that well, but she stood on the baseline and fired shots back, just over the top of the net, which were absolutely impossible to do anything with. But Ben managed it very well.'

Francis Barton, who had been a close friend at prep school and for some while afterwards, lost touch for a long time. In 1972 they met again at the Red House, when Britten (then aged fifty-eight) invited him to lunch. In his letter of acceptance, Barton said, 'I'll bring a tennis racquet too, shall I, in case there's time to fit in a set or two!' He knew, without being asked, what was required. All visitors to the Red House also knew before the game began that there could be only one winner. Humphrey Maud, as a young teenager, found he was given no quarter – 'absolutely none. We played quite fiercely, and there was no question of him being beaten.' There was 'something almost sadistic in his cool destruction on court', according to another teenaged friend, Jonathan Gathorne-Hardy. 'I took games off him but I don't remember ever beating him at tennis, nor at squash, which we played later. And being beaten by Ben was quite literally like that.'

While he was writing the *Spring Symphony* during the winter of 1948–9, he used to play squash with Eric Crozier for an hour or more every afternoon. 'I was no real match for him: he was faster than I was and had more stamina, and he always played to win, delighting to outwit his opponent by a series of unexpected shots that were impossible to return.' A few years later, Imogen Holst noted how an energetic game of squash had brightened his mood. He told her 'how he enjoyed the relaxation, not only of games, but of being with ordinary normal public-school people'. On another occasion he relished the 'glorious Indian summer' when he played 'quite a bit of good tennis & enjoyed it hugely', and 'abit of squash – bad but gay* with Nipper, & good & exhausting with David Row'.

* The word 'gay' was a favourite of Britten's: like many of his contemporaries, he used it in its long-standing sense of 'joyous' and 'lively'.

It was no coincidence that most of Britten's children were keen on sport, and he would enquire about it encouragingly – partly because he knew it was on a schoolboy's daily agenda, and partly because he loved it himself. He wrote to the twelve-year-old David Bedford:

I'd love to see you, & play you ping-pong, although I expect you've been practising so hard that you'd beat me easily! I've been playing squash once or twice; do you play that? It's a lovely game – <u>very</u> fast. I think you'd be awfully good at it. How go the cricket coachings?

Cricket was always a fascination, if not his prime sporting skill. David Layton recalls his 'cunning bowling' in the Gresham's nets, where he kept his right arm (illicitly) low, which caused great amusement. Humphrey Maud remembers playing cricket with him on the lawn at Cliveden in the 1940s. Ben was delighted when the boy hit a six off Pears's bowling – the ball smashed a dovecote, which tumbled down to the ground. Imogen Holst recorded one occasion in 1953 when Britten and Pears attended a prep school match, at which 'he and Peter had umpired and scored for the small boys – the winning team never made more than 3 runs, but there were 39 byes'.

But not every ball game suited him. At school he 'only quite liked football (although he kicked a pretty "corner")', and David Layton remembers that 'he wasn't much good at hockey', which was confirmed in one of Benjamin's letters to his parents:

Do you know, I did something the other day, which will surprise you, nearly as much as it surprised me! I shot a goal in hockey – I did really! I hit the ball (for once, I must admit) and after it had rebounded off about two of my opponents, it went, carefully avoiding the goal-keeper straight into the net. Don't you think it good? I could & would scarcely deign to touch another ball for the rest of the game.

Buoyed up by his success, he told his sister Beth a fortnight later that he was 'getting quite a star at hockey now; quite brilliant is the game I play now'. But he quickly admitted that quite often the ball 'completely evade[s] contact with the stick I use'.

Although he lived next to a golf course for twenty years, and golf had been his father's Saturday pastime, Britten had little interest in the game. Even his fondness for Paul Rogerson did not lead him to contemplate taking up 'your wretched golf' himself.

> Glad you're playing golf so well (or was your opponent rather dim that you got a bottle of Cydrax* off him?) – but don't forget your cricket & tennis . . . You must be good when you come here next holidays!

> Glad, in a way, about the new golf clubs – but rather wish it had been a new cricket bat or tennis racquet. But I see I shall have to take up golf, unless you can play tennis with golf clubs, or I can play golf with a cricket bat . . .

Almost twenty years later, Ronan Magill found Britten's sporting enthusiasms were unflagging: 'He always wanted to know about my rugby at school – rugger and runs, because he obviously knew about the public school life and he saw that it hadn't changed a bit. Luckily I was good at games, and enjoyed all that rough and tumble too.' But his interest in rugby was wholly vicarious: after Roger Duncan suffered 'a bad kick in the head at Rugger' during his second term at Harrow, Ben's comment was 'horrid game – I never liked it'.

He remained proud of his *victor ludorum* award at South Lodge, and it was the athlete in him that took delight in staging beach sports in his final opera *Death in Venice*. He knew the shadow of serious heart illness was hovering over him as he completed it, which gives his stage athletics an extra poignancy. Never again, after the opera's première, would he wield a

* A non-alcoholic fizzy apple drink.

tennis racquet and cut his serve with a fiendish spin. Some critics have wearied of the Greek pentathlon at the end of Act I, and recommended it be cut. But, for Britten, it was of immense importance. Aschenbach, the ageing writer, is not obsessed with Tadzio as a statuette, or a pretty face – but with an animated boy on the move. He first watches him walking into the dining room, then playing games on the Lido, strolling round the city of Venice, or joshing with his friend Jaschiu, and finally walking through the waves. The Games of Apollo, in which the fair-skinned Tadzio ('Phoebus of the golden hair') repeatedly prevails, watched by the hotel guests and his devoted mother, have the flavour of ancient Greece about them: this is the acme of physical beauty for a youth who would have won the admiration of Alcibiades. Apollo speaks of the youths contesting

> in strength, agility and skill
> the body's praise.

After watching Tadzio's exertions in the pentathlon, Aschenbach is excited and liberated by 'the power of [Tadzio's] beauty'. But Tadzio is, as well, young Benjamin winning all the races and throwing the cricket ball furthest – to the adulation of the school and the plaudits of his adoring mother. He is the junior tennis champion of Suffolk. He is also the blond Emil that Britten had seen, back in 1933, returning home in triumph, surrounded by cheering crowds, to the intense pride of his beaming mother.

The presence in Britten's music of an unrelenting competitiveness and the sheer thrill of bodily exertion strikes Humphrey Stone forcefully. His memory of Britten on the tennis court is that 'he had a nervous energy about him, rather like a coiled spring. The quickness and deftness of his playing comes into his music, in the way so much of it is highly sprung, taut, percussive and very unlimp!' The same was true in the demon games of ping-pong. 'You felt the coiled spring was ready to leap on you! His spontaneity and his ability to be totally engaged with you while you were playing were the same when you watched him conduct or perform. The energy was about his love of giving life to something – whether it was children or his music.' The accumulation of nervous energy before a public performance sometimes led to an attack of nausea, and Britten would steady himself with a glass of whisky or brandy before going on stage. Colin Graham particularly remembers an acute attack of nerves before the première of *Curlew River*, when Orford church was blacked out by a power failure, and Britten was 'in a terrible, terrible state', being sick in the churchyard.

The surviving recordings of Britten rehearsing with orchestra are proof of his nervous efficiency as a conductor – in terms of the clarity of his beat and musical thought, but also of his use of rehearsal time. When he stopped the orchestra, he always knew exactly what he wanted to say, even if it was a list of nine or ten points, and he never wasted a moment. The Canadian film of the *Nocturne* rehearsal shows this – indeed at the end, Peter Pears had to walk on to remind him gently that it was time to start the performance. His Purcell rehearsal with the London Symphony Orchestra (also in the early 1960s) reveals the tension of Humphrey Stone's coiled spring in his voice, his body language and his beat – and then, of course, in the music. I remember much the same thing when he was recording Elgar's *The Dream of Gerontius* with the same orchestra and its chorus at the rebuilt Maltings in 1971. From my position in the tenors, I watched him hunched over his music stand as he conducted the eleven critical bars leading up to the one moment that Gerontius sees God, a dramatic orchestral *crescendo* which built – not, as I had expected, to the huge dissonant chord (when Elgar's unique instruction is that ' "for one moment" must every instrument exert its fullest force'), but to the silent pause which Elgar had marked in the score immediately before-hand. Such was the verve Britten brought to that *crescendo* that it extended into the silence as he brought the orchestra off – the pause seemed, giddily, to last for ever. It was as if he had been running at full pelt towards the edge of a cliff, and then had stopped at the last moment, teetering on the brink (perhaps caught out by the lack of a twelfth bar), unsure whether he would avoid toppling over. So the triple *sforzando* chord, when it came, was one of simultaneous terror and relief. That, surely, is what Elgar intended. When that recording was issued, some of the critics of the day who could remember Elgar conducting the work in his old age avowed that Britten had got closer than anyone (Boult, Barbirolli or Sargent) to the fire in Elgar's belly.* But then, although Elgar is often visualised as a sedate Edwardian gentleman, the reality is that, in much of his music, as in his demeanour, he shared Britten's restless, nervous energy, as well as his acute ear for orchestral colour and spacing.†

The connection between that physicality and Britten's music-making was perceptively made by Eric Crozier.

This enjoyment of the sheer physical pleasure of playing games and of winning by a combination of swift thought and economy of effort, was reflected in his piano-playing and his conducting. From the first bar he was on top of his form, like a trained athlete beginning a race, nervously intense, poised, determined to succeed, and revelling in his mastery – and at such times he radiated a kind of magnetism that inspired everyone who played or sang with him.

Sue Phipps, who often turned the pages for him in recitals, observed an intense energy which was with him 'through almost every moment of life': he hardly ever relaxed from it. She found it 'quite terrifying watching his hands coming down on to the keys, because they came down absolutely a-quiver. You thought,

* The composer William Alwyn, who had played the flute in Elgar's 1927 performance in Hereford, said that Britten's reading was 'as near as possible Elgar's own'.
† The two composers, so apparently unlike, had other points in common. They shared a passion for riddles and conundrums; they both composed away from the piano; their company was either charming or impossibly prickly; and the pattern of their working day was similar.

"how is he ever going to put a key down?" and then finally the finger met the key and this glorious sound came out. It was just extraordinary. Imogen Holst used to say that he could make *vibrato* on the piano, which of course you can't, and that he could make the sound increase once he put the key down, which of course you can't. But such was the intensity of what he felt inside himself when he was making music, that he conveyed that to you, whether it was physically possible or not.'

Others who witnessed Britten's piano-playing were mesmerised by the colours he achieved. His occasional pupil Ronan Magill says the way he touched the keyboard to make a phrase speak, to achieve a particular colour, was evidence of his physicality. 'It wasn't scientifically programmed with him – it was completely natural, it was something that just happened.' Magill observed the bodily vitality at close quarters during the intermittent piano lessons Britten gave him in the early 1970s. 'You could see his long, spindly fingers slightly shaking as they played, as if his body was carrying a sort of live wire of feeling through it. There was a kind of intensity, a kind of vibration – you'd feel almost that he was crucifying himself by his own electricity, and that he would not seek to preserve himself from this. On the contrary, he would look for it.' Magill was particularly struck by this in a performance of Schumann's Piano Quartet: 'I will never forget a colour he got in the Scherzo where he made a sort of shimmer of sound. It was just like a shudder of electricity through the body.'

There is a similar effect in the 'embroidery' aria in the third Act of *Peter Grimes*. Ellen Orford has found a boy's jersey washed up by the tide: she recognises it as the one she knitted for Grimes's apprentice – and that therefore the boy may be dead. It is a moment of great poignancy as Ellen's faith in Grimes is destroyed, and she too feels he may be a murderer. As she sings

> Now my broidery affords
> the clue whose meaning we avoid

the orchestra abandons its *legato* accompaniment to play a succession of *staccato* wind chords, uncannily spaced to create a feeling of hollowness: the effect is of a series of sharp sobs, or electric shocks. Magill points to Britten's love of *staccato* sounds: 'He was very particular about precision and clarity'.

His thrill of the physical chase matched his nimble mental gamesmanship. It resulted in a facility for fast music – Robert Saxton sees him as one of the few twentieth-century composers apart from Stravinsky who could write 'convincing fast music'. The 'Dies Irae' movements in both *Sinfonia da Requiem* and *War Requiem* have this quality, as does 'Rats away!' in his orchestral song-cycle *Our Hunting Fathers*. Throughout his life he was fond of marking his scores 'quick': whereas the word 'fast' indicates nothing more than rapidity, the word 'quick' has extra connotations, of being vital, responsive, sharp-witted and effective – all essential parts of Britten's nature. The second of his *Five Walztes (Waltzes)* for piano (written when he was ten and revised at fifty-five) is marked, 'Quick, with wit'. The word crops up frequently in his operas (*Gloriana, Noye's Fludde* ('quick and excited'), *Death in Venice*), as well as in his children's quartet *Gemini Variations* and in two of his children's songs *Friday Afternoons*. He also uses it in later songs such as 'The Tyger' and 'The Fly' in his *Songs and Proverbs of William Blake*, and at several points in *Winter Words*. Even in his final years, pieces such as the Burlesque in his Third String Quartet, 'Cakes and Ale' in his *Suite on English Folk Tunes*, and the Jig in his last completed work *Welcome Ode* show that he had lost none of his characteristic vigour and excitement with speed, despite his frailty. It had been there at the outset of his career, with the Tarantella in his *Sinfonietta* or the 'Alla burlesca' in his *Alla quartetto serioso*. Just to make the athletic significance of those 1933 quartet movements absolutely plain, Britten gave them the Shakespearean subtitle *Go play, boy, play*,* and marked two of the movements 'P.T.' [Physical Training] and

---

* Leontes's line in *The Winter's Tale*, Act 1 scene 2.

'Ragging'. These musical revisitations of his schoolboyhood were performed when he was just twenty, and the Burlesque was later dedicated to his South Lodge friend, Francis Barton.

His fascination with speed and movement led naturally in adult life to skiing, which he took up with great success. It also lay behind his favourite toys – his cars. The term 'boy racer' might have been invented for him. He bought a Lagonda, the first of many cars, for six pounds at the age of twenty-two. (He wrote off another in 1937, was charged with dangerous driving, but was acquitted.) He knew that speed impressed his young friends, who would usually sit with him in the front, while any adult passengers were confined to the back. Humphrey Maud used to take the wheel of his open-topped Rolls Royce while Britten was driving: 'I would say, "Ben, do let me steer". So I would lean over and steer away, and the car would do everything it did. It was obviously pretty frightening for my parents or whoever else was sitting in the back.' On other occasions, Humphrey and his sisters would sit on the folded hood as Ben roared around Regent's Park. Later it was a Mercedes, again with a collapsible hood, which Ben volunteered to keep down even when it was wet. He told Humphrey that 'if you drove it fast enough, the rain would go over you in a complete curve and you were absolutely dry inside'. Speed was an essential part of driving, partly for its own sake, but also for the thrill it gave his young companions. For Humphrey Stone, there was 'a certain dash' to his driving. The rides in the open-topped Rolls were about 'wind in the hair, his dog [Clytie, the dachshund] climbing all over him and licking his face, and the smell of leather'. David Hemmings recalled the same smell in the Alvis convertible in which Britten collected him from Saxmundham station in 1954: they drove along the lanes to Aldeburgh with the hood down, talking about 'tea and trains and fishing and East Anglia'. Imogen Holst experienced a similar journey in the same car, to her great excitement.

It was absolutely <u>thrilling</u>, and felt just like flying: my skirt filled like a balloon and nearly lifted me out of the back, and the hedges made a marvellous whooshing sound as we rushed past them.

Wulff Scherchen remembers the excitement Britten got from the AC sports car lent him by Lennox Berkeley in the spring of 1939. 'It was the proper sports car, practically totally hand built, twelve horse-power,* but, as Ben said, it could easily do ninety, and he proceeded to demonstrate this on the highway to Brighton. I was worried about this, because I knew that the brakes weren't all that good. He'd only demonstrated to me the previous day that if you stomped on the brakes the car didn't necessarily run straight. So I didn't really enjoy being driven at ninety, but he thought it great fun – "Brighton in twenty minutes instead of half an hour", you know, a real achievement!' Britten boasted to Pears that he was handling the car 'like a schoolboy', and teased Berkeley:

Everything is going well with the car – I did 85 in her on Saturday just to show that the wheels were going round properly. But don't worry I'm very careful!

But speed had its more earnest, obsessive side as well. During his American stay in the early years of the war, he suffered from a musical version of writer's block, which was depressing him. He was in 'the blackest of moods', and his surrogate mother on Long Island, Elizabeth Mayer, suggested a visit to Jones Beach to clear the air. It was winter, the beach was deserted, and the friend who had driven him there allowed him to take the wheel, even though he was not licensed to drive in America. She was scared to death as he drove 'like mad', up and down the beach at high speed for several hours. The next morning, Mrs Mayer came to thank her. 'He's writing again', she said.

His most important sporting pastime was not always available to him. When he moved from the Old Mill in Snape in

* According to Britten it was 16 h.p.

1947, he chose a large house in Aldeburgh, overlooking the seafront. Although the Old Mill in its renovated form had been his own original and unusual creation, he said some months after the move that he did not really regret leaving it, and that he had always felt most at home by the sea. It certainly suited a composer with such a maritime empathy, as evinced in *Billy Budd* and, most famously, in the Sea Interludes in *Peter Grimes*. But it was not enough to be beside the sea. He liked, above all, to be in it.

His new garden gate was literally no more than twelve feet from the shingle on the beach, and from his composition desk in the bay window on the first floor he could look out at his beloved North Sea, which had not been a part of his daily life since he left the family home in Lowestoft. In a letter to Pears shortly after the move, he made clear that it was not only the sea that held his attention: 'The waves look grand in the sun, & the swimmers very pretty!' Some years later, he remarked humorously on the distraction of 'all the little naked figures disporting on the beach'. It was his equivalent of Aschenbach's vantage point at his hotel window, overlooking the Lido. But, unlike Aschenbach, he was always happy to take the plunge himself.

He had a passion for swimming, or, as he usually called it, bathing. This could be expressed in the bath, the shower or the swimming pool. But the sea was the ideal place, and living that close to the water meant that he could very often swim naked without attracting undue public attention. If friends were staying, adult or adolescent, they were expected to join in. 'At night we'd strip off, run naked from the garden door, across the road, over the pebbles, and leap straight into the sea', remembers Humphrey Stone, who stayed in Crag House as a boy. 'I'm sure he loved living there for that reason.' Roger Duncan's sister Briony remembers him going for midnight swims with Ben: she thinks she was too scared to join in herself.

One of the attractions that Britten wanted his guests to experience was the nocturnal phosphorescence in those East Anglian waters, as the opera producer Basil Coleman vividly recalls: 'Our bodies were covered in it when we all went in on one occasion late at night without any clothes on – it was quite marvellous. We'd never seen anything like it.' For a skinny boy like Humphrey Stone, the excitement of watching each other glow in the water was offset by the other characteristic of the North Sea: 'You'd say, "Isn't it beautiful?" as you were shivering away'. David Hemmings had similar memories: 'We used to dash out of the back door, splash, splash, splash – straight into the surf. I loved it up there. It was bloody cold though – I mean bloody cold.'

Stone never felt awkward about these bathes. 'We rushed in, without thinking twice. He did it with great spontaneity – that was the way he was – and I didn't feel self-conscious about it as a result. He had the boyishness in him which related to me as a boy, and we were just having fun together, rather than there being any sinister overtones.' He laughs when he considers why Britten was so keen on it. 'I don't know – it gave him a thrill, perhaps. It's quite different – swimming in the sea naked and the waves pounding in. And it's a sort of boyish prank, isn't it? Although I'd never done it before, I didn't think it was in any way strange. Perhaps I should have done!' As so often with Britten, innocence was combined with sensuality: a diary entry from a Cornish holiday in 1936 (when he was twenty-two) articulates the thrill he got during a walk along the cliffs.

The climax is when I find a colossal chasm in the rocks – miles away from civilisation – climb an enormous distance down to rocky shore & undress & bathe stark naked. The sheer sensual exstasy [sic] of it! . . . Utter bliss!

There had presumably been little opportunity to swim naked when he plunged into the North Sea off Lowestoft as a boy. The routine was to use the Britten family beach hut just below their home in Kirkley Cliff Road. Basil Reeve says that 'Beth came along and, somehow or other, we would all go and swim in this darned sea'. Just a short distance up the road, South Lodge was equally close to the beach. But when he moved to Gresham's there was early morning skinny-dipping in the pool. His school friend David Layton says that in the summer they always bathed before breakfast in the nude – 'we never bathed with costumes at all except when other people were about'. So the nude bathing at Aldeburgh was, in part at least, a return to his boyhood. His brother Robert recalled going for a picnic with him and Peter Pears on Havergate Island, near Orford. 'It was a lovely hot day, and, as we were watching, Ben said, "I think I'm going to have a swim", so he stripped himself to his new-born clothes and leapt into the water, whereupon he was attacked by a number of sea birds, and it was quite alarming for him. They didn't actually touch him, but they got very close!'

In a letter to his young friend Roger Duncan, he gave some idea of the importance to him of swimming, even when the day was crammed with composing, performing and entertaining. He elaborated his rigid self-discipline – though he would no doubt have been disappointed to manage only four dips, compared with his optimum five.

> It was quite a busy day. I started with a bathe before breakfast; then I worked [composed]; then Peter & I went to the hall to rehearse; then another bathe; then some old friends of mine came to lunch; then I went and had some hard singles with Andrew Potter (another bathe to cool off); then Peter & I went to rehearse with the other singer (Nancy Evans) in the concert; then dinner and changed; then the concert, & after that, we gave a party to about 50 people here, & then to complete the day a lovely moonlight bathe!

It would no doubt have delighted Britten to know that, two years before, Imogen Holst had commented on his youthful physique after seeing him go swimming with two companions. 'When they were standing at the edge of the water, it was impossible to tell from their back views which was Ben & which were the two young boys in their late teens or early 20s.'

It is entirely characteristic that the first piece in his piano suite *Holiday Diary*, written when he was twenty, was entitled 'Early Morning Bathe'. The ginger barefoot walk across sharp shingle, the first tentative steps into ice-cold water, the decisive immersion of the whole body, the realisation that the water was not as cold as it had seemed, the purposeful swimming in deeper water, and then the awkward exit across painful pebbles . . . It is all there in the music.

Duncan remembers those early morning and late-night dips. They dashed across the garden in their dressing gowns, stripped off and jumped into the freezing water, did a few strokes and then came out again. It was a bit like the cold baths that Britten encouraged him to have: 'three-inch bath, cold water, stay in for at least 30 seconds – then it was just delightful to get out again. It was just to wake you up.'

Britten's love affair with cold water was another way in which he kept his own childhood alive. At Gresham's, when it was too cold to swim in the winter, there were communal cold showers, 'designed to wake you up', as David Layton recalls, 'and I suppose keep you clean too. We never had any hot water, apart from a hot bath once a week. Those who were good at it knew how to avoid the cold showers – they went in and came out without getting wet, but rubbing themselves excitedly with their towels. The others got wet and didn't mind.' Britten was clearly one of them. He disliked the luxury of hot baths: they made him 'feel dead for hours'. Colin Graham sees it as part of Britten's puritanical lifestyle: '. . . healthy mind and healthy body, and all that stuff. It was an interesting side of him.'

There cannot be many composers who have featured baths and bathing in their music. But Britten did not rest content with *Holiday Diary*. He expanded on the theme in two works of the late 1940s, just after he had moved beside the sea: *Saint Nicolas* and *The Little Sweep*. 'The Birth of Nicolas' delineates the saint's progress from infancy to boyhood to manhood, and, in Eric Crozier's words, bath-time is an essential rite of initiation:

Innocent and joyful, naked and fair,
He came in pride on earth to abide:
God be glorified!
Water rippled *Welcome!* in the bath-tub by his side;
He dived in open-eyed: he swam: he cried:
God be glorified!

Piano and percussion let rip with increasingly frantic, syncopated runs, as though the boy saint is 'slipping on the soap' (in Robert Saxton's imaginative description) 'and crying out "God be glorified!" '. In *The Little Sweep* the following year, the boy chimney sweep achieves redemption through the cleansing of 'Sammy's Bath'. Ten years after writing the *Holiday Diary* pieces, he had 'an awfully soft spot for them still'. He said, 'They just recreate that unpleasant young thing BB. in 1934 – but who enjoyed being BB all the same . . .!!'

His move a short distance inland to the Red House in 1957 was a welcome release from the prying eyes of passers-by on the seafront. But it did entail a divorce from his beloved sea. Bathing, however, continued in the same way in the pool he built at the Red House shortly after the move – indeed it was never heated. One summer, Pears told Britten that he envisaged him 'in wonderful hot sunshine in the garden sunbathing & then cooling off in the pool surrounded by Miles's and such. Am I quite wrong?'

Twenty years earlier, he had set up his first home, the Old Mill, at Snape. As part of his extensive renovations, he put in twin showers in the bathroom, side by side ('a very copious space', Wulff Scherchen recalls). This may have seemed a rather avant-garde idea for a young bachelor in the late 1930s, but he probably wanted to recapture the schoolboy camaraderie of taking showers in company just as much as to make a statement about his new independent lifestyle. One of the first he invited to stay was Piers Dunkerley, who sent this unusual message from Bloxham School, in response (presumably) to enquiries from his intended host:

My usual bath routine is as follows:–
(i)   1 shower (cold) on getting up
(ii) 1 hot bath before dinner
(iii) 1 cold shower after tennis or digging
I hope the well will stand up to it.

When Britten's rebuilding of the Old Mill was featured in *Ideal Home* magazine a decade later, a different version of the architect's drawing was used, which showed (incorrectly) two separate bathrooms.* He was clearly aware of the potential delicacy of the design of his plumbing.

---

* The double shower lasted in the Old Mill for more than sixty years. It was finally removed in renovations in 1999/2000.

CHAPTER 12

Malo . . . than a naughty boy

On 12th December 1953 a small choirboy with a round, angelic face, but a none too angelic glint in his eye, stood on the stage of the Royal Court Theatre in London for a singing audition. He recited Robert Browning's 'Home Thoughts from Abroad', and sang 'Where'er you walk' from Handel's *Semele*. 'He looked so tiny – I can remember clearly', says the opera producer Basil Coleman. 'He had a small voice – a nice, sweet voice. He was nice-looking, and he made an impression.' Coleman's assistant at the time, Colin Graham, adds: 'He had such zinging personality, even at the age of eleven – such self-assurance on the stage. And yet he had this sweet look in his face, and this beautiful sound.' As the boy stopped singing, a bass voice rang out from the stalls. 'Thank you, thank you *very* much. That's really very good.' When he heard that, the boy knew he'd got the part. The deep voice belonged to Britten. The boy was the future actor and director David Hemmings.

If truth be told, the auditions had not yielded much talent. Basil Coleman says they were 'rather depressing'. Britten was looking for a boy to sing the role of Miles in the opera he had not yet begun to write, based on Henry James's ghost story *The Turn of the Screw*. Miles was a complex character far removed from the normal walk-on role for a child. David Hemmings, one of the more bumptious boys in the choir of the Chapel Royal at Hampton Court Palace, had been encouraged to apply by his music-master. Although his voice was actually a little thin, he had a winning way at festivals, and often walked off with the prize. He knew how to sell himself to the judges.

He certainly sold himself well to Britten. He could sing top C 'without thinking', and managed the E above that 'with great ease, and he thought that was extraordinary. But I wasn't the traditional soprano, I had a very different kind of voice. Not great – not by any means great – just different. He spotted that in me. I was an actor rather than a singer and I think that quality in me drew a kind of breath with Britten.' It was a guise he had frequently assumed at school: from the age of six he would entertain his classmates, who used to beg their form-master, 'Please, Sir, let David tell us a story'. So he did, making it up off the top of his head. David and his father did not get on, but when Hemmings senior played the piano in his local pub, he was proud to show off his chorister son, so the boy went with him to sing along.

Within a few months of the audition, David Hemmings left school, left his home in the London suburb of Tolworth, and arrived in Aldeburgh for voice-training and to learn his part in the opera. For the next two or three months, he lived at Crag House. He was given the 'blue-chintz bedroom at the end of the first-floor landing with a chess set underneath the window' and Molesworth books on the bedside table. He became the darling of the household. 'It was one of the most wonderful times of my entire life', Hemmings told me shortly before he died. Britten was still working on the score, so 'we all gathered round the piano – Peter Pears, Jennifer Vyvyan, Joan Cross, Arda Mandikian, Olive Dyer and me'.* Britten played, 'and we all sang to it. He really constructed the opera round our voices.' Time was short: Britten had started writing it in March, and he was not to finish it until early September, just two weeks before the English Opera Group's opening night at Teatro la Fenice in Venice.

In Suffolk, Britten laid on academic tuition for his protégé, under the aegis of Basil Douglas, who managed the EOG. But it did not amount to much, once time had been allowed for singing lessons and instruction in his opera role – let alone croquet,

* They sang the roles of Peter Quint, the Governess, Mrs Grose, Miss Jessel, Flora and Miles respectively.

tennis, swimming and other extra-curricular activities. Douglas had promised David's father that there would be four hours of schoolwork every day. But Hemmings reckoned that it amounted to no more than that for the whole duration of his stay. 'If Ben gave me time off, which he did quite frequently, I would wander out along the beach. The fishermen would be mending their nets and I used to ask them if I could help. It was just adorable: they taught me how to repair the nets, and they taught me to drink, because they said, "Well, we're going up to The Mill* and you must come up and have a drink", and I said, "Well, I'm under age", and they said, "Not for us, you're not. You can mend a net, so you can come and have a drink with us." '

Britten also set out to broaden David's musical experience beyond the confines of church and pub. When he first arrived, Ben played him the recording of his *Young Person's Guide to the Orchestra*, which almost fifty years later Hemmings hailed as 'just the best piece ever written for kids'. He told me it should be played in every classroom 'just once a week', and his hilarious, unprompted – half-spoken, half-sung – exposition of the piece was all delivered at the correct pitch. 'Michael Tippett, eat your heart out!', he concluded. 'Britten is, without question, the best English composer of the 20th century.'

As the boy worked on the opera, his 'nice, sweet voice' quickly developed and he began to fit the role. 'It was fascinating', says Basil Coleman, 'how the voice grew and grew with his confidence. Working with him in rehearsal, I found it was no problem for him to do what I asked of him. Imogen Holst taught him how to play the piano in the piano scene and I think she loved those sessions. So did he. It was masterly: he'd do precisely what she wanted and did it splendidly.'

Britten's choice was vindicated. But, before long, his friends began to notice that he was captivated by David the boy, as well as by David the performer. This is all the more remarkable for happening when *The Turn of the Screw* was being composed at

* The pub on the seafront at Aldeburgh.

fever pitch, with little time, presumably, for any distractions. The opera had already been delayed a year to accommodate *Gloriana* for the Queen's coronation. But Britten always compartmentalised his life: the time he devoted to his friends, to his letter writing, and to his boy companions, did not impinge on his fecundity; if anything, it enhanced it. *The Turn of the Screw* is arguably the most tautly and ingeniously constructed of all his operas, both musically and dramatically. Britten had been ill for several months with bursitis in his right shoulder, which meant he was unable to use his right arm. He had not composed anything of substance since the completion of *Winter Words* the previous September. His infatuation with David Hemmings perhaps spurred his creativity after a period of enforced idleness, just as Aschenbach's creative paralysis was unlocked by his obsession with Tadzio. It was another foretaste of *Death in Venice* some twenty years later.

The infatuation (and it is Hemmings's own word) lasted for most of the two years he worked with Britten. Charles Mackerras, who conducted at Aldeburgh in the mid–1950s, saw it at first hand. 'David Hemmings was an extremely good-looking young chap and he also very much played up to Ben's obvious adoration of him, and drank it in. You know how a person looks at someone if they're in love with them – their face lights up when he or she comes into the room, and they give them precedence in everything. Ben's behaviour was so much that of the besotted lover that one thought that maybe he might have behaved improperly with him eventually. But if we can believe David Hemmings (and I do), there was no "hanky-panky" at all. Obviously it was a sexual attraction but I'm sure that it was never actually fulfilled.'

Basil Douglas had no doubt that Britten '*loved* David – he was in love with him', but he admired his self-restraint, because he was 'really smitten* and didn't David know it!' The boy

---

* Basil Douglas used the same word to describe Britten's attitude to Wulff Scherchen in the 1930s.

David, just like Tadzio, enjoyed his hold over the older man. Hemmings later felt Peter Pears had been jealous of him: Pears, after all, had to come and go because of his other singing commitments. David was there all the time.

Basil Coleman was another house guest during the later stage of rehearsals. 'Ben got very fond of him, of course. But it was more than that – it was the need to make sure the boy trusted him completely. There was a rapport between the two of them which gave him confidence, and would ultimately draw out a brilliant performance from the boy, because he was safe, as it were.' Coleman says everyone in the cast was devoted to David, and insists that it is wrong to exaggerate the attraction Britten felt to children. He rejoices in the devoted friendships Ben had with boys, friendships that he feels would have been hard for him to sustain in today's more censorious climate. But he does admit that one singer, in particular, was concerned that the composer was getting too fond of David. Asked if he felt that was a risk, Coleman paused for a while before replying: 'Not really. No – I trusted Ben . . . No. And I was staying in the house too, so I would have been aware of anything untoward.'

A rare eyewitness account of a meeting between David and Ben conveys the flavour of their friendship.

> No one could have doubted the innocence of the relationship who, like me, was on Aldeburgh seafront one day when David, just arrived from London, spotted Ben among the many people enjoying the sunshine, ran to him, and with a shout of greeting took a flying leap into his arms. He received in return a laughing kiss on the forehead before Ben set him down. The audience had recently emerged from a concert in the Jubilee Hall, so there must have been several dozen ordinary Festivalgoers looking on, and clearly they were amused, not shocked.

This vignette, written by Maureen Garnham, secretary to Basil Douglas at the EOG, confirmed her perception of Britten's relationship with children:

Ben loved and understood children – all children, girls as well as boys – and frequently composed for them. Much has been made of his physical attraction to boys, which undoubtedly existed but which he always had under firm control.

Half a century on, Hemmings himself had no reservations. 'He was not only a father to me, but a friend – and you couldn't have had a better father, or a better friend. He was generous and kind, and I was very lucky. I loved him dearly, I really did – I absolutely adored him. I didn't fancy him, I wouldn't have gone to b . . . – well, I did go to bed with him, but I didn't go to bed with him in *that* way.' He admitted Ben was infatuated with him: 'Everybody asks me whether or not he gave me one, whether or not it was a sexual relationship. The answer to that question, as I have often said, is: no, he did not. I have slept in his bed, yes, only because I was scared at night* . . . and I have never ever, ever felt threatened by Ben at all because I was more heterosexual than Genghis Khan!' I asked him whether he felt Britten's feelings for him had been those of a father for a son, or whether he had been in love with him. Hemmings's response was elliptical: 'That's a very good question, but I think both are entwined in one. If you are in love with a young man, certainly you can consider him your son. He certainly wanted to bring me up, he certainly wanted to send me to an appropriate school where I could learn music and learn to play the piano, and, yes, he loved me, he did, he did. But he loved me like a father, not like a lover.'

If some twelve-year-old boys might have been too innocent to appreciate sexual danger signs, David Hemmings was not one of them. As a choirboy travelling from Tolworth to Hampton Court, he had (like David Spenser) been molested several times

---

* Jean Maud noted in an interview (transcribed at the Britten–Pears Library) that, when the Maud family was staying at Crag House in the late 1940s, the children were often frightened at night because of the noise of the North Sea waves crashing on the beach only a few feet away, and needed to be comforted.

by a man on the bus, 'so I knew what the goings were'. Before leaving home for Suffolk the first time, he had been warned about Britten by his father, 'strangely enough in Leicester Square men's lavatory. He told me – his exact words – "You know he's a homo, don't you?" ' But in the event, Hemmings said, Britten was 'as clean as kingdom come in that regard – I couldn't fault him, not for one single second'.

It does seem remarkable that his parents were content for their son to move to Aldeburgh for several months to live with Britten. I asked Hemmings whether they had been concerned, and he seemed genuinely surprised by his own answer. 'No, they weren't, really! I think that's quite extraordinary now, I really do – because they weren't. They thought I was well out of the home. I wasn't a great kid, you have to understand: I was not what you might call a 'come home at night' kid and I'm talking seven or eight years old. I'd be in the alleyway and I'd be up little girls' trousers – I'm serious – and always it was my mother that would come storming down the alleyway and say, "Why aren't you at home?" And I've continued that life really ever since.'

His mother did go to Suffolk for occasional visits, and his father joined her for one weekend. The boy was nervous about how his father would behave, because he knew he disliked Britten, and there was apparently one tense moment when they were all walking on the beach together, and Ben patted David on the head. His father took umbrage at this, but nothing was said, and the ménage continued.

David's sexual awareness merely heightened the concern of some of those around him. In the context of this particular opera, in which he was to play such an important part, it was hardly surprising. Myfanwy Piper based her libretto on the Henry James story, but, as with all his operas, Britten was closely involved in both its overall shape and the actual words used. The essence of James's plot was unchanged, revolving as it does around two orphaned children, Miles and Flora, being brought up at Bly, a large, isolated country house. Their uncle and guardian, who lives in London, has arranged a new governess for them, who arrives at Bly full of good intentions. But she soon becomes aware that the house contains ghosts of two recent employees: Peter Quint, a former manservant, and Miss Jessel, her predecessor as governess. Before their deaths, Quint and Jessel had also been lovers. The new governess seeks to protect Miles and Flora from the ghosts, who she realises are trying to corrupt them. But she discovers (without much help from the slow-witted housekeeper, Mrs Grose) that the apparently innocent children are attracted by the ghosts, and colluding with them. She manages to send Flora away with Mrs Grose, but herself takes on Peter Quint in a heroic battle for the soul of Miles. Her apparent triumph crumbles as the boy dies in her arms. His rejection of Quint has been too much for him. But so has the suffocating embrace of the Governess.

The production team originally understood the work as a straightforward ghost story. 'But it was only really during rehearsals', says Colin Graham, the stage manager in 1954, 'that we became (at least I became) aware that there was more to it than that – the relationship between Miles and Quint. And the way Basil [Coleman] was directing it was making that quite clear.'

Although the only overt sexual reference in the story is to the previous love affair between Quint and Jessel, *The Turn of the Screw* has a latent sexuality that adds to the tension and the spookiness. Right at the start, it is clear from the Governess's musings that she is drawn to her employer, the children's guardian (whom we never see). He himself is a Jekyll-and-Hyde character. He is apparently noble and kind-hearted, but as the story unfolds we develop the suspicion that he is aware of what is happening at Bly, and is in some way complicit. The Governess's concern for Miles becomes almost passionate, and her obsessive, meddlesome desire to protect the boy moves beyond the maternal to the unnatural. In some modern productions of the opera, there has even been a hint that the children, brought up in their distorted environment, have an incestuous affection for each other.

Malo, Miles's song in the schoolroom, sets the context for the discomfiting relationship between the boy and Peter Quint which pervades the rest of the drama. We realise that the boy, consciously or not, is advertising his own emotional and psychological complexity on the brink of adolescence. He and Flora have been fooling around, to the exasperation of the Governess. Everything then stops, and Miles's haunting melody emerges to the eerie accompaniment of the cor anglais. He is apparently reciting a classroom jingle designed to remind pupils of the different meanings of the Latin word *malo*. But the words suggest a deeper awareness of temptation and evil:

> *Malo* . . . I would rather be
> *Malo* . . . in an apple tree
> *Malo* . . . than a naughty boy
> *Malo* . . . in adversity.

It is a pivotal moment in the opera. We realise there is much more to Miles than a larky little boy. This song is both simple and complex, poignant and unsettling, and it encapsulates Britten's interest in the co-existence of innocence and sensuality. Some productions have made the mistake of pre-empting this chilling moment by portraying Miles as a knowing child from the start. In those early rehearsals, Basil Coleman did not try to explain its significance to David Hemmings. '*Malo* is full of all sorts of overtones and so on which I'm not sure that we made him aware of necessarily. He was just made to sing it quite beautifully which he did.'

The potential sexual charge between Miles and Quint undoubtedly stems from the Henry James original, but it is given sharper focus by Britten's decision to allow the ghosts to speak. We first see Peter Quint as an apparition on a roof-turret but, brilliantly, Britten contrives to delay his first vocal appearance until the momentous final scene of the first act. Then he makes contact with the sleeping Miles for the first time, and his appeal to the boy is expressed in the melismatic, seductive way he calls his name. Miles has spent his life surrounded by women, thanks to his absent guardian. His claustrophobia has been compounded by his expulsion from school for some unexplained wickedness: he is now virtually interned in his own home. Peter Quint is the first man he has recently encountered (and indeed he must remember him in life), and Quint is (unusually for Britten) the only man in the opera. Furthermore, Miles the treble has been surrounded by sopranos (there is not even a mezzo-soprano, let alone a contralto): this adds to the brittle tension of the piece, and gives it a unique sonority. So, when the tenor voice of Quint tantalises the boy with visions of 'the hidden life that stirs when the candle is out', Miles is only too ready to respond. The boy, imprisoned by women in his nursling state, cannot but be excited by Quint's romantic depiction of himself:

> I'm all things strange and bold,
> The riderless horse
> Snorting, stamping on the hard sea sand,
> The hero-highwayman plundering the land.
> I am King Midas with gold in his hand.

As Miles cries, 'I'm here, oh, I'm here' (the word 'oh' is surely a sign of longing), he thrills to the mentions of gold, secrets and 'the long sighing flight of the night-winged bird'. These fantasies recall the allurements with which the Erl-King enticed the boy in Schubert's setting of Goethe, which Britten and Pears had rehearsed together before the war:*

> Dear child, do come with me!
> Wonderful games I'll play with you!
> Many bright-coloured flowers are on the shore,
> My mother has many a golden garment.

There is also a parallel with Britten's favourite film of twenty years before, *Emil and the Detectives*. During his train journey to Berlin, Emil is both excited and frightened by the grotesque

---

* See page 77.

images of the big city with which the stranger in the bowler hat (who turns out to be the villain) humourlessly teases him. The polarities of attraction and repulsion are confused, just as they are in the extraordinary music which closes the first act of *The Turn of the Screw*. It is both enchantingly beautiful and profoundly disturbing, and leaves the audience emotionally drained.

As the first rehearsals of the opera progressed, Colin Graham came to realise that, although the character of Miles still had 'an underlying innocence, because of who he is and the age he is', he had been 'got at'. This was where there was an awkward crossover between the fictional part of Miles and the real boy they were working with, David Hemmings. David's horizons had certainly been expanded by the romance of spending weeks on the Suffolk coast as Ben's favourite. The production team had come to realise why Britten had chosen the cherubic Hemmings to play Miles, and why that decision was so shrewd. There was a knowingness in him that worked. 'There sure was', says Graham. 'David was years ahead of his own age. The way he behaved with young women was quite louche and suggestive. I don't know where he'd learnt it from, his Dad or something, but it was pretty advanced for a boy of his age.'

During rehearsals in summer 1954, Britten never spoke about the sexual undercurrents in the story. There was too much practical work to be done. But he had discussed them with Pears and with his librettist, Myfanwy Piper. At one stage, her draft said that Quint 'made free' with Miles. Britten told her that Pears thought this was 'too suggestive', and went on to refer back to the original wording: 'James merely says "Quint *was* too free with the boy". I think the sexy suggestion should only refer to his relationship with Miss Jessel, don't you? Incidentally, it may help to avert a scandal in Venice!!' In the final version of the libretto, the distinction is all but invisible: 'Quint was free with everyone, with little Master Miles [. . .] Hours they spent together [. . .] He made free with her too, with lovely Miss Jessel [. . .] He had ways to twist them round his little finger. He liked them pretty, I can tell you [. . .] and he had his will, morning and night.' The music achieves the same result, with its claustrophobic sense of encroaching evil.

Ten years later, in a letter to another of his librettists, William Plomer, Britten did marvel that he was able to engage boys who just 'got on with the job' to sing Miles. 'Thank God', he added, 'most children don't put two and two together'. Plomer had just drawn his attention to a remark of Henry James, handed down by Siegfried Sassoon: James had been asked what construction should be put upon *The Turn of the Screw*, and he replied, 'the worst possible construction'. Basil Coleman points to the hostile reactions that James received when his original story was published. 'He got a great many letters afterwards, accusing him of all sorts of evils, and he said, "Well, then I've succeeded. Because you read into it the evil that you know".'

Britten was intrigued by the corruption or disintegration of innocence, and none of his works addresses this so directly as *The Turn of the Screw*. A further fascination for him was the unspoken question of whether the innocent himself had become complicit in the corruption, and therefore whether the 'innocence' of the treble voice had curdled. In the opera itself, the answer is clear. It comes in the final bars of Act I, after Miles's rendezvous with Quint and Flora's with Miss Jessel. The boy says to the Governess: 'You see, I am bad. I am bad, aren't I?' Britten relished this line. He wrote to Myfanwy Piper in January 1954 that he liked Miles's remark 'because it is clear, bright, and in short phrases, which I think is right for the boy's character and his manner of singing'. This letter demonstrates that Britten had instinctively perceived the parallel between Miles and David Hemmings at the December audition, long before he got to know him well in Aldeburgh. The decidedly unmonastic Hemmings made the connection himself without hesitation. 'I wasn't exactly what you might call a "prior-boy" myself – choir-boy yes, prior-boy no. Did I know Miles? Yes I did. He was me. And I think Ben saw that in me. He saw the wickedness in me, he saw that evil sense of countenance about me. He thought I was naughty, and that's why Peter Pears was afraid of me, because *he* thought I was naughty too!' There is no equivalent line for Flora, who has also been caught out of bed: perhaps Miles is speaking on behalf of both of them, perhaps it is the 'wickedness' in him that has drawn Flora to meet Miss Jessel. Or perhaps, for Britten, Miles was the only one that mattered anyway.

At the start of Act II, Myfanwy Piper's libretto is inspired in its use of a quotation from Yeats's 'The Second Coming': 'the ceremony of innocence is drowned', which conveys a sense of ritual inevitability in the unfolding drama. Both Quint and Jessel use this phrase as they each set out their desire for 'a friend' or 'a soul to share my woe'. Quint rejects Jessel's reproaches over their previous affair. It is quite clear that he has Miles in mind when he sings:

> I seek a friend –
> obedient to follow where I lead,
> slick as a juggler's mate to catch my thought,
> proud, curious, agile, he shall feed
> my mounting power.
> Then to his bright subservience I'll expound
> the desperate passions of a haunted heart,
> and in that hour
> 'the ceremony of innocence is drowned'.

At this point the music echoes Quint's earlier seductive call to Miles. In the final struggle between Quint and the governess for ownership of the boy, Quint calls out: 'Beware of her!' It is an uncanny reminder of Longfellow's warning against female allure in his poem 'Beware!', which the young Benjamin had set to music close to his ninth birthday (and had frequently revisited during his schooldays to make small adjustments). The Governess may have appeared 'a maiden fair to see', in Longfellow's words, but she could 'both false and friendly be'.

David Hemmings's horizons at the age of twelve were defined by Tolworth, Margate and Aldeburgh. So the première of *The*

Turn of the Screw was not only his stage début: it gave him his first taste of foreign travel. In early September the whole cast set off for Venice to perform in the Biennale. Hemmings, as the star turn, enjoyed a feast of publicity photographs, on a gondola, at a water fountain, with fluttering pigeons, all of them revealing a feisty young boy with a wicked twinkle in his eye (see plate 19). Mrs Hemmings was there as chaperone, but almost fifty years later her son recalled with special satisfaction a headline in *The Children's Newspaper*: HEMMINGS THE MENACE SINGS OPERA IN VENICE.

No other Britten opera, apart from *Paul Bunyan* in America, was first heard outside his native shores, and the première of *Bunyan* was scarcely a happy precedent. *The Turn of the Screw* was to be broadcast live on radio in Britain and parts of Europe, and the composer's nerves, never steady before a performance at the best of times, were a-jangle on this occasion, thanks to a strike by the Venetian stage hands and then a delayed start on the night, because the previous broadcast had overrun. The full-feathered audience of La Fenice began a slow handclap in the stifling heat of a mid-September evening, made more sultry by the heavy scent of roses which bedecked the auditorium.

It was not a happy start. But David Hemmings was to find that the climax of his first professional stage appearance would be indelibly imprinted on his memory for the rest of his life. The very process of reliving the opera's momentous conclusion, and almost acting it out as he spoke, brought a lump to his throat almost fifty years later. 'This may be emotional for me, but that tells you how much I really admired it and him. At the end of the piece, Jennifer Vyvyan as the Governess sings a reprise of my song, *Malo*. She is bending over my dead body after I've been split from Peter Quint, and then the orchestra play four soft chords (berm, berm, berm, berm), and Jimmy Blades hits the timpani one last time, ber-berm. End of story. Curtain comes down. Not a sound in the audience – *not a sound*! And I'm lying in Jennifer Vyvyan's arms – who has just done this *unbelievable* aria – and then there are one or two faint claps in the audience.' As he talked, Hemmings demonstrated how those faint claps grew into a swelling tide of applause: 'And it's absolutely *sound*-throbbing. Well, if that's not great music, I don't know what is. And I am *so proud* to be a part of it, and I'm sorry that I'm sort of weeping about it, but it was pretty magnificent stuff.'

Once the curtain calls were over, the whole cast attended a reception given by the Mayor, who gave David a Märklin train set. The evening was still young, and the cast set off to carouse in the alleys of Venice. It culminated in an *al fresco* rendering of Greek folksongs by Arda Mandikian, who had sung the role of Miss Jessel. Hundreds of people stopped and stared at this impromptu display. The boy David was in his seventh heaven: no wonder the stage hooked him that night.

Shortly afterwards he sent Britten a horseshoe charm, with a touching little dedication: 'For Ben, with best wishes and good luck for future performances of the "Screw". With love, David xxxxxxxxxxxxx' They came in profusion. In October, the opera opened in London at Sadler's Wells, then it travelled to Holland and Sweden, and in January it was recorded by Decca – the first time a complete Britten opera had been committed to disc. He also took the opportunity that year to record *The Little Sweep* and *Saint Nicolas* while he still had David's treble voice and cheeky character available to him. 'David is lovely as Sammy', he told the first producer of *The Little Sweep*, 'simple & touching'.

Sometime in November 1954, David found time to go back to school, though not for long. He took the opportunity to show off a leather belt that Britten had given him (remembering perhaps the snake belt the young Benjamin had proudly owned at prep school), and in his thank-you letter said, 'I would like to spend a few days at Aldeburgh with you, the first weekend after Christmas, or whenever it is convenient with you. Please give my best regards to Peter (Quint you devil!*),

* These words are Miles's final utterance in the opera.

and all at Aldeburgh. Lots of love to you! Yours always, David xxxxxx'

He did indeed go to stay, and Britten sent him a present afterwards, which prompted a further letter.

Dear Ben,
Thank you, Thank you for the lovely game 'Dover Patrol'. I enjoyed playing it so much at Aldeburgh with Richard, that I have been trying to get it (in vain chiz.,), therefore you can imagine my joy at receiving your parcel. This is also an opportunity to thank you for my lovely stay at Crag House, I don't think I have ever enjoyed a holiday so much – even Venice. It was so good to have somebody you were fond of with you all the time and for this Ben, I thank you indeed. I most certainly will – if it's all right with you, stay with you again sometime. [. . .]

Yours, with all my Love, David xoxoxoxoxo (1,000,000 times).

A bureaucratic problem developed early in 1955 about taking the boy on overseas tours at his age. He wrote to Britten that he was 'extremely disappointed at the prospect of not being with you [. . .] "Turning the Screw" ', and added: 'But you may borrow my screwdriver if you like!' The problem was resolved, and Basil Douglas's secretary Maureen Garnham noted his 'remarkable performance, dramatically as well as musically, and had I been his mother I might have been worried about its effect on him. Probably, however, he was already enough of a professional to be able successfully to separate his stage role from real life, and not to "get the horrors" as I probably would have done at the same age.'

David's absorption into the Britten canon was enduring. He retained such a regard for *Let's Make an Opera* (the 'entertainment for young people' that incorporates *The Little Sweep*, in which he had taken the part of Sammy) that, decades later, when the Metropolitan Opera asked Hemmings which opera he would like to produce for them, he replied without hesitation:

'*Let's Make an Opera*'. An awkward silence followed, because this little show was not quite what the grand sophisticates in New York had had in mind. Then they parried with: 'What about *Macbeth*?'

As the performances of *The Turn of the Screw* continued, David's now fruitier treble voice survived miraculously into his fifteenth year. Britten tried to map out a career for his young star. He wrote to his old school, Gresham's, to see if they could take him, and received an encouraging response. He also wanted to send him to Florence for coaching as a tenor, once his voice had broken. But the opera had launched Hemmings's stage career rather than a musical one, and he forsook Britten's plans in favour of more attractive film offers that were already coming his way.

The end, when it came, was sudden. The EOG took the *Screw* to Paris, to the Théâtre des Champs-Elysées, in 1956. In the middle of his keynote aria, *Malo*, David's voice broke – just like that. A mortified Britten brought the orchestra off, waved his baton at David in a fury, and put it down on his music stand as the curtain was lowered. 'I was Spanish-archered immediately (got the El Bow). As I walked off the stage, I passed Robin Fairhurst (who'd been my understudy for two years) walking up the stairs. I thought, "You little bugger, you're going to be playing this for weeks". But', he added with glee, 'his voice broke the following night!'*

Hemmings remembered it as the last time he had any dealings with Britten. When I asked him whether this father-figure whom he so adored had said anything to him, he surprised me – and I think himself – by the answer that sprang to his lips: 'No. No, he didn't. That was a bit sad, I have to say, but from that moment forward, I was history. . . Sad isn't it? The idyll was all over.'

---

* Maureen Garnham dates the breaking of Hemmings's voice to later in 1956, rather than at the Paris performances in May.

CHAPTER 13

For I am but a child

Nearly three years before David Hemmings's triumph in Venice, Britten had written another work, on a much smaller scale, about a tussle between a young boy and an older man. In this instance, however, he did not devise the boy's role for a child singer, but assigned it to the foremost British contralto of the time, Kathleen Ferrier.

In January 1952, some five years or so after she had sung *The Rape of Lucretia* at the Glyndebourne première, Ferrier joined Britten and Pears in a six-city tour to raise funds for the English Opera Group. Shortly before they set off, Britten tossed off a new concert work for the three of them to perform, whose theme of sacrifice must have been poignant for Ferrier after her recent cancer treatment. For a while Britten had been intrigued by the naïve language of the medieval Miracle Plays, which were designed to present Bible stories for street performance. Just as he responded to boys' voices from the street or the playground rather than the chancel, so he preferred his sacred themes earthy rather than ethereal. With his own enduring interest in paternal relationships, the story of Abraham's readiness to sacrifice his son Isaac as proof of his obedience to God was a theme that resonated with him. He was perhaps reminded of it during the long gestation of *Billy Budd,* which was first staged the previous month. In the original novella, Herman Melville surmises that Captain Vere 'may in the end have caught Billy to his heart even as Abraham might have caught young Isaac on the brink of resolutely offering him up in obedience to the exacting behest'. In any event, Britten quickly marked up this story in his copy of the Miracle Plays with cuts and pencil annotations. The result was what he called a Canticle for alto, tenor and piano, *Abraham and Isaac.*

Britten had been impressed by the 'true innocence and purity of her character' as well as by her voice* when Ferrier created the role of Lucretia in 1946, and had at that time contemplated writing a cantata for her. Perhaps this encouraged him, against what might have been expected, to cast a woman in the boy's role of Isaac. Unfortunately no recording of the Ferrier performances survives. After her early death the following year, Britten recorded the piece with Norma Procter and Peter Pears. After hearing it through, he said it was a 'really <u>wonderful</u> record'. But for some reason he never consented to its public release.

The first time he performed it with a boy alto as Isaac was in December 1960, when John Hahessy took the role. As head chorister at Westminster Cathedral he had taken part in the première of *Missa Brevis* the previous year, and Britten was shrewd enough to spot how well his voice would suit the part, which ranged from A flat below middle C to top E flat. Hahessy (today the tenor John Elwes) says that at that point his voice was 'sinking rapidly to the tenor range and was ideal for the role. I was never an alto except at this precise moment. I could still reach higher notes but the lower ones were definitely appearing with strength.'

Britten inscribed his score in gratitude for 'a wonderful first performance' and gave him his first watch as a present. They recorded it shortly afterwards. So Britten's only commercial recording of the work is with a boy alto, not with the contralto he had originally envisaged. Professional performances today with a boy are extremely rare: concert promoters and record producers are unduly fearful of the unpredictability of a boy's voice when it is on the verge of breaking, and not flexible enough to take advantage of a boy's voice when it is *à point*. They resort instead to the safety of a counter-tenor. But there

---

* For Britten, voice and personality were always intertwined. In paying tribute to Ferrier after her death, he said: 'The thing – the only thing – that moves me about a singer is the way the voice communicates the personality'. He loathed a voice that was simply beautiful, 'like an overripe peach' (BBC *Omnibus* 6.10.68).

is nothing to beat the impact of a boy's voice in this music, as attested by amateur performances in schools. Not even the radio recording of Janet Baker's Aldeburgh Festival performance with Britten and Pears in 1968 has the raw intensity that a boy's voice brings.

For the television documentary *Britten's Children*, Philip Langridge as Abraham was joined as Isaac by Nicholas Daly, a former chorister at King's College, Cambridge. His top treble notes had become vulnerable, but his middle register and bottom notes were rich and strong, particularly his bottom C sharps in the scene where the boy almost eggs his father on to kill him. The two octave leaps in 'Ah, mercy, father, why tarry you so?' were heart-rending. There is a powerful parallel between the boy Isaac on the verge of being slaughtered in his prime, and the boy singer with that special bloom and richness of the voice in the weeks before it breaks and is lost for ever. In both cases, the boy is on the threshold of adult experience and knows he has to be brave – yet he also knows his own vulnerability and is afraid. From his own knowledge of this piece, John Elwes stresses that a boy alto singing at full volume has 'fear and worry' in his voice. 'He is at his limit and fragile.' Adults cannot convey that childish fear, because their vocal limits outstretch those of boys, allowing them to 'override even the "bullying" of Abraham!'

The contrast in vocal strength between man and boy adds to the drama. Britten clearly sensed that. That was why he picked out John Hahessy for the role at exactly the right moment. But whether he had always envisaged that, after Kathleen Ferrier, Isaac might be sung by a boy is unclear. The score is ambiguous: the voice is specified as 'alto', rather than 'contralto'. In 1952 he had not yet put a boy's solo voice on equal terms with an adult's: *The Turn of the Screw* was yet to come, and at that time boy sopranos never stepped outside the chancel, let alone that rare creature, a boy alto. Even in church choirs, unbroken alto voices were not valued, but consigned to a waiting room on their way down to the tenors or basses.

The extraordinary power of *Abraham and Isaac* rests upon a mixture of naïvety with an almost supernatural profundity, nowhere more so than in the opening. Britten was faced with the challenge of representing the voice of God calling Abraham, which he achieved by a synthesis of the two voices, tenor and alto, sometimes in unison, sometimes in close harmony (often in spooky seconds). The accompaniment, a series of extended rising arpeggios on the piano, manages a *Rheingold*-like sense of timelessness and security through an unabated wash of E flat major. But there is also a peculiar fragility in the arpeggios, achieved by the omission of the fifth interval in the chord: there are no B flats, only the ripple of E flats and Gs, which lends the sound an unforgettable translucency. No wonder, as Michael Tippett admiringly recalled, Britten said the opening was 'worth a million dollars'.

In these first pages, the piano refuses to move from E flat major (the 'clear, resonant' piano arpeggios at the start of Schubert's *Trout* Quintet have a similar rootedness). If the three flats of this key are sometimes used in music to represent the Christian doctrine of the Trinity, the composer Robert Saxton describes the lack of movement as 'an E flat halo, an all-embracing sonority, in which the music sits'. When the music modulates to the three-sharp key of A major for the start of the human drama, it is all the more remarkable. It is the polar opposite to E flat major, yet Britten manages the transition in a mere five bars.

The 'million-dollar opening' is worth even more when a boy takes the alto part. At once the vocal lines are no longer a duet, but contrasting and complementary aspects of the divine nature – innocence and experience, frailty and strength, naïvety and wisdom. This is a more complex and subtle congruity than the simple masculine-feminine balance when a contralto is used, and a counter-tenor fares little better. At the climax of the human drama, the intended moment of sacrifice, the voice of God is heard again, and the re-coalescence of the two voices carries even greater power. Philip Langridge was intrigued to sing the piece with a boy for the first time. He found that he had to rebalance his top notes in reaction to Nick Daly's vulnerability at the bottom of his register. The emotional dynamic was quite different too, and the infusion of audible innocence changed the character of the work.

The ingenuity of Britten's realisation of a familiar Bible story owed much to his instinctive concern for the plight of the boy. He himself spoke with admiration of the way Kathleen Ferrier had characterised him: 'the boyish nonchalance of the walk up to the fatal hill, his bewilderment, his sudden terror, his touching resignation to his fate'. This piece, perhaps more than any other of Britten's, expresses the tenderness of a father-son relationship, a tenderness which he had never known in his own family situation. His own father was a remote, formal character with little understanding of what music meant to his son: indeed Britten called him 'almost anti-musical'. But, as an adult, Britten repeatedly assumed for himself a paternal role, particularly with boys whose natural fathers were absent or difficult. In the years that followed the Ferrier performances, he did not ask any of the boys who had sung Miles, or Sem and Ham in *Noye's Fludde*, to try their hand at Isaac. It was only after his boys' mass *Missa Brevis* in 1959 that the idea seems to have struck him, or that the right voice presented itself. But the 'rightness' of the boy alto was there in the writing all along. He so identified with Isaac's predicament that he wrote the part for a boy singer, perhaps without consciously realising it.

Ten years later he returned to the story in his *War Requiem*. In the context of war, he naturally sympathised with Wilfred Owen's mordant poem 'The Parable of the Old Man and the Young', in which there is no reprieve for the boy. Isaac's slaughter by his father is Owen's bitter emblem of divine brutality in the First World War. For Britten, it embraced both his own pacifism and his devotion to children, so it was an appropriate choice for Peter Pears to read at his memorial service in Westminster Abbey. In his musical setting of the poem, Britten took the (for him) rare step of quoting his own music, with a poignant reference back to the rippling arpeggios of the

Canticle's opening, as if to say that the honest, simplistic human faith which they represented had been betrayed by God.

Britten could sometimes be almost flippant about his most moving pieces. He dismissed his *Serenade* for tenor, horn and strings as 'not important stuff, but quite pleasant, I think'. *Abraham and Isaac* was, in his view, 'a naïve little piece': with Isaac's attempt to use 'every wile to try & escape' his plight, 'I don't think there'll be a dry eye in the place– – –!'

This self-deprecation does of course contain some truth. The words of a Mystery Play, designed for the market square, were neither particularly pious nor subtle, and one of Britten's hallmarks as a composer was that he did not shy away from apparent naïvety or banality. One of the more amusing episodes in the Canticle is the agitated D minor section when Isaac appeals to his father for leniency – corporal punishment any day, rather than capital, he seems to say:

> If I have trespassed in any degree,
> With a yard [rod] you may beat me.

As Abraham cites divine authority for his plans, the boy pleads that his mother would come to his rescue if she were there – accompanied all the while by hectic contrary-motion scales on the piano, that daily grind for any schoolboy doing his music practice. As the slightly discrepant scales come unstuck, and the boy tries uncertainly to get them going again, we hear him insist: 'For I am but a child'.

Britten often toyed with the idea of adopting children, so that he could be a real father to them. Shortly after setting up house at the Old Mill in Snape in the mid-1930s, he offered a home to a twelve-year-old Basque refugee from the Spanish Civil War, Andoni Barrutia, and before his arrival was buying him clothes and a football and 'enjoying the responsibility tremendously'. Piers Dunkerley wrote to Ben from Bloxham in April 1938 to find out how the newly arrived Andoni was behaving, and hoping that 'he hasn't crashed the car, or killed Caesar [the family dog Britten had inherited from his mother] or anything terrible like that!' It was rather close to the truth. Andoni was a nui-sance: he spoke little English, was of little help around the house, and the cause of no little friction with the housekeeper. After only a fortnight, Britten decided he would have to go – 'which bleeds my heart but it is better on the whole'.

He returned to the idea some years after moving to Aldeburgh. Again he wanted to adopt victims of war – in this case two German orphans. The plan never came to fruition, but he told Imogen Holst that he had been thinking about it 'for ages because he realised that it was unlikely that he'd ever marry and have children of his own, and he'd got such an immense instinct of love for them that it spilled over and was wasted'. He talked of finding the right school for them (he clear-ly had boarding-school in mind), and then scheduling his con-cert tours for term-time, so that he could be with them in the holidays. He said he wanted to adopt a girl and a boy 'but it would probably have to be two boys because of regulations about a predominantly male household' – an interesting com-mentary on the more relaxed social attitudes of the early 1950s, long before adoption into gay households had become such an apparently modern and controversial idea.

At much the same time, he was thinking of adopting Robin Long, the local boy known as 'Nipper', whose rather anxious face has become familiar in the photograph of him beside Britten aboard Billy Burrell's fishing boat (see plate 16). Burrell regarded the boy as 'a sneaky little devil' who 'didn't care a damn about nothing. [. . .] He was that sort of boy that the girls would strip him off, with nothing on at all, and he didn't care a damn!' Britten took him on a boating holiday across the North Sea and up the Rhine with Pears and a group of friends, and he was thinking of paying for him to go to private school. Burrell, who reckoned Britten wanted 'more or less to adopt him', told the composer: 'You want to forget that! That's the biggest mistake you'll ever make.' Britten was very upset a year or two later when Mrs Long intervened to stop her son going sailing with him and Burrell.

Colin Graham, who knew Britten well for the last twenty years or so of his life, believes that he 'desperately would have liked to have children of his own'. His agent Sue Phipps once broached the subject with him: 'He said, "Well, of course, if circumstances had been different, maybe I would have had some and maybe I would have been very happy".' Her impression was that Britten's true offspring were his compositions. But there was one boy for whom he became a surrogate father. 'I think he really felt a great need to help that boy in a most major possible way', says Colin Graham. 'And Roger was the closest . . . I mean right up to the very end of his life, he always regarded him as a lost son.'

Roger was the son of the librettist of *The Rape of Lucretia*, the mercurial poet and playwright Ronald Duncan. Britten is sometimes said to have been Roger's godfather, which he was not. He is often said to have adopted him, which he did not. But he was, in a sense, a father to him, because Ronald Duncan and Benjamin Britten reached a strange informal arrangement to share the boy between them.

They had first met in 1935, and had collaborated on several musical projects before and after the war. But their initially close friendship became somewhat fraught as the years went by. Duncan was a self-absorbed man, who had many difficult relationships, not least with his wife, Rose-Marie. The marriage was never broken, but its intermittent cracks were at the expense, Britten thought, of their two children, Briony and Roger. So he began to take Roger under his wing in 1954, when the boy was eleven and Ben was forty. He felt he had an opportunity to brighten his life and give him a framework that was otherwise missing. 'Roger needs love', his sister (now Briony Lawson) says today, 'and perhaps he didn't get a sufficient amount from my parents. Ben coming along, showing him attention and giving him special treats, meant a lot to Roger.' Roger himself says Ben was 'just very caring. He was in many ways what my father wasn't.' Ronald Duncan seemed to acknowledge that in a note he once wrote Britten: 'Please give Roger the love he needs'.

At the start, Britten was preoccupied with writing *The Turn of the Screw* and training his new discovery, David Hemmings. But he began corresponding with Roger at his Somerset preparatory school, All Hallows, and visiting him there, and their friendship blossomed. Roger was good-looking, intelligent, conscientious, curious, wide-eyed, affectionate, expressive, and good at maths and sport. He was not particularly musical, but in other ways he reminded Ben of the boy he imagined himself to have been, and of his own schooldays. He wrote to him at the start of term in January 1955:

> I expect you are safely back at school now, & getting used to all the old things again. I thought about you quite alot on Wednesday when we were travelling around, & saw lots of boys going back to school, armed with tuck-boxes, and wearing bright school caps. I must say I felt I'd rather be going back to school than doing the kind of concerts we were doing [. . .] – but I daresay you wouldn't agree!

Britten's infatuation with David Hemmings seemed to subside as his regard for Roger rose. 'David H was a good boy', he told his producer after completing the recording of *The Turn of the Screw*. 'I've seen quite alot of him & am fond of but puzzled by his two completely opposite sides. He's no Roger, I'm afraid!' More than once he wrote to Roger about 'little David Hemmings' or 'Master David Hemmings, aged 13, but jolly good', but his main concern was to offer fatherly advice and sympathy about tennis and cricket. Roger's sportiness was a delight to the athlete in Ben.

> It was rotten luck for you being out third ball in that match – that's what I don't like about batting in cricket; after all if you serve a double-fault in tennis, you don't have to leave the court, however much your partner may swear at you! I think one should be allowed two or three lives.

> I hope the back-hand is improving – don't forget to stand sideways to the net when you hit: it is much easier to hit

that way, & the same with forehand & serving [. . .]. I must really give you some coaching in the summer!

[. . .] Lots of love & kisses, old thing, & hope everything goes well – Ben ooxxooxxoo

That summer Britten took Ronnie Duncan aside and put a most unconventional proposal to him – that they should 'share' Roger. 'I want to be as a father to him', Duncan reported Britten as saying. 'Will you allow me to give him presents, visit him at school, and let him spend part of the holidays with me – in other words share him? [. . .] That fills a gap in me.' Duncan was not remotely put out. Apparently without consulting his wife, he readily agreed, and added (as if happy to demonstrate he was a defective father): 'We've always got Briony'. Britten, according to Duncan, was delighted: 'It was as if I had given him three opera houses'. Briony Lawson says some people, even today, are rather shocked by the arrangement, which lasted throughout Roger's schooldays. 'But I think it's OK, because he didn't harm Roger at all. He just wanted to give – and to give not only good times but love as well is a lovely thing.'

Ben continued to take an interest in Briony too. Both children went skiing with him. He took them to concerts at the Wigmore Hall. Briony paid some visits to Aldeburgh with Roger. But for the most part Roger went there on his own. He spent a quarter of each holidays with Ben. The first-fruit of the 'agreement' was a two-week visit in the summer holidays, in Aldeburgh and then in London, at Pears's flat. Britten noted it to Basil Coleman.

I had little Roger here for a fortnight – which was enchanting. He is a dear child, & a most sweet & gay companion. [. . .] His is not an easy home life, as you know, & I think it's a relief to him to have an avuncular refuge!

For part of his visit, Roger was joined by another young friend of Ben's, Humphrey Stone. Ben took copies of some of Roger's photographs. 'I like the photos very much', he told him, 'especially the one I took of you & Humphrey dressing! That is a funny one. But that one is particularly valuable to me because do you know I had a <u>disaster</u> with <u>my</u> photos? [. . .] So that's the only photo I've got of you.'

When the time came for Roger to leave, the parting was 'pretty tearful', because in the middle of the autumn term Britten and Pears were leaving on a tour of Europe, India and the Far East, which meant that Ben and Roger would be separated until Easter. But Roger's father wrote to Britten on his travels, to consult him about Roger's education as if they were jointly responsible without any input from his mother.

Roger is going to Harrow in May, a term before the other new boys. I've agreed to this because the housemaster wanted it. Was I wrong? I dunno. It'll mean he's the <u>only</u> new boy. But it does give him a summer term extra & surely the <u>whole</u> of the school won't turn and bully him?

While he was travelling, Ben wrote a series of long, descriptive letters to Roger, which he asked the boy to keep safe. They were in effect his travel diary, and remain a fascinating account of his reactions to new cultures as he journeyed through India, Singapore, Indonesia, Hongkong, Japan, Thailand and Ceylon. He was particularly eloquent about how his senses had been 'knocked sideways' by the sights, sounds and smells of Bali.

The air is always filled by the sound of native music – flutes, xylophones, metalphones and extraordinary booming gongs – just as it is filled by the oddest spicey smells, of flowers, of trees and of cooking, as one's eye is filled by similar sights plus that of the really most beautiful people, of a lovely dark brown colour, sweet pathetic expressive faces, wearing strange clothes, sarongs of vivid colours, and sometimes wearing nothing at all.

He was charmed by the dancing – 'most of it by little girls aged about 10 or less – wonderful little creatures, doing dances of tremendous complication lasting $\frac{1}{2}$ hour or more!' – and by the gamelan music which would from now on have a significant influence on his own: 'what would have amused you was one Gamelan (the Balinese orchestra), made up of about 30 instruments, gongs, drums, xylophones, glockenspiels of all shapes & sizes – all played by little boys less than 14 years old. Jolly good they were too & enjoying it like fun!'

Roger was writing back regularly to Ben, who was properly inquisitive about the prep school rhythms of Roger's final year. 'So your voice is breaking!', Ben wrote on his way home. 'I wonder if you'll be talking a deep bass over the telephone when we talk these next days!' Roger received the call soon after Britten and Pears reached home in the middle of March.

My Darling Ben,
It was simply lovely to hear your voice again. It seemed so long that I almost felt nervous.

I do hope that you come to some arrangement with Mummy. I liked your idea about my meeting you somewhere then going on slowly to [the family home in] Devon. I can't believe that it is only six months since I saw you, it really seems like two years. But your letters were so interesting that they slightly relieved your absence especially during the holidays.

I am looking forward immensely to going to Harrow [. . .]
All my love, Roger xxxxxxxxxxxxx
PS I'd love to see you as soon as poss. Ring me after you've rung Mummy. It's simply lovely to have you back in England – in easy writing distance.

The reunion was arranged for Reading, and confirmed in a rather off-hand note to Britten from Roger's father.

He is terribly excited to see you & is off to Reading on Wednesday to meet you. At any rate, that's what he says. I do hope that won't be a bore. Say if it is, & I'll lock him up in a pig-sty.

Ben was now safely back for Roger's first term at Harrow. He knew from his own experience what a rough time that might be, and Roger knew where to turn for advice and sympathy. 'I know exactly what you mean about your Freud and Mathematics', Ben wrote early in that summer term. 'It is one of the most infuriating things I know, to be ahead of your class – much more maddening than being behind really! Did I ever tell you that I <u>never</u>, all the time I was at my public school, caught up with the Maths standard that I'd reached at my Prep school. Gosh, I was bored!' (No wonder one of his prep school masters said of Britten: 'It was a pity he took up music, because he would have made a wonderful mathematician'!)

Britten quickly relayed to Duncan senior that the new Harrovian 'seems to be OK then; I have had a very funny and highly critical letter from him – certainly quite a confidant! But what hell those first days must have been.' In June, Ben visited Roger at Harrow – one of a surprisingly large number of excursions that he found time to make to the schools of his boy companions. 'Roger was a charming host, & showed me around', he told his father. 'He seemed happy, & busy.'

When Roger's school report reached his parents while he was away with Ben, Ronald Duncan sent it on – not to his son, but to his father figure. 'Give my love to Roger', he said. 'I hope he is not in yr way too much. I enclose his report! It's quite good, don't you think?' Britten replied by return:

> Roger is a great dear – I like him more & more & love having him here. He is really quite intelligent, & always good company. Thank you for sending the report – what an odd document! It's years since I'd seen one. I suggested to Roger he might write a report on the masters . . . Bet it would be much more interesting!

In 1957, Britten told Basil Coleman he was seeing 'more & more of little (now quite big!) Roger, as his parents get more & more unhappy. He spends about ½ his holidays from Harrow here, & is an enchanting & deeply affectionate boy.' He mentioned to Pears (who was usually away performing when Roger was visiting) that he had stayed the weekend just before the end of term: he was 'very sweet, & affectionate, bit worried about his exams I think – felt sick (familiar feeling – ??!!) going back & all'.

In the mornings the boy was expected to entertain himself while Britten was composing. He bought Roger a new Raleigh bicycle so that he could explore rural Suffolk on his own. In the afternoons he made time for Roger: they would go off church hunting, which encouraged his interest in architecture, or they would play tennis. In the evenings, he was impressed by the way Ben would sit with a score on his lap, 'flipping the pages, hearing the music in his head just by reading it' – just as he had all those years before at prep school.

The following year, Britten dedicated his children's opera *Noye's Fludde* to his nephew and nieces, Sebastian, Sally and Roguey Welford, and also 'to my young friend, Roger Duncan'. It was a surprising combination, unless the intention was to indicate that Roger was 'family'. Peter Pears used to pay special attention to Briony, to make up for Ben's concentration on Roger. But to cast Britten as Roger's quasi-father is too simplistic. There was another dimension to their relationship, something that made it distinct from the affection he had for many other adolescent boys. There was a fervent edge to Ben's love for Roger, which was returned in a relationship that was ardent, but chaste. It lasted through his schooldays until he went to Cambridge, where precipitately he got married as an undergraduate.

Roger Duncan readily admits today that Britten's interest in him was homosexual. When I asked him about his own feelings at the time, he replied: 'I admired him and enjoyed being with him. I enjoyed and liked his affection, his care, and the attention he gave me. But I wasn't attracted to him physically.'

'But perhaps he was to you?' I ventured.

'Oh I'm sure. That was quite plain. But he respected the fact that I was not.'

Duncan today is a little reserved about publicly discussing his response to Britten. But his private letters of those years glow with profound feeling.

My darling Ben,
[. . .]I have an essay to write and five other letters and some Maths prep to do, and to learn some Milton. [. . .] We must do some longer walks around Aldeburgh or Welcombe [his home in Devon] together. I do so enjoy those walks with you over the marshes, but it's not the same at Welcombe, because you're always talking to Daddy as I know you have to.

I am longing to see you Ben. I think of you a great deal and miss you. Please keep writing in between arias of the opera. [. . .]

All my love to you, and Love to Peter, Miss Hudson* & the angels,† from Roger oxoxoxoxxoxx

For the first two years of Roger's teens, Ben was writing to him at least once a fortnight – highly unusual for an adult outside the family. Humphrey Stone says there was 'a strong bond' between Roger and Ben: 'Roger was rather good-looking – which may have had some bearing on it'. With a philosophical shrug, Briony admits that 'Ben just had this fascination for younger boys. And Roger was very, very good-looking.' Ben made no bones about the appeal that the male body held for him. Roger remembers him empathising with Michelangelo or Leonardo da Vinci – or indeed Alexander the Great: 'he used to talk about men's and boys' bodies being much more aesthetically pleasing than women's, which were rather bulbous and curvy'. Although Roger briefed him about his girlfriends in Devon, Ben was 'not very interested'.

As a boy, Roger became aware of homosexuality only after he had gone to Harrow, where he was teased about his friendship

---

* Britten's housekeeper in Aldeburgh.
† Britten's dogs, Clytie and Jove.

with Britten, and became embarrassed about it. He did not dilute the effusion in his letters, but 'we talked about it and I told him I wasn't homosexual, and he respected that. He used to kiss me, and that was about all.' To avoid any awkwardness, Britten would sometimes call Roger his godson. On other occasions, he introduced him to eminent musicians staying in Aldeburgh as 'my friend Roger Duncan'. Roger was 'too innocent to be embarrassed by that. I wasn't aware of them thinking "Well, he's the latest boyfriend".' Briony says there was nothing embarrassing about their relationship. 'It was just innocence, to be honest. It's nice to have some innocence in this world.'

Duncan remembers Britten as 'very proper. He wasn't fey at all. He didn't appear to be homosexual. He was very strait-laced – he always wore a tie, and changed for dinner.' He says he wanted 'to relate to someone who wasn't always asking him questions about his music. Ben could relax with me: he wasn't on show, he wasn't conducting.' On their walks he talked to Roger about Schönberg and twelve-tone music 'and how dreadful it was'. He liked Stravinsky's music, and admired Shostakovich's.

But there were whispers in Aldeburgh. Charles Mackerras, who was conducting there in the mid-1950s, remembers apprehension that a scandal was brewing. But Roger's parents were not particularly curious about what was going on. 'I think my father trusted Ben not to . . . seduce me, to be straightforward. And my mother likewise. I was a pretty precocious, articulate person, and if I'd had any concerns I would have told them, and I didn't.' It was only many years later, after the composer's death, that his mother enquired whether Britten had misbehaved: 'She did ask me, because she was never quite certain whether there had been any homosexual relationship, and I said to her, "No: he just used to kiss me occasionally, and was very affectionate".'

Duncan believes that, although not sexual, it remains one of the most important relationships of his life. 'I was very honoured and privileged to spend so much time across eight years with such an interesting person'. Although his sister knew the bond was special, Roger never discussed it with her, and she had no idea, until I showed her copies, of the depth of feeling in their correspondence. 'That's news to me – I've never seen or heard of these letters', she told me. 'Roger was very, very fond of Ben. I feel a bit sad about that.' Her sadness was born not of disapproval, but of the realisation that Roger's deep adolescent involvement had been doomed. 'It was real devotion, wasn't it? Real love, really.'

Roger Duncan was married at the age of twenty, while he was still a law student at Cambridge. In Briony's eyes he looked only 'about fourteen years old' – but not this time in Britten's. Ben wrote to congratulate him, gave him an antique pedestal desk as a present, but declined the wedding invitation, and had little contact thereafter. His attitude had been the same when Dunkerley became engaged. Weddings of his favourites were not his natural métier.

Roger did see Ben again shortly before the composer died. Afterwards he wrote a letter of condolence to Pears from his adoptive Canada:

> You must know how much influence he had on my early years, for which I will always be most grateful and the memories of which I will always treasure. He was such a kind, wise, loving, knowledgeable person. He was indeed a second father to me. He always made me feel an equal, which I could never be of course, by not talking down to me, or treating me as a child. He gave me my enduring love for architecture, parish churches, and old buildings, which is still the thing I miss most of England. I loved him dearly as an adopted father/friend, and I consider myself so very honoured to have known him well for ten of the most impressionable years of my life.

A small oil portrait of Roger by the artist Mary Potter still hangs in the Red House. After Britten's death, Pears offered it to Roger. But he declined it. He wanted to feel that some part of him would remain among Ben's personal things.

CHAPTER 14

The coming of the fludde

An important part of Britten's composing routine was his afternoon walk – beside the river at Snape, along the beach or across
the marshes at Aldeburgh. On one occasion he met three small
boys standing beside the railway line which then ran between
Aldeburgh and Saxmundham. He passed them as he crossed
the line on his way to the sea, and they were still there when
he returned. One of them was holding a jam-jar containing
some tadpoles. They told him they were waiting to see the train.
Britten then asked them what they were going to do with the
tadpoles. The boys replied: 'We want the tadpoles to see the
train'. With glee he regaled Rosamund Strode with the remark
when he returned to the Red House for tea. 'That's the kind
of thing he enjoyed so much – the "sidewaysness" of children's
thinking.'

Although he engaged best with children on the verge of adolescence, he knew how to communicate with younger children
too. Without a family of his own, he was generous with his time
and attention to his five nephews and nieces as they grew up.
Even at the height of his fame and in exalted company, he was
unabashed in playing with children at their level. After giving a
recital with Peter Pears in New York in 1969, he was invited to
a large reception at a private house, but vanished soon after
arriving. He was discovered in the nursery, 'giving his second
performance of the evening'. He was 'romping on all fours
across the floor' with his host's five-year-old son and the family
dog. 'While graciously apologetic, he seemed as regretful as his
playmates about their interrupted idyll.'

This understanding of children at their different stages of
development meant that his writing for them was always

highly practical. He knew how far he could stretch them within their capability, and he also constructed the children's sections in his concert pieces so that they were detachable for separate rehearsal. The boys' choir in the *War Requiem*, for instance, sings off-stage and with its own conductor. All his stage works, with the exception of *Paul Bunyan*, *The Rape of Lucretia* and *The Beggar's Opera*, include parts for children. He was heartened by the reaction to the opera he wrote in 1949 expressly for them, *The Little Sweep*, and collected 'all the photographs I can lay hands on' of the various productions of it around the world. He therefore knew what a healthy venture it had been commercially. His producer Basil Coleman remembers him saying 'Well, it's not a gold mine, but it is a little copper mine!' The auditions for the child soloists in the first production gave him great pleasure. 'I heard 37 Ipswich children', he told John Maud, '& was enormously impressed. It was all organised by the Co-op, & all sorts & conditions of children turned up. But the combination of skill & assurance was staggering. I feel the next generation of Britons is going to be a knock-out, in the best sense too!'

Britten considered writing another children's opera to pair it with – Beatrix Potter's 'The Tale of Mr Tod', perhaps, or an original science-fiction story provisionally entitled 'Tyco the Vegan'. But neither project materialised, and it was not until 1957 that he returned to the idea – this time on a much more ambitious scale.

Whereas *The Little Sweep* had required six child soloists, his new piece *Noye's Fludde* called for ten. It also had a children's orchestra, with only a minimum of professional stiffening, and a vast chorus of child-animals, played by both girls and boys (some with broken voices). Forty-nine different species were listed in the text – from leopards to peacocks, from camels to curlews – and Britten envisaged that the whole ensemble would comprise several hundred Suffolk schoolchildren in a pioneering example of community music-making. 'I like the child approach to performance very much', he said later. 'I think the main reason for my writing for children is because I believe in the artist being a part of society and I like the idea of being used by the young.'

Britten took his libretto from the volume of Chester Miracle Plays which he had used five years before for *Abraham and Isaac*. The directness of expression appealed to him: the original play had evolved as a medieval market-square dramatisation of the story of Noah's Ark, complete with anachronistic Christian language and a touch of slapstick humour – an early example of educational drama. Britten's opera at one stage had a similar intent. It was commissioned as an opera for television. But the ITV company Associated Rediffusion lost interest and abandoned the project. By then Britten was fully engaged with it and the opera went ahead at the 1958 Aldeburgh Festival in the confined space of Orford parish church.

According to its producer Colin Graham, Britten conceived it as a vehicle for harnessing the unbalanced musical talents in Suffolk schools. In the late 1950s, recorders and violins proliferated, rather as saxophones do today, and Britten relished the idea that any number of players could join in – they did not have to be in a normal orchestral balance. It resulted in a completely fresh, distinctive sound.

He did provide for a nucleus of adult professionals: a string quintet, treble recorder, timpani, piano and organ. But the rest of the unorthodox orchestration is designed to evoke the naïve notions of childhood, and to enable children of the slenderest musical ability to join in. The wind section consists of four bugle parts and a host of descant and treble recorders,* but no traditional woodwind or brass. The strings include three violin lines graded by difficulty, to give a chance to elementary fiddlers who have not graduated beyond first position. The unpitched percussion is elaborate and noisy: a range of drums, tambourine, cymbals, triangle, whip, wood-blocks and gong – plus wind machine and sandpaper (both drawn from his *Night*

---

* Britten himself frequently played the recorder as an adult.

Mail experience twenty years before). The pitched percussion consists of two arrows new to his acoustic quiver: slung mugs and handbells.

Merlin Channon, one of the county music-masters press-ganged into service by Britten, witnessed the first incarnation of the slung mugs. His school, Woolverstone Hall near Ipswich, was supplying the percussion section, and Britten arrived for the first rehearsal with a carful of instruments and a photographer in tow. 'It was like God coming to my music room', says Channon, who regularly used Britten's *Young Person's Guide to the Orchestra* as a teaching aid. After setting out the various percussion instruments, Britten produced a large box. To Channon's surprise, it contained a disparate collection of teacups and two wooden spoons. He then placed two music stands six feet apart, and joined them with a piece of string ('he even brought his own string'), on which he hung the teacups by the handles. He explained that each cup had a different pitch, to provide the right plip-plop of raindrops to start and end the storm. As Britten talked to the boys, Channon realised he was 'absolutely brilliant' at it. 'He'd have made a wonderful prep school master. He just clicked.' The photographer captured the début of this new instrument, and the pleasure young performers had in playing it – which, as Britten said himself, was an important part of his calculation.

The cups had presented some practical problems. Britten had begun by tapping some at his own tea-table – without much success. He was about to give up on the idea when Imogen Holst suggested stringing them up and hitting them with a wooden spoon, a trick she had learnt while working for the Women's Institute during the war. She took Britten shopping in Aldeburgh, and they both tapped away at any cups they could find, in the hope of identifying the pitches he needed. But Aldeburgh did not carry a wide enough range to supply a full scale, so they had to shop further afield. In a later rehearsal at Woolverstone Hall, which was being filmed by John Schlesinger for the BBC, three of the sacred cups fell to the floor and were smashed. But the resourceful boys raided the school kitchens for more – very much in the spirit of Britten's practical approach as imagined by Robert Saxton: ' "Once we've had a cup of tea, let's wash up and then use it as a percussion instrument." ' But, by the time of the performance, the delicate teacups had been wisely converted into the sturdier slung mugs of Britten folklore.

His experiment with the teacups was not an isolated one. Some ten years earlier he had delighted Enid Slater's seven-year-old daughter, Bridget, when he came to supper and filled eight wineglasses with different amounts of water to create a complete scale, and then got the family to strike them with teaspoons. 'Ben conducted, and we played (I think it was *God Save The King*); and we, after having disciplined ourselves for a while, fell about laughing [. . .], my sisters and I in the paroxysmic, abandoned, teenage way of laughter.' Eric Crozier recorded a similar experience during the war, as a token of the 'happy and harmonious' atmosphere in Britten's and Pears's London flat. 'Very soon we were all busy emptying and filling our water-tumblers to get a musical scale, and then we played tunes by striking them with our spoons.'

The magical sound of handbells was reserved for the climactic moment in *Noye's Fludde* when God seals his promise to mankind with a rainbow in the sky. It would have been simple to use the more common tubular bells, but Britten had an acute ear for bells, whether those of Mahler's symphonies, his school chapel, East Anglian churches, or his beloved Venice (which he represented so evocatively in *Death in Venice*). He came across the gentle, unsophisticated timbre of handbells, albeit with a hieratic authority, almost by chance. He used to invite children of the Aldeburgh Youth Club round to his house, where he would give them the stamps off the many foreign letters he had received. On one visit, a boy said he had to leave for his handbell practice. Britten was intrigued by this, and invited the handbell group round to play to him. He was so struck by their rendering of *Little Brown Jug* in his garden that he gave them this special moment in *Noye's Fludde*. Their discovery came quite late in the composition process, but Britten felt they were 'a gift from God. So', he said, 'we have to use them'. They add an exotic flavour of the Far Eastern music that Britten had relished on his world tour of 1955–6: he did not write rounds or changes for them in the manner of an English campanologist, but gave them unearthly clusters outside the experience of any church ringers, except perhaps when rounds have gone awry.

The bells had practical problems too. The particular set used by the Youth Club came from Aldeburgh Parish Church, which had invested in them to enable ringers to learn peals for the big bells in the church tower. Britten was quite unaware that this set was unusual in being cast in the key of E flat, rather than the customary key of C, and so his handbell parts in *Noye's Fludde* presume the scale of E flat. Many school performances of the work have been complicated by the difficulty of finding six pairs of bells in this key – a requirement that owes more to accident than to artistry. The publishers, Boosey & Hawkes, eventually had a special set made in E flat, which they could then hire out together with the orchestral and vocal scores.

The logistical challenge of mounting a performance that involved different schools around the county was far tougher than anything Britten had yet attempted. He played his part in travelling round to school rehearsals, where he treated children 'as adults in the making, so he never talked down to anybody'. While he was indulgent to them and did not get cross, 'he never soft-soaped them. He'd be quite firm about "what I need" and "what you need to do". He was just very professional.' To help things along he made an informal private recording of the whole work on vinyl long-playing discs, for distribution to each participating school. He gathered Peter Pears, Imogen Holst and Colin Graham round his grand piano in the Red House, shared out the singing roles between them, and played the orchestral parts himself, adding a few sung contributions of his own.

Imogen Holst's wobbly soprano enlivened proceedings, particularly when squeaking the part of the mice as they entered the ark. All the singers craned forward towards the microphone on the piano as they recorded it at sight and without stopping. 'Quite a bizarre record', Colin Graham says. 'But Ben was nothing if not practical.'

The music itself was technically within the reach of his young performers. The main challenge for the conductor, Charles Mackerras, was co-ordination, particularly when the animals, in masks and costumes, processed two by two into the ark, singing 'Kyrie eleison' to a simple two-note phrase.* Britten provided for some flexibility in the score, to accommodate varying lengths of procession. Even then, with children moving some distance through a reverberant church, the synchronisation of sound was always going to be relative. His extraordinary talent was to allow for some imprecision and errors, which somehow came to belong to the weft of the work. The animals' procession was interspersed by rather showy bugle fanfares. At one of the first performances, the bugle boys attached to a local Army barracks were not available, owing to a prior military commitment, and professional brass players were brought in instead. Mackerras remembers this as a disaster: the adults were of course far better players than the bugle boys, but they brought a professional precision which made the fanfares sound quite wrong. 'Normally Ben was quite a tyrant in getting exactly accurate performances of his works. He would say, "I don't wish to be interpreted, because I want you to do exactly what I've written". But somehow in *Noye's Fludde* it was the opposite. The fact of it being slightly inaccurate and slightly out of tune and not together seemed to be part of the effect that he wanted.' Britten himself admitted that, for amateurs, he tried to write music which, 'even if they get it wrong, doesn't sound too awful – where the actual polish of the performance isn't the ultimate aim'.

* In a letter to his friend James Bernard some weeks before the première, Britten wrote: 'Thank God I have not got to control them myself'.

This was not an excuse, however, for inadequacy. He was in despair after attending *Noye's Fludde* at Lancing College in 1959, under the direction of John Alston.* But he was never tempted to blame the children.

> It was unadulterated HELL. John Alston is quite, quite hopeless – he hasn't a clue as to how to beat the simplest bar, & that coupled with the fact he's totally unmusical, got no sense of rhythm, & found the music impossible to remember (when he took his eyes out of the score) etc. etc. made the performance as agonising as any I yet remember. Ditto the production, which was inane & incompetant [*sic*] – & really made no use of that lovely place. What was doubly infuriating was that the material was <u>excellent</u>, the kids knew it backwards, were really gifted; & to see their efforts so sacrificed made one mad. [. . .] Hell, Hell, Hell – why must children always have the 5th rate to guide them? That's what makes the Westminster Choir so exceptional.† One good thing – it has brought all those schools, state & private, girls & boys together for the first time; and they are doing 8 performances, all sold out!

When his old schoolfriend David Layton heard the bugle calls in *Noye's Fludde*, he knew immediately where they had come from. His mind leapt back thirty years to their days at Gresham's, when he and Benjamin were idling away the afternoon with bat and ball in the nets while the school's OTC band marched up and down the other side of the cricket field. They had managed to win exemption from the OTC, and instead could dream of hitting a cricket ball neatly between the lines of uniformed soldiery (though they never actually achieved this). The band music reached them several times, as it ricocheted off different school buildings in competing echoes, with the bugles

---

* The son of his first viola teacher Audrey Alston, through whom he had met Frank Bridge.
† This letter was written the day before the boys of Westminster Cathedral Choir gave the first performance of his *Missa Brevis* under George Malcolm.

predominating. If Layton is right, their importance for Britten was as a link to his schooldays, rather than as a symbol of militarism, and certainly their benign role in *Noye's Fludde* bears that out. Colin Graham remembers the first orchestral rehearsal with the bugles, which were 'pretty devastating' in their impact, and regards the appearances of handbells and bugles as two 'magic moments' in the score.

Britten's practicality asserted itself again when the voice of one of the three treble soloists broke during the rehearsal period. The role of Jaffet had been assigned to Michael Crawford, in one of his very first stage roles: he fared better than David Hemmings, in that Britten simply tweaked his part to suit a tenor voice – and so it has remained. During what turned out to be Britten's last appearance in public, at an Aldeburgh cabaret evening six weeks before his death in 1976, Peter Pears as compère happened to mention Crawford. But he could not remember which role he had taken. Britten, by then a very sick man, loudly called out 'Jaffet!' from his seat in the Jubilee Hall.

In the final stages of rehearsal for the first performance in June 1958, the children were ferried by coach to and from halls in Aldeburgh and Thorpeness, and eventually to the parish church in Orford. It meant that Aldeburgh and its environs were visibly flooded with young boys and girls, and several of the adult musicians started to snigger about the number of boys surrounding Britten. 'Some of us mocked the idea', Mackerras recalls, 'and we said, "Well, now this is Ben's paradise!" We were rather derisive about the whole thing.' But Mackerras fatally miscalculated the lattice of loyalty in Aldeburgh, and his mockery reached the ears of the choreographer John Cranko, who immediately passed it on to Britten. Mackerras counted himself not just a colleague but a friend of Cranko, so he felt cruelly betrayed. Perhaps, as a fellow homosexual, Cranko felt a greater loyalty to Britten. But his action, which was bound to cause Britten great distress, was a strange way of showing it. It resulted in the only recorded instance of Britten directly confronting the gossip about his fondness for boys.

For Colin Graham, the first sign of something amiss that day came when he was directing 150 children in the first orchestral rehearsal. 'Ben suddenly appeared in the doorway like a black thundercloud. He wasn't going to interrupt the rehearsal, which he needed to hear, but he was so upset because he'd just heard about it. Everybody wondered what was wrong. It was a bad moment, and it blew up into something enormous.' As conductor, Mackerras was too preoccupied to sense the storm cloud at the door, and it was only later that the storm broke. When Britten returned home, he sent for Mackerras, twelve years his junior, using Pears as his intermediary.

Almost half a century on, Mackerras sounds hesitant and awkward in describing the interview. 'I had a message to present myself at the Red House and I of course had just no idea what it was all about. I found Ben and Peter there. They told me what it was about and how upset Ben was, and he said, "Am I a lecher just because I enjoy the company of children?" He was extremely calm – but in an icy kind of way. He was obviously furious. And Peter gave vent to his fury a great deal more than Ben.' Pears told Mackerras that he had utterly spoilt the pleasure in *Noye's Fludde*. 'So I became terribly nervous and I tried to explain. But, I mean, how *can* you explain that, although we all revered Ben's musicianship and loved him as a man in many ways, we were slightly amused by . . . by the homosexuality. And I think that the chief thing that shocked him was the fact that here was I, a friend, talking that way about him. I don't think it had ever occurred to him that we found any of this amusing or unusual. I was terribly upset myself then. And I couldn't really explain it clearly to him.'

For Mackerras at that time, as for many of his generation, Britten's homosexuality was inextricable (and barely distinguishable) from his attachment to children. They were two sides of the same coin. Today's conventional wisdom frowns on mockery of homosexuals and the gay lifestyle, because they have become more socially acceptable. Yet at the same time paedophilia has become too heinous a crime for humour.

Britten's confrontation with Mackerras did not lead to an immediate parting of the ways. The première of *Noye's Fludde* was almost upon them, and it would have been foolhardy to dispense with its conductor, who was also involved in other concerts at that year's Festival. So he and Britten were 'extremely polite' to each other, and the performances went smoothly. 'He seemed to have forgotten it or to have got over it. But of course I was never engaged in Aldeburgh again – not for a long time.'

Despite his dismay over the Cranko incident, Mackerras still delights in the memory of *Noye's Fludde*. He describes Britten as 'the best musician I have ever worked with', and says that *Fludde* was 'yet another manifestation of the diversity of Ben's genius. It's an absolute masterpiece.' He believes that Britten responded to the naïvety and rusticity of the original mystery play, performed as it would have been by 'rude mechanicals': despite the sophistication of the writing, it retains a surface 'roughness, or down-to-earthness'. He also points to the ease with which Britten took familiar tunes – like the hymn 'Eternal Father, Strong to Save' in *Noye's Fludde*, or the nursery rhyme 'Tom, Tom, the Piper's Son' in *The Turn of the Screw* – and recreated them in his own style. 'By means of his harmony and very typical orchestration, he managed to make the music sound his own.' He pulled a similar trick in his setting of 'The Choirmaster's Burial' in his Thomas Hardy song-cycle *Winter Words*. Without any fuss, he weaves in the choirmaster's favourite hymn-tune 'Mount Ephraim' (traditionally sung to 'For all thy Saints, O Lord') at the appropriate points in the poem. The tune is at first evident on the page, but is later concealed amid a characteristic triplet sequence: it emerges in the notes played by the pianist's right thumb – a tune as translucent as the angels who sing it in the churchyard, while Hardy's stiff-necked vicar watches them through his bedroom window. Many singers (including some professionals) are unaware of Britten's artifice, so subtly is it achieved. It is another of the challenges that he liked to set himself. But it is not just a trick: it is at the wistful, elegiac heart of one of Britten's finest songs.

The use of familiar Anglican hymns as part of a work's structure was a device he had used in *Saint Nicolas* in 1948, and was contemplating again at the end of his life in a projected opera about the Christmas story. In *Noye's Fludde*, they are moments of high emotion, as the audience (or, as Britten put it, the congregation) find themselves required to join in with tunes they first learnt as children. The concluding hymn, set to Tallis's Canon, goes round and round in endless eight-part canon, with the child performers processing out through the singing audience. There are few whose eyes do not prick as, literally, they see and hear the passing of childhood. The accompaniment with flattened sevenths from jazzy bugles and unearthly handbells is unmistakably Britten, but the tune comes from Tudor England – a brilliant trick, as Robert Saxton has observed. 'Everybody's in tears at the end, and there's not a note of Britten being sung!' It was Britten's rare and peculiar gift, through his own daily re-encounter with childhood, to transmit direct to the inner child in each of us, bypassing the jamming device that is so often interpolated by maturity.

Five years later, Britten disclosed some of the pride he felt in *Noye's Fludde*. He had been asked to open a new building at one of the schools which had taken part, Kesgrave Heath School in Ipswich. In his speech he referred teasingly to Stravinsky's recent twelve-tone work on the same theme, *The Flood*. Stravinsky, he told the children, was 'perhaps the most famous composer living today' and 'very old'. (Great composers, he added, should be 'old if possible'.) His music for *The Flood* was 'frightfully difficult', and needed 'the greatest singers and the greatest players in the world to perform it'. Britten said he was not jealous of Stravinsky, 'not at all. I was much happier with my performance in Orford Church', sung by Suffolk boys and girls.

At the time of that first performance, he was ebullient about working with children. 'I think they get, perhaps unconsciously, a great kick out of doing something brand new. I find them also as audiences highly receptive – very choosy perhaps, but if they like something, and it can be music as new or as old as you like, then their reaction is spontaneous and encouraging.' Rosamund Strode saw the way young performers responded to him. 'He knew that children liked a challenge, and that if they were interested in something, they'd bring it off.' For Charles Mackerras, it was obvious that 'children really loved him and were fascinated by him, and by the fact that he spoke their language and, in a way, entered their world.'

CHAPTER 15

Keep on writing

The singer James Bowman memorably identified Britten and Pears as a couple of prep school masters, because of the decorous and inoffensive nature of their relationship, and their proper, slightly fuddy-duddy way of life. Peter Pears had in fact tried his hand as a prep school teacher before embarking on his singing career, and Britten was certainly a schoolmaster *manqué*. He once told Imogen Holst, after visiting Lancing public school (where his young friends David and Steuart Bedford were pupils, and Pears had been in his time), what a good school it was. He then went on to say that 'if he didn't get so involved with other things he'd like to be a schoolteacher'. If her journal, written up the same day, is to be believed, he did not even say he would 'like to have been' a teacher. The man who had just completed an opera commissioned by the Queen, no less, was idly imagining a change of career, just as he had in David Rothman's hardware store on Long Island when he was in his American doldrums twelve years before. Imogen Holst tried to tell him how exhausting it was to be a school-master (compared with his life as composer, performer and festival organiser, no doubt). 'But', she recorded, 'he didn't sound convinced'.

Britten scarcely ever did any formal teaching. He was indeed far too busy. But Sue Phipps says that simply playing a piano duet with him was 'such an extraordinary musical experience that you went away feeling you'd had fifty lessons'. He did take a number of aspiring composers under his wing. David and Colin Matthews between them worked for Britten for the last decade of his life. Years earlier, a young music student, Arthur Oldham, helped with the preparation of *Peter Grimes* at weekends during the war. In return Britten advised him on his own compositions, although he added that composition could not be taught: 'You either have the gift or you haven't, but by working with a composer quite a lot can rub off which could be useful to you'. One evening Oldham told a friend excitedly that 'my session with Ben tonight was the most wonderful one I've ever had'. They had discussed the Variation form in general, and Oldham's new piece *Variations on a Carol Tune* in particular.

> For the first time, I was able to talk easily to him, on the same level. He wasn't tired, or pressed for time; everything was perfect. He asked me to describe what I'd done, and my plans for the piece, in detail and then asked me to play them. And (again for the first time and to my intense delight) I was able to play them calmly, and just as I do to you; pointing out the good bits as I went along, and with Ben agreeing and looking as pleased as me with a right chord. He [. . .] made some excellent suggestions which I agree with completely. He wants the Theme lengthened by repetitions because the later Variations are longer and complete pieces in themselves. Then he played me the Mozart Variations on *Ah! vous dirai-je, Maman* with great poetry and intelligence.

Britten was invariably generous to musical children who sought him out for support or advice. During the war James Butt helped him with proof reading, transposition and scoring work, in exchange for composition guidance. Imogen Holst recorded a decade later that Britten had spent an hour advising two school-boys from Ipswich Grammar School about the opera they were writing. Robert Saxton, the tongue-tied little boy who met Britten backstage at an Albert Hall Prom in 1963, had originally made contact with him earlier that year, in what he now recognises was a 'very pushy' letter. His mother had suggested he contact either Stravinsky or Britten and, undaunted, he did what she said.

Dear Mr Britten,
I am 9 years old. I learn the recorder & violin, and am
trying to compose little minuets and short tunes. What I am
writing for is should I compose from my head or with my
instrument? When we come on holiday, (we is my parents
and my small sister of 6) we come to Norfolk to see my
grandparents in Norwich. And we pass through Ipswich.
From Robert L.A Saxton.

In other hands, such a letter might have been passed to a secretary
for acknowledgment, or simply thrown away. To Saxton's abiding amazement, Britten not only replied, but did so promptly on
a postcard from Switzerland, where he was on holiday.

Thank you for your letter. I should try to write your
music 'from your head' and then try it over on one of
your instruments. I think that's the best way round.
Perhaps I shall see you on one of your journeys to
Norwich.[. . .]

This encouraging response led to further requests for advice,
and at the end of the summer term the boy sent him his first,
very large, manuscript.

I enclose the 'Lament for the Dead in G major'. This piece
of music is scored for:-
    WOODWIND:- 3 flutes, 5 oboes, 3 A cls[clarinets],
3 Bb cls [. . .], 1 cor anglais and 8 bassoons,
    BRASS:- 6 corni, 6 trombes, 2 tenor trombones, 1 bass
trombone, 2 Bb tubas and 1 BBb tuba.
    PERCUSSION:- 3 timpani, 2 bass drums, and 1 piano.
    STRINGS:- Vlns I, Vlns II, Vlas, Vlcs, and contrabassi.
    SOLOISTS (INSTRUMENTAL):- 1 oboe.
    SOLOISTS (VOCAL):- 1 soprano, 1 contralto and 1
tenor. P.T.O.
    I certainly understand that you are a very, very, busy
man, indeed; and really you are probably the busiest
composer living.

His choice of soprano, contralto and tenor soloists (even if not the orchestration) was perhaps modelled on the *Spring Symphony*. He had been listening to this on disc, and passed its composer the news that he had found it 'as enjoyable as Händel's "Messiah" '.

The volley of Saxton manuscripts had begun. Britten thanked him for his 'splendid' *Lament*: 'My! You <u>have</u> worked hard at this piece. I expect your father was very pleased that you wrote it* – & I am very pleased that his operations were successful!' Signing himself 'Benjy Britten', he suggested a visit to one of the Promenade concerts at the Royal Albert Hall, when Robert could 'come & say "hullo" afterwards? I'd like to meet you, & perhaps we could make a plan.' The correspondence continued after their meeting backstage. Robert felt emboldened to send his mentor a Christmas card, on which he had drawn a picture of Santa Claus. His message inside spoke truer than he knew: 'I don't believe in Father Christmas, but I'm sure you do!' In the spring Britten invited him for a lesson and tea at the Red House.

The still small boy was dropped off by his mother: they stood on the front step and rang the bell. She was impressed that the composer himself opened the door and said unceremoniously, 'Hello, I'm Benjamin Britten'. In the same way, after she had collected her son again, Britten ran down the drive calling after her, because her coat was stuck in the car door. He opened it and made sure it was tucked in.

Left alone with the great man, Robert helped get the tea in the kitchen. Saxton today is impressed by the easy way that Britten, then aged fifty, engaged with him. 'He warned me not to put my fingers in the parrot's cage. He said, with that rather schoolboy humour that he liked, "What would your mother say if she came to pick you up and your fingers had been bitten off?!" ' When the boy took the plate of strawberry jam sandwiches into the sitting room, Britten suggested he did not put it on the sofa in case he sat on them. He also asked Robert to use

---

* The *Lament for the Dead* had been written when his father was undergoing surgery in hospital.

bellows on the fire. 'He said, "Have you ever done this before?", and I said "No", and of course I set off pumping away and he suddenly said, "No, stop!" because sparks were flying on to the carpet. But I think he almost did that because it would be funny.'

Once they moved on to music, he became the professional. Before accompanying Robert on the violin, he asked him if he'd tuned the instrument. 'I said, "Oh yes", and as he tested the strings his face was twisted in agony. He retuned it and said, "You must tune your violin properly". There was no pat on the head and saying, "Well, you're only ten".' They discussed a composition Robert had brought with him – a setting of Gray's 'Elegy' for '1 soprano (voice) & 1 violin'. Robert was surprised to discover that Britten could not sing. 'He sort of groaned it, which I found rather amusing. But he was very, very strict about which syllables came on which note, proper word-stresses in relation to the bar line.' He pointed out that Robert had the stress wrong on 'the curfew tolls *the* knell of parting day', but he knew how to sugar the pill. 'Instead of "the curfew tolls the knell . . ." he said "the curfew knolls the tell". After saying this several times, he asked me, "Have I been saying that wrong all the time?" I rather coyly said, "Oh no", and of course he had. I thought I'd better not say, "Yes"!' Saxton says the lesson probably lasted for ninety minutes at most, but seemed to him to have taken up a whole afternoon. It has remained a golden moment, suspended in time.

They met only a few times, but the letters and manuscripts flowed spasmodically for six years. Britten's advice was always practical and encouraging. One Saxton piece, for unaccompanied violin, began with a rising scale of G major. Britten sent it back with a piano accompaniment:

It is a little empty in places I feel, & think you could make something go with it nicely, like a scale going <u>down</u> at the beginning??! (I have scribbled out the start in pencil for you, but you needn't do the same, of course.)

By this contrary-motion device, he turned Saxton's tune from G to E major. 'If anybody wanted me to give them an example of genius, that's it!' says Saxton. 'It's completely magical, like something out of *A Midsummer Night's Dream*. He's teaching me a lot of technique in a short time – the contrary motion, descending bass, the unconventional key-change, the idea that I've done something in 3/4 which doesn't really make the most of the metre, so he's turned it into a hint of a waltz . . . Looking back, I'm actually ashamed that I didn't continue what he'd done and send it back to him.'

Saxton feels today that Britten was '100 percent' influential in his decision to become a composer. It was what he already wanted to do, but his instinctive response to Britten's sounds, and to his sense of light and space as a fellow East Anglian, confirmed it. Britten saw the problems he was having, and empathised with them through his own experiences at Robert's age.

The young Saxton was still in difficulty over whether or not he should compose at the piano. Unlike the young Britten, the piano was not his first instrument, and his keyboard technique could not cope with the swirling sounds he had in his head. Britten encouraged him to stay away from the piano (as he did himself): 'If you [are] miserable without a piano to write with – well, use one; but plan in your head well before! The thing that matters is genuinely sincere music!'

When the boy told him that he had written an opera about Cinderella which was being staged at school, Britten replied with a telegram which must have made Robert feel a mile high: 'GOOD LUCK FOR TWO VERY HAPPY PERFORMANCES TODAY TO YOU AND ALL TAKING PART BENJAMIN BRITTEN.' His letters were still larded with simple, practical advice, always supportive of his music teachers at school:

> Sounding right is the only thing that matters in
> writing music. If you get tired of just writing the
> same kind of music – try & find out other <u>forms,</u>
> such as Studies, Marches, dances (lots of different

kinds) that other composers use, & try them yourself. But keep on writing!

As Robert developed, so the advice became more specific. Every time Britten received a manuscript, he clearly gave it some attention.

Thank you for your letter & for the Barcarolle & Prelude. I like the first the better of the two because it seems to have more of an <u>idea</u>. But isn't the last note (left hand) of bar 2 a G <u>natural</u>? If it isn't – listen carefully & see if it ought not to be!* I should have liked more ideas (as I said) – the Prelude – it perhaps ought to be <u>more</u> like J.S. Bach! Look at some of his 2 part Inventions & see how he keeps his music interesting. Anyhow I'm glad you are finding time to write so much.

At the age of fourteen, the vexed issue of the piano was still bothering Robert. Britten's response was detailed and practical:

If it worries you too much to work away from the piano, I should go back to it. Only try to think what kind of thing you want to write <u>before</u> you sit down at it. And remember that there won't always be 10 fingers playing the music – that violins, oboes & voices work differently from pianos. But that I am sure you realise. Try & think of the melody, the rhythm, the accompaniment, the colour of it all (what instruments) as far as possible <u>all together</u>! Certainly not always the tune first (I am sure that in Schubert's Trout he thought of the <u>accompaniment</u> first). Go on writing, play & sing as much of what you write as you can, & find out <u>why</u> you don't like the bits that don't work. (I shouldn't like to be a Tenor in the last 7 bars of no. 2 carol, – why did they get left out? – or at the end of no.3 – phew! That's high!)

---

* This echoed Britten's own composition lessons with Frank Bridge. 'When Bridge played questionable chords across the room at me and asked if that was what I meant, I would retort, "Yes it is". He'd grunt back, "Well, it oughtn't to be".'

Saxton overlapped with another boy who would become one of Britain's leading tenors, Adrian Thompson. He began his singing career in the Wandsworth Boys' Choir, where he sang for Britten as a soloist in *The Golden Vanity* (which was recorded and filmed) and the first performances of *Children's Crusade*. He was also learning the double bass, and had the nerve to ask Britten to write a piece for him. He somehow sensed that the famous composer would not mind being asked.

Dear Mr Britten,
[. . .] I know you are a busy man, and you may think I have a cheek asking you this, but would you write me a little Piece for a Double Bass. I am a Double Bass Player in our School Orchestra [and] in my own orchestra the Barnes Chamber Ensemble. At the moment we are tackling Bach Brandenburg Concertos 2, 4 and 5. I have tried composing for myself but my harmony teacher throws a wild fit when I show them to him.
    Your friend, Toss.

Within a few days, back came the surprising answer.

My dear Toss,
[. . .] I am a fearfully busy person, & I'm rather up to my eyes in composing at the moment; but who knows I might one day dish up something for you & your double-bass! Tell me, how good you are at it, what pieces you play, & what are the instruments in the Barnes Chamber Orchestra? Do you want it with strings, only, or with percussion or wind too – that's to say if I did ever write something for you!
    Love, Benjamin Britten.

His canny questions horrified 'Toss', because he was barely beyond first position, and the matter of a composition for the double bass was quietly dropped. But the interesting thing is that Britten was ready to contemplate it, rather than dismiss the idea out of hand. 'It was lovely', says Thompson today, 'that he didn't make me feel small for having asked such a ridiculous question – but then I'd never heard of *Peter Grimes* or *Billy Budd*. To me he was just someone who wrote music.'

That initial exchange led to an extended correspondence between Ben and 'Toss', reinforced at the start by personal contact when Britten was working with the Wandsworth choir. Britten presumably knew that 'Toss' was short for 'Tosser', an abusive nickname given him by contemporaries at Wandsworth because he sang in the choir. But Britten adopted it without embarrassment and turned it into a term of endearment.

'I wrote letters to him, and almost by return of post or within a couple of days, a letter came back, carefully responding to what I'd written, which encouraged me to write another one. So I wrote for years and years.' It was Britten's regular technique, which in part explains why the correspondence held in the Britten–Pears Library is so voluminous.

The only occasion when Britten wrote a work for named child performers was in 1965. His *Gemini Variations* were designed for the twin boy prodigies he had met in Hungary the previous year, Gábor and Zoltán Jeney. Their prowess on violin and flute respectively, and at the piano, resulted in his 'quartet for two players', and the score came complete with stage directions, telling each boy when to change instrument. Britten was clearly very struck by the thirteen-year-old twins, and invited them to Aldeburgh to give the first performance. They recorded a rehearsal tape for him, which they sent from Budapest, and he responded with a detailed critique. He also took a keen interest in the practicalities of the performance.

> What we want to know <u>urgently</u> is – how high do you like to sit at the piano? Get someone to measure your most comfortable piano-stool & let us know quickly, as we want to have a nice bench made, so you can move quickly from one position to another.

The boys wrote long and charming letters to 'Uncle Britten', then 'Uncle Benjamin' and 'Uncle Beny'. They told him at

Christmas 1964 that 'by the first sip of champagne in 1965 in thought we are on your side, with two kisses on your cheeks, for evidence of love and friendship of your twins'. After the *Gemini Variations* première the following summer, the emotion in Britten's farewell as they took their leave at the Red House has stayed with Zoltán ever since.

He kept up a correspondence with the Jeneys for a while. 'Sometimes things go wrong, and we get very cross and depressed', he wrote in October 1968, '[...] but I expect you know all about that too, and how one never feels one will cheer up again – but one does, eventually! Please don't stop writing to me about what you are doing . . . I always enjoy photographs too, and I see that you are growing bigger and handsomer every day!'

Some years later, as a result of Britten's intervention, the violinist, Gábor, won a scholarship to the Royal College of Music. This was not just a flash of enthusiasm on Britten's part, but a calculated assessment of the twins' characters. He told Sir Keith Falkner, principal of the RCM, that he was keen to help Gábor, and not Zoltán, because he felt Gábor would benefit both personally and musically from being separated from his stronger twin brother.

The boys' father wrote Britten a touching letter of thanks. 'Your large-scale generosity turned a helpless, sad boy – our Gábor – into a young man abounding in joy and vitality. As the father, I simply thank you.' Britten had indeed been supporting them financially, as he did a number of his protégés – and he had written to the Minister of Education in communist Hungary to secure Gábor's exit visa for study in London. But later he became stern with them both when he learned they were seeking political asylum in Britain, and accused them of 'abusing' his support. He said that he would have nothing further to do with their problems 'financially or otherwise' if they cut their ties with their own country. Perhaps, as the Jeneys believe, he was anxious not to jeopardise the important contacts he had with eminent musicians in the Soviet bloc. Although he did continue to support Gábor at the RCM, and the twin émigrés did remain (nominally) Hungarian citizens, the flow of correspondence dried up.

A generation earlier, another budding musician who sought Britten's guidance was the eleven-year-old Benjamin Zander. He has now become a renowned Mahler conductor, but at that time was a promising cellist. His early efforts at composition had been derided at a local arts festival, and he had been advised to stop composing until he had had some lessons. Britten was aghast. He had not met the boy, but he was emphatic (as he would be later with Robert Saxton) that a composer had to keep composing.

> Of <u>course</u> you should go on writing. It is like everything else, cricket or swimming, you must get used to it. You will of course need some help, but that can come later. Write as much as you possibly can. I hope to be able to see you & talk to you soon – when my present rush of work is over. Perhaps your mother can bring you to Aldeburgh in August & then you can bathe & play on the beach as well as talking & playing the piano to me.
> With love from
> Benjamin Britten.

Contact with Britten had been established six months earlier by Zander's mother, who pressed her son's musical talent on his attention. Britten delighted in dealing with a namesake – especially when the boy even shared his own boyhood nickname, Benji. Mrs Zander took Britten at his word, and the whole family decamped to the Suffolk coast: for three years they took their holidays at Thorpeness, only two miles from Aldeburgh. Britten would often arrive with his viola, and Pears with his bass recorder, to play chamber music with Benji and his siblings. 'It was a magical time', Zander says.

Britten involved himself in decisions about Benjamin's education, promising 'to help in any way I can the development of a boy I think so promising'. He said he was always interested to see young and talented children growing up, '& one as brilliant as Benji is, is really exciting'. He suggested that he apply for a scholarship, and listed Lancing, Sherborne and Radley as possible schools. He also sent off a testimonial to the music-master at Oundle, which Benji's parents had been to inspect. '[It] seems to be a conventional, but not hide-bound, public-school', Britten told them, 'with plenty of music & generally a civilised artistic policy. I think the firm discipline which this school will have will be good for Benji (I am <u>always</u> an advocate of it!).'

The talk about education prompted Britten once again to relive his own schooldays in his correspondence with the boy. 'Hope all goes well with you, 'cello, composition, and rugger tackles – not forgetting algebra!' In the end, Zander went as a boarder to Uppingham, from which he joined the National Youth Orchestra cello section as its youngest-ever member. His mother heard that Britten was annoyed by a cocky letter the boy had sent him from his new school, and wrote to apologise. Britten found the time to reply immediately, even though his house on the front had just been inundated by the sea during the East Anglian floods of January 1953. It is a letter of striking perception, reassurance – and, to an extent, admonition.

Benji is such an attractive boy that there is a great danger of his becoming 'spoiled'. By this I do not want to seem unaware of his recent troubles at school: the 'spoiling' that matters comes from those most near and dear to him, in which I include myself. Benji has a real problem, & that seems to me to be one of <u>specialisation</u>. He is extremely musical, as musical a child as I have ever met, but in no particular direction are his gifts quite remarkable enough yet. I am sure they will become so, but he must not be encouraged to think that he has already achieved something, or that his life is going to be easy. The letter he wrote to me is entirely unimportant, and I will not mention it to him when I write for the simple reason that I wish him to write to me always exactly as he feels without any sense of restraint – I certainly hope you will not mention it to him either. [. . .] Please do not worry about the matter nor think that I have in any way retracted from my opinions or affection for the boy. I will continue to help him in any way that I can, and I feel certain that our high hopes of his future will be justified.

Much earlier in his career, when he was living in the United States, Britten met another schoolboy, Gordon Green – a wartime evacuee from Suffolk living on Long Island. Their friendship bore artistic fruit when Britten returned home in 1942, and made a point of meeting Gordon's father, the artist Kenneth Green, who as a result became the set designer for *Peter Grimes*. During the war, Green was on the staff of Wellington College in Berkshire as the art master, and Britten went there in July 1943 to discuss the sets.

It came completely naturally to him to ask Green if he could meet some of the boys, just as he had at his brother's school at Prestatyn before the war. In this gesture of what might be called 'selfish altruism', he spent time talking to pupils who were considered musically bright, among them James Bernard, who had already begun what would become a lifelong career as a composer.

'I already hero-worshipped Britten', Bernard said. 'I was seventeen, and at that age full of confidence, and I remember chatting away. I'd written a piece for the inter-house music competition, a piece for piano, trombone and a number of percussion instruments. This greatly intrigued Ben, who even invented a new percussion instrument when we needed an extra one. He found a bit of old drainpipe and banged a stone against it – it made a splendid resounding noise. We then had an instrument called "stone and drainpipe"!' Bernard kept the score all his life, with Britten's annotation: 'Composed by James Bernard, Edited by Benjamin Britten'. It was one of his most prized possessions.

On the strength of that single encounter, Britten began a correspondence with the boy and invited him and some of his friends to the opera after the end of term (to see Pears singing the role of Alfredo in *La traviata*). 'Love to all my friends', he wrote, 'including Lowe who made the faces, & the boy with the drain pipes, & of course Skinner! – & to you'.

The friendship continued during Bernard's national service in the RAF, after which he went to the Royal College of Music to study composition with Herbert Howells. Britten was ready with advice on the basis of his own unhappy time there almost twenty years earlier.

> Your experiences at the R.C.M. seem to be identical with mine. But all the same, dreary as most of it is, there <u>are</u> things to be got out of it. The thing which helped me was always to <u>insist</u> on dropping classes which were boring & a waste of time (it took some insisting, but worked in the end); & also to insist on changing professors who were useless, or who neglected one. [. . .] The other thing which I should insist on is <u>more</u> time for composition. I don't know how this can be worked, but Howells might help. I hope he's sympathetic & will help you to get things performed.

Britten added: 'I agree that the scruffy girls are a nightmare & a pest – it is maddening to have them around & in the way, but it's possible to ignore them'. But the comment probably stemmed as much from the typical irritation of an immature boy as from the predilection of an adult.

When he left music college, Bernard was telephoned by Britten, who needed help in preparing the full score of *Billy Budd*. ' "Jim", he said – he always called me Jim – "would you like to come and do it?" I went to Aldeburgh and spent a year with him while he was writing his new opera. I got to know Ben extremely well. We just clicked. I would copy out while he wrote feverishly.' Britten later complimented him on his intelligence, his ability and his concentration. 'It has also been a very great pleasure in having you about the house. I can think of very, very few people I could have borne here during that wretched time of composition – you were the soul of tact, & good company to [*sic*].'

The awe-struck Bernard dreamt that he 'would stay with Ben forever as his personal assistant'. But, like so many others, he found instead that he was suddenly dropped. A letter arrived, which (in Bernard's words) said: 'Jim, now that *Billy Budd* is complete, your work with me is finished. Now is the time for you to break out on your own. If you stay with me, I shall swamp you and you will never make a career for yourself as a composer.' Bernard was upset at the time (as Saxton was to be almost twenty years later) but came to appreciate Britten's wisdom. It was another instance of his ambivalence between a thoughtfulness for Bernard's future and his own selfish need to prevent people staying too close to him for too long. They remained in touch: Imogen Holst records a sunny August morning in 1953 when she found Britten, Pears, Jim Bernard and Paul Dehn sitting in the garden at Crag House, 'drinking coffee, naked to the waist, in shorts, looking as if they were in the South of France'. She was worried that Bernard might think she had done him out of a job in copying out *Gloriana,* 'but he was the very last person who'd ever have a grudge: easy, and good to look at'.

Encouraged by the writer Paul Dehn, who was to be his partner for almost thirty years, Bernard became a prolific composer for the cinema – in particular for many of the Hammer horror films. Although Britten's own experience of feature film work was unhappy (*Love from a Stranger* was his only such score), he professed his admiration: 'I think you have done splendidly – a real example to other composers who are often too grand (or too incompetent) to accept commissions of the sort that you have always done'. When he heard that Bernard was writing an opera for pupils at his old school Wellington, to mark its centenary, he became highly excited. He himself had just written *Noye's Fludde*, and he was apparently thrilled to think that his protégé could embark on an opera in similar vein, strengthened by his share of the birth-pangs of *Billy Budd* eight years earlier. 'I look forward to it with impatience', he wrote. 'Do you think I should be allowed in if I can manage to get there? Don't make it too difficult, Jim, will you? I am so pleased you are doing this piece; it is a very wise operatic start for you, & we hope for great things in that direction from you.'

The opera *Music from Mars* was performed by the boys of Wellington College in June 1959. Britten did not manage to attend, but Bernard told him of its success 'with boys, parents, staff & even governors!' and sent him cuttings from the national press. He even reported that Paul Dehn (who had written the libretto) had overheard a woman in the audience saying, 'Doesn't it remind you of Benjy Britten?' Britten had offered his help in getting the piece taken by his own publishers, Boosey & Hawkes, and Bernard sent him the full score for inspection. The response, when it eventually came, must have been shattering.

My dear Jim,

It didn't need a chance glimpse of you in Sloane Street the other day to remind me I hadn't written to you about, nor yet returned, 'Music from Mars'. It has been on my conscience a long time – altho' there are extenuating circumstances [. . .] I know I should have written before, altho', I fear, what I want to say isn't easy.

I don't honestly feel I can recommend your & Paul's piece to Boosey & Hawkes. You know, I'm sure, how very sympathetic I feel towards you & the kind of music you write, & I'd love to have you published by them – but I don't feel that this is a suitable work to start off with, & if I am going to introduce you to them it must be with something in which I am completely confident.

It would take a long time to tell you exactly my reactions. Most likely they would bore you, especially as you've had the work done & most likely were very pleased with it, & judging by the photos you sent you should have been pleased with the <u>look</u> of it. But were you honestly pleased with the <u>sound</u>? Did the young people <u>really</u> make an effect with their voices – didn't you really want more power & incisiveness than they could give you? You have written

some technically <u>very</u> difficult stuff, & must have had some
very special children if it really worked. From my experience
in giving young people stuff to sing, I've come to the
conclusion that the music must be lyrical (not rely on
dramatic expression), well 'boiled', ideas clear & precise – o,
& many other things too long to go into now. I feel it is all
abit too complicated, elaborate for young people.* This is,
anyhow, what <u>I</u> feel – many people I am sure may feel
differently, & I see no reason at all not to try B&H off your
own bat, & of course, Jim, I wish you, sincerely, luck with
it! Another thing which, alas, may fight abit against it is it's
[*sic*] very particular, public school, background – it does all
seem abit too 'Wellington' for the bulk of the schools who
do this kind of thing – alas, practically no public or private
schools.

I wish I could say this rather than write it [. . .] But one
day we <u>must</u> meet, & you must tell me you forgive me for
being difficult, narrow-minded, short-sighted, but – at least
honest?

Bernard took it on the chin. He remained devoted to Britten,
and appreciative of his earlier guidance. But he had the courage
to spring to his own defence by return of post:

I am truly grateful to you for telling me what you really feel
about the piece – as I'm sure you know how much I value
your advice and judgement. But will you forgive me if I
impertinently answer you back a bit?

The proof of the pudding is at any rate partly in the eating,
and I do promise you that the opera came off triumphantly!

Of course there were plenty of rough corners musically:
one of the trebles' voices broke just before the first

* This reproof might have been hard to sustain a decade later, when the (rather
younger) singers of the Wandsworth Boys' Choir were struggling with the
technical challenges of his *Children's Crusade*. But at this stage Britten was
flushed with the success of *Noye's Fludde* in which he had treated his child
performers more gently.

performance, so that his most lyrical number was, to say the least, <u>not</u> very lyrical, and some of the cast were perpetually inclined to sing flat – but none of them seemed to find the music too difficult, they caught on very quickly both to the recitative and the songs, and put the whole thing over with great confidence and verve. [. . .]

The libretto (quite apart from the music) was a tremendous success – I wish you could have heard the laughter – and I'm sure that for teenage boys it was absolutely right to have plenty of action and visual excitement and not too much lyricism, specially in view of the speed with which teenage voices break and balls drop!

With regard to the opera being too 'Wellington', there is not one private joke in it, and all the characters could equally well be grammar-school boys, apart, perhaps, from the cricket-playing boy, who in any case gets 'sent up' along with his cricket. In fact a number of public-school traditions are quite gently mocked [. . .]

I'm quite prepared to admit the music may be <u>bad</u> as music, but it does work.

James Bernard remained a (highly successful) film composer throughout his life, but after this experience only seldom ventured beyond the cinema.

The Scottish composer Ian McQueen approached Britten for advice at the age of seventeen. In April 1971 Britten invited him to send 'two or three of your best works, obviously the most recent', and promised to look at them and respond frankly. The boy sent him a *Sinfonietta* he had written in 1968, at the age of fourteen – it shared the same title as Britten's Opus 1, published when he was eighteen – as well as three newer pieces. He also sent him an audio tape, which Britten returned: 'It is not easy for me to play tapes; I think anyway that I can judge music pretty well by reading the score'.

Britten did him the honour of taking his music seriously and giving his reactions in detail, with no punches pulled.

He did not patronise him with comforting platitudes, and yet the boy must have found some of the remarks painful to read. Today they provide a fascinating commentary on Britten's own compositions, as well as an insight into his views of contemporary music beyond the Aldeburgh fastness. So it is worth quoting them at length. He began by noting that McQueen's music had 'made great strides' since 1968.

The *Sinfonietta* is very naïve, both in technique and conception, although it has qualities of imagination and sensitivity which I am glad to find in all your work. [. . .] One finds a surer touch in the *Horn Duo*. This is, of course, rather lacking in personality since I suppose you were deliberately trying to 'write down' to a certain occasion. That is not at all a bad thing to do, but it takes experience not to lose individuality in doing so. The *Altenberg Songs* attempt something much more difficult, and of course I don't think that you can be said to have quite succeeded. But here I am delighted to see that you don't eschew certain 'outworn' (so-called) devices, such as common chords. However, those of us who use the greater, non-academic freedoms have considerable problems in giving our works a consistent intensity. That can come with experience, of course, and with careful <u>listening</u> to your music, and noting with severity what doesn't sound exactly right and inevitable. [. . .] I am glad to see that you have a sensitivity to the setting of words. The last *Septet* is difficult to comment on. It is of course more sophisticated than the other pieces, but how successful it is depends on what it is you are really trying to say. Have you heard the work? I note several clear moods, and resourceful writing for the instruments. But I suspect some bravura in the writing of the notes on paper, which may not always be dictated by the sound imagination. That is what I personally always demand (and where I quarrel with some of my contemporaries). This is also the case with 'improvisation',

which I seldom find works, except occasionally and
accidentally – and art should never be accidental or vague.

Britten ended on a note of encouragement:

Anyhow, Ian, as you see there is much I can query in your
music, but you have imagination, energy, passion and
character – all essential things for composers. The other
things – control, shaping, an acute ear – can be acquired by
experience, and of course hard work, which I feel you have
the capacity for.

The 'energy, passion and character' which Britten found in his
music was fully evident in McQueen's vigorous four pages of
self-defence which came in reply. The boy bridled at the accusa-
tion of naïvety, and at the criticism of the 'improvisation' in
his septet. He explained his thinking in detail, and pointed out
(not unfairly) that aleatoric techniques had become part of
the post-war musical language. (He might indeed have observed
that Britten had devised his own in the Church Parables.) A composer as prickly as Britten often was might well have resented
McQueen's presumption. But the correspondence continued for
the rest of his life, and it is not hard to imagine a sneaking admiration for the boy's persistence and self-belief at the very age
when he himself had met faint praise, indifference, or even
hostility in his first year at the Royal College of Music. McQueen
himself today acknowledges Britten as one of his role models.

It was at this time that Britten said he was shy about teaching composers, and 'frightened' of imposing his own solutions
on their problems – though he did admit that it gave him 'great
pleasure' to go through the works that young composers
brought him.

I do think that at this moment of acute change in music
that I perhaps am not the right person to guide young
composers. My methods, which are entirely personal to me,
are founded on a time when the language was not so
broken as it is now. I think this is a moment of lack of

confidence which I shall outgrow, but at the moment I feel that the young composer would not be interested in my criticisms. Because virtually really all a teacher can do to help a student is to say, 'Is this what you mean? And if not let's try and find out what it is'. In other words, to shine a brighter light on the music than the scholar really has . . . is yet in possession of.

He did however advise his godson Michael Berkeley in the early stages of his composing career. Michael was following in the footsteps of his father Lennox, who had remained on good terms with Britten after their close but volatile friendship before the war. As a treble in Westminster Cathedral Choir, Michael had taken part in the first performance of the *Missa Brevis*. He fondly remembers Britten's natural understanding of a child's mentality. He had gone to stay at the Red House, along with three older fellow choristers. Britten said he would take them to the Aldeburgh Fair, and gave each of them a ten-shilling note to spend. As Michael was getting himself ready to leave, he found he had managed to mislay the money, and in embarrassment said he was not feeling well and would stay behind. Ben sent the other boys out to the car, put another ten-shilling note in Michael's pocket, and told him to join them. 'He knew perfectly well that I'd lost it', Berkeley recalls. 'The really intuitive thing was that he got the other boys out into the car first. So he never embarrassed me in front of them.'

As a young composer, Berkeley was amazed by the way Britten worked. 'He had a very, very good ear. He wrote music straight from his head on to the page, and only tried things out on the piano afterwards. All of us aspire to that, but he really could do it. He could look at a score of yours and say straight away, "That horn is playing the wrong note there surely", and he would always be right.' He would 'point out things that he liked, so that one was encouraged', and he would also notice if there were 'infelicities in the scoring' or if he was 'pushing an instrument [to a point] beyond where it would sound good'.

At the age of twenty-two, Berkeley sent him a score for a brass octet entitled *De Profundis*. Britten reacted with practical points marked in pencil on the manuscript. 'I wouldn't say he needed to spend days on it, I wasn't really advanced enough for that. But it was enough to make you realise that he'd bothered to look.'

Even for his own godson, there was a point at which Britten's encouragement suddenly dried up. Towards the end of Britten's life, when he could no longer play the piano, Pears asked Berkeley to write a song-cycle for him and the harpist Osian Ellis to perform. When the manuscript reached them, Pears and Ellis sang the songs through and Ellis told Berkeley they were delighted with them. But the cycle was never performed, and Pears never mentioned the songs again. Berkeley was 'utterly devastated' by this, because he had confidence in what he had written, and could not understand the silence. Some years later, he happened to tell his fellow composer Nicholas Maw what had happened. 'He said, "Ah, which poet did you set?", and I said, "Hardy", and he said, "There you are, you can't set one of Ben's favourite poets – moreover one that he's set himself".' Maw said he had once made the same mistake with some songs for tenor and guitar, and they were never performed. Berkeley points out how demoralising it was for a young composer to get no response, 'completely cut off'. At the same time, he marvels at Britten's apparent insecurity. 'After all, if you're one of the greatest setters of the English language [to music] since Purcell, why should you worry about a youngster in his twenties doing the same poet*?'

The experiences of Berkeley and Maw are borne out by a revealing document in the Britten archives. To mark the bicentenary of William Blake in 1957, the Aldeburgh Festival ran a competition for young composers to set to music a Blake poem of their choice. Now Blake was almost as much Britten's poet as Thomas Hardy was. He had not yet written his *Songs and Proverbs of William Blake* for Dietrich Fischer-Dieskau: they

---

* The cycle *Wessex Graves* has been successfully performed and recorded.

were eight years off, although ideas and subjects often germinated in his mind for many years before being committed to paper. But he had famously set Blake's 'The Sick Rose' in the *Serenade* for tenor, horn and strings in 1943 ('O Rose, thou art sick'), and his poem 'Spring' in the *Spring Symphony* six years later ('Sound the Flute'). In between came his song-cycle *A Charm of Lullabies*, which featured Blake's 'Cradle Song'. There had also been two Blake settings for voice and piano when he was still in his twenties.

The competitors might have supposed that, since it had been organised by the Aldeburgh Festival, the contest had Britten's support, even perhaps enthusiasm. They can have had no clue that they were trespassing – or perhaps, more accurately, competing with one of the adjudicators. And, in Basil Coleman's words, 'Ben had to win'. They had, all unwittingly, entered a trap. Britten gave no quarter in his adjudications, which have lain undisclosed in the Britten–Pears Library until now. 'Pretentious nonsense . . . quite hopeless & naïve . . . just dull & conventional & no ideas . . . <u>vile</u> vocal writing . . . No song at all – no lyricism . . . illiterate & babyish . . . incredible ineptitude & squareness . . . no feeling for words or shape of phrase . . . awkward & ugly, finally accademic [*sic*] & narrow – no ear.' Sometimes the entries were damned by comparison with the rogues in his musical gallery: 'Brahmsy . . . R.V.W.ish* . . . van Dieranish [*sic*]† . . . uptodate Parry . . . arid & Hindemithy'. Britten's comment about two competitors in their early twenties who were about to make a considerable impact in the contemporary music world was terse: '12 tone'. Perhaps, in his mind, there was no need for further evaluation. Perhaps there was a gut distaste for serial music, compared with his more circumspect public utterances. The composers concerned were Alexander Goehr and Cornelius Cardew. A song by the

---

* The initials of Ralph Vaughan Williams, who had been on the panel which awarded Britten a scholarship to the Royal College of Music a quarter of a century before.

† Bernard van Dieren, the Dutch-born English composer (1887–1936).

young John Ogdon (four years before his gold medal in the Moscow international piano competition) drew the withering reaction: 'ridiculous vocal line, illiterate, no idea of piano'.

The severity in these notes sits ill with the early encouragement he gave Robert Saxton and Michael Berkeley. But then the Blake competitors were mostly adult composers who had long since left both school and Britten's instinctive protection zone. At their age, he himself had faced brickbats from his critics. But there had been plaudits too.

Britten did relent for one or two entrants: one was 'if young, promising. But no technique as yet, but some ideas & mood, but no vocal line'. Another was 'sensitive, but no discipline as yet. Not the worst.' There were occasional flashes of encouragement: 'some ideas, too long, symphonic feeling for voice – no contrasts for verses. But one of best'. A setting of 'Merry, merry sparrow' was 'rather dear – "comic" – but finally not enough ideas – but quite atmospheric'. Only one competitor won any real praise: Malcolm Williamson was noted as a 'real composer'. His setting of 'The Fly' was a 'good idea, dull middle section, but well-shaped'.

It was presumably a simple task to reduce the fifty entries to a very short shortlist. When the results of the competition were announced, Williamson was one of four joint winners. Despite any initial misgivings Britten may have had, the two twelve-tone composers Goehr and Cardew shared the prize, along with Michael Nuttall, whose setting of 'Cradle Song' Britten had deemed to be 'simple, rather naïve, not eventful, but complete in expression, dullish vocal line, but singable'.

Robert Saxton's association with Britten came to a sudden end at New Year 1970, when he was sixteen. All Britten's letters so far had been handwritten: this one was typed.

Dear Robert,
Thank you very much for sending me all your new music.
[. . .] I am afraid, not being well and having to go abroad immediately on my recovery, I really cannot look at the

pieces at the moment. You do really need someone who can give you clear and regular advice now. [. . .] You are writing well enough now to deserve first-class tuition.

I am always interested in what you do and I should be pleased to see in the future how you develop, so do not forget from time to time to let me know and show me what you think is representative of your achievements so far.

This comes with every good wish for 1970 and all the other years in the future.

Yours sincerely,

Benjamin Britten

P.S. I really think it is better if I return to you the manuscripts which you have written out so clearly for me to see. I am sure you will have good use for them elsewhere.

'I can't say I was pleased to receive that letter!', Saxton chuckles ruefully. 'But I needed it.' He believes Britten may have sensed that he had been seeking his approval more than his advice. What he now needed was a teacher with more time to be much tougher with him. The letters stopped. So did the birthday and Christmas cards. But Saxton took Britten's final recommendation, and began to study composition under the tutelage of Elisabeth Lutyens. He went on to become one of the leading British composers of his generation, with a continuing regard and admiration for the man who had taken his early aspirations seriously.

CHAPTER 16

No one should be smiled at like that

Britten's attachment to the children's card game of 'Happy Families' was a sign not only of the childhood he always carried with him. It also exemplified the family life which he had enjoyed as a boy and to which he still aspired, even without children of his own. His sisters Barbara and Beth would often stay with him in Aldeburgh, and some of his friendships with children gave him privileged access to their families, as in the cases of Humphrey Maud, Humphrey Stone and Roger and Briony Duncan.

But part of the fun of 'Happy Families' for Britten was its requirement of good manners. As befits a Victorian game, the rules insist that the transfer of any card must be prefaced by 'please' and acknowledged by 'thank you'. Any failure to do so can result in the return of the card being requested, again with the words 'please' and 'thank you'. This was tremendously important to Ben, according to his agent Sue Phipps. 'He took great delight in catching anybody out who failed to say "please" or "thank you" – which was all part of the man, because he had the most beautiful manners, and he expected everybody else to have good manners as well.'

This corresponds with the conventional pattern and rhythm of his life. Although his long relationship with Pears was itself unconventional for its time, it was largely concealed in a wrapping of middle-class normality. At the time of the trial of Lord Montagu of Beaulieu, Michael Pitt-Rivers and Peter Wildeblood on charges of homosexual indecency, the police interviewed a number of suspected homosexuals, Britten among them. If they visited his home, it is easy to imagine they would have been disarmed by the unexceptionable, humdrum nature of the household – rather in the manner of Mayor Swallow in *Peter Grimes*, at the head of a suspicious search party set on inspecting Grimes's hut. It was almost as if Britten had anticipated the moment.

> Here we come pell-mell,
> Expecting to find out – we know not what.
> But all we find is a neat and empty hut.
> Gentlemen, take this to your wives:
> Less interference in our private lives.

He was orderly and punctilious in both dress and behaviour. His was in many ways the antithesis of the stereotypical gay lifestyle of today. In his twenties he had experienced the bohemian chaos of the Brooklyn house which he and Pears shared with Auden, George Davis and others in New York, and it was not at all to his taste. The Protestant work ethic might have been invented for him: he disdained wasting time* – everything in his day, whether work or relaxation, served his professional purpose. Merlin Channon had a glimpse of this when he was invited to bring the boys of the percussion section in *Noye's Fludde* to tea at the Red House. When Britten left the room to fetch more cakes, they spotted a timetable for the day on his piano. 'Every single hour was carefully planned, and we noticed that we had been allocated one of these. So we knew when to go.'

Beyond the level of officialdom, the whisperings about Britten's relationships with children continued unabated. Richard Kihl, a schoolboy who lived locally and often used to join Britten for tennis doubles, remembers being teased mercilessly by fellow pupils when Ben 'bowled up in his Rolls' to fetch him from school – such was Britten's reputation. Sue Phipps recalls tongues wagging all the time. 'It was something that, as a family member (and because I'm Peter's niece, I felt part of Ben's family as well), I was tremendously aware of within my own

---

* In a light-hearted letter to his old schoolfriend John Pounder in 1963, he looked back to the occasions in his childhood when he had been 'happily wasting time' on the beach at Lowestoft.

family, which was the most worrying part. What the rest of the world felt didn't seem to matter nearly so much, but even family members were very upset and disturbed by it. They put together homosexuality and friendship with boys in one and the same package, when of course they had nothing to do with each other at all, but that's just how it was. Yes, tongues wagged like mad.'

In the mid-1950s, he invited a rather shy teenager, Dermot Bowesman, to stay the weekend in Aldeburgh. He was the nephew of his old schoolfriend Francis Barton, and was considering a career in music publishing. The boy's mother, Joy Bowesman, later said that one of her relatives had tut-tutted about letting Dermot stay with 'people like that'. But Joy said with emphasis that she knew Ben: as a girl she had played duets with him, and he had been to stay with her and Francis at the Barton family home. Her faith in him was rewarded: he wrote her a long and thoughtful letter of advice about her son.

My dear Joy,
We have just posted Dermot off back to you, and enjoyed the weekend with him a great deal; although he was naturally rather overawed to start off with, he got much gayer, and soon was chatting quite freely, especially after his ping-pong successes!! [. . .]

I think it would be a great mistake at this point to say definitely what he is going to do when he grows up. He is very young for his age and has not yet developed the knack of handling people that he indubitably will sooner or later. Until we see how this knack develops I think it would be a mistake if he meets a director of Boosey & Hawkes. They might so easily not understand each other, and Dermot's diffidence might be misunderstood as lack of keenness.

Can we not see how this goes for one term, and then if he is consistent in his plans he might come here for a few days next summer and I will casually invite down one of the publishing directors who could talk to him and give us his unofficial advice.

Eight years later, Dermot Bowesman died of cancer in his twenties. Britten gave a recital with Peter Pears in Dermot's memory, and out of affection for his childhood friends Joy and her brother Francis.

Michael Berkeley believes that Britten's social conformism meant that there was no real risk of 'anything wayward' happening to the boys in his charge. He says there was 'a kind of vicarage feel' to life at the Red House. 'Things had to be just so.' This stemmed from the faith-based values instilled by his mother, which found continued expression in his censorious attitude to marital infidelity. Britten found himself on the cusp between the old and new morality. The strict moral code of his upbringing contended with his choice to live his life in a homosexual relationship, about which he was entirely open among his friends. Jostling for position within that contention were his strong, and separate, feelings for adolescent boys. This created a turbulence in his mind, evident (without any attempt at concealment) in the edgy tension of works such as *The Turn of the Screw* or *Death in Venice*. It made his music unique.

'It was never anything which one felt had the air of something sordid or dangerous about it', says Berkeley. 'That, in a way, is the innocence of Ben's childlike nature. He rejoiced in their presence. I don't think he was desperate to get in their trousers – or maybe, deep inside, part of him would have liked to, but he would never have presumed to have done that.' Berkeley feels we will never know 'where sexual drive – imagination – took off, to create works of art. The turbulence that he himself clearly felt comes out in the music. So there obviously was a very creative by-product of this strange mix in him, and we have to be grateful that it was there, because we have a series of masterpieces as a result.'

The last song-cycle he wrote for Pears and himself to perform was *Who are these children?* It was triggered by sight of the wartime newspaper photograph which had first prompted the Scottish poet William Soutar to write those words. This showed a troop of huntsmen riding down a bombed-out street, while a boy stood to one side with his bicycle, watching with several children in blank incomprehension. It was the boy's face which caught Soutar's (and then Britten's) breath, as the haughty procession passed insentiently through his shattered world.

> Who are these children gathered here
> Out of the fire and smoke
> That with remembering faces stare
> Upon the foxing folk?

These songs belong to the encircling gloom of *Children's Crusade*, and Britten's despair at the thought of the young being tossed about on the wreckage of adult lives.

Britten was more powerfully involved in the individual suffering of children. In his beautiful schoolboy work for soprano and orchestra *Quatre chansons françaises*, he foresaw his own trauma at the death of his mother (as children often do) when he set Victor Hugo's poem 'L'Enfance'. A five-year-old boy sings and plays all day long, unaware that inside his mother lies dying. As a boy himself, Britten envisages the heartache to come when the child is strong enough to bear it. That maternal bond, which was so real to Britten from his own experience, is the central feature of *Curlew River*. His involvement with the 'Madwoman' is deeply felt, deranged as she is by the disappearance of her twelve-year-old son, abducted into slavery. On her fenland journey, she imagines her son as a bird torn from the nest, or as an innocent lamb devoured by the carrion crow. Her poetic refrain, in William Plomer's libretto, captures her isolation and loneliness in heart-rending music:

> Birds of the Fenland, though you float or fly,
> Wild birds, I cannot understand your cry,
> Tell me, does the one I love
> In this world still live?

The climax of this 'church parable' builds when she finds her son's grave, and her mad-song is peppered with curlew cries, as she wrestles with her distress. Because the Madwoman is sung in this all-male cast by a tenor, there is a parallel with the mad-song of that other visionary Peter Grimes, driven insane by the death of his apprentice. In *Grimes* we only hear the boy crying out as he falls to his death: in *Curlew River* there is a transcendent moment of redemption as the voice of the boy's spirit (a treble, of course) emerges faintly from the plainsong hymn loudly chanted by the woman's companions. At first it is almost an aural illusion, but the boy's voice gathers strength, and with his benediction the mother is released from her insanity. The intensity of this scene is heightened by the sound of high-pitched bells, a reminder of the handbells which accompanied another divine intervention in *Noye's Fludde*.

Colin Graham, the producer of *Curlew River*, believes that the work was very personal to Britten, and the Madwoman's predicament expressed the 'passionate yearning' he had for a child of his own. There is some corroboration for this in Britten's attitude to the boy who sang the Voice of the Spirit in the opera's second cast, John Newton. He was indeed a favourite at the time of the work's première, and for some years afterwards. For this thirteen-year-old boy (as for David Spenser), the fifty-year-old composer was always 'Ben'. John stayed the weekend at the Red House during the summer holidays after the work's first staging, and then went on tour to Russia with Britten and the English Opera Group, where he performed Miles in *The Turn of the Screw* and Harry in *Albert Herring*. He was then invited back to Aldeburgh for a November weekend while Pears was away.

> Little John has cheered me up a bit. He is a sweet
> affectionate child – makes one feel rather what one has
> missed in not having a child . . . John is a little bit of a
> substitute, and I'm really lucky!

The boy stayed there again over New Year, shortly before he started at a new school. Britten and Pears set off in January for a long trip to India, but Ben – always sensitive to the trepidation caused by a change of school – wrote to him from Delhi.

> My dear Johnnie,
> By the time you get this you will be back at school. Things will seem rather strange, but soon they will all straighten out, and you won't remember that you were ever a 'new boy'. You must write and tell me all about it – what dormitory you are in, what the boys in it are like, how you get on with the Headmaster and Mr Watkinson (?) and of course Dr Forster and the music. [. . .] I was glad to see you before you went back, even for just that short rushed time – but I was a fool over the stop-watch (getting the wrong kind).

From this it is clear that Ben had taken a close interest in his new school – Cawston College in Norfolk: indeed he helped fund the boy's education there. He had also managed to see Johnnie again between New Year and his departure for India, armed with a present. Now he was the latest young friend to be honoured with Ben's travel diary from exotic parts. That first letter from Delhi captured a moment familiar to many visitors to India, but presumably more powerful in its impact on Britten, who was accustomed to boys 'attaching' themselves to him. In this case it was 'a serious young boy, about 12 or 13' who followed them wherever they went, 'but seriously not cheekily. I smiled at him once or twice, and when we finally got into the car to go off, I waved to him'. The boy followed them at a run as they drove through the streets of Old Delhi, and when they had to stop in the mêlée 'he came right up to the car window, looking appealing'. He was well-dressed, 'so it wasn't money he wanted, and he didn't look unhappy'.

A few days later, he wrote from Udaipur to report on his encounter with two crocodiles, 'one a baby and one the biggest creature I've ever seen – like a great tree trunk, lying there basking in the sun! Not attractive creatures, and looking as if they'd like to chew us all up, boat as well. Once as we were just passing the beach, where the biggest one was grinning at us, the engine of the motor boat refused to start and we drifted helplessly on – I wondered if I'd ever see Aldeburgh, or you, or Cawston College again!'

In Madras they visited two children whom Britten and a friend had 'adopted' as babies on his previous visit to India.

> I have been writing to mine occasionally, and we have a very touching reunion. He is a sweet boy of about 13, very dark, good looking, but shy. Funny thing is, his nickname is Bim, and I have a group of god-children who always call me Bim! We go to the home where he lives, and they all perform for us, doing some dances and gymnastics – they are very lithe creatures, and perform brilliantly and neatly.

Britten was struck by the beauty of the people in general. He wrote from Bombay:

> It has been a pleasure to watch them moving around – their graceful bodies, and dark skins, beautiful eyes and appealing smiles. You have only got to glance at them for a fleeting second with friendship on your face, to get an immediate reaction of pleasure.

Soon after Britten's return from India, John Newton was invited for a week to Aldeburgh, the first of six stays at the Red House over the next year. At one point, Britten wrote to Pears: 'Johnnie went back to school, & is very proud now that he has been made a Monitor. He's a dear boy, & was very sweet to me here.' Although he later scaled down the friendship and today prefers not to discuss it, John Newton became for several years the most regular visitor to Aldeburgh of all Ben's young friends, apart from Roger Duncan in the 1950s.

Overlapping with him was another boy soprano, Stephen Terry, who recorded the role of Harry in *Albert Herring* and later the speaking (and acrobatic) role of Puck in *A Midsummer Night's Dream*. He maintained a lively correspondence with Ben, and at the age of thirteen he asked if he could regard the

Red House as a refuelling stop on a cycling tour he and some friends were planning. Ben replied that it was 'quite OK for you to come & use this house as a Youth Hostel!' Like many of the boy companions, Stephen (nicknamed 'Terrymins') was not aware of any sexual interest from Britten. He himself would like to have been his son 'because of the whole richness of his intellectual, aesthetic and emotional life'. He said there was 'an incredible tenderness' and 'a great sense of gentle, almost fragile being'. He found Pears rather severe and judgmental and, like David Hemmings had before him, felt he was 'a slightly hostile presence'.

Britten's protective instinct towards children is amply demonstrated in the third song of his *Nocturne* for tenor and orchestra. This sets words of Coleridge from 'The Wanderings of Cain' about a 'lovely Boy' clothed only in 'a twine of leaves', plucking fruits by moonlight in a wilderness. In a moment, Britten conjures up the moonlit scene by means of delicate harp arpeggios, and soft harmonics from the strings, with occasional plucked chords. The boy seems to tiptoe through the wilderness to what might be called the *staccato* cantilena of the tenor – the *staccato* quavers once again providing the characteristic physical energy. The movement is once again in A major, the key of *Young Apollo* and *Death in Venice*. It was the key he naturally turned to when describing a beautiful boy. The whole dream-like movement is limpid, gentle and innocent, with the exception of the final outburst of indignation that a small child should have been left to wander on his own.

> But who that beauteous Boy beguiled,
> That beauteous Boy to linger here?
> Alone, by night, a little child,
> In place so silent, and so wild –
> Has he no friend, no loving mother near?

Moments like these convince Colin Graham that Britten never had any ill intent towards children. 'Ben was so concerned with the corruption of innocence all the way through his works and through his life that it would be incredible for him to be corrupting innocents himself.' The tenor's remonstrance and the harp's furious *glissandi* do indeed express Britten's concern about an unprotected child on the edge of danger. Just as in *A Midsummer Night's Dream* two years later, he saw nightfall as a time of mystery – whether magical or perilous – and he had had a 'strange fascination' with the world of night and dreams since he was very young. Indeed he connected it with his own schooldays: he claimed that, last thing at night, he used to remind himself of the problem he had to solve before his algebra lesson the following morning, because he had been told that, while his conscious mind was asleep, his subconscious could carry on working. He also felt that dreaming could have a long-lasting effect, for good or ill. 'It can release many things which one thinks had better not be released; and one can have dreams which one cannot remember even, I find, in the morning, which do colour your next day very darkly.'

Both the *Nocturne* and *A Midsummer Night's Dream* have a recurring motif in the strings which suggests the breathing of someone asleep. For Britten, this was another return to childhood. At the age of sixteen, he had written to his parents from Gresham's to say that he was kept awake at night because he was mesmerised by the sounds of breathing in the dormitory.

> There were two boys snoring in bed next to me; one of them snored taking breath both in and out, while the other only when breathing in. For about five or even six times they agreed, & then gradually they got out of time, & they took quite a time to get in again. It fascinated me so much that I could not go to sleep.

The precision of his description indicates how intriguing he found it, as both a mathematical and a rhythmic conundrum.

In the late 1960s Britten was increasingly weighed down by the pressures of performance and administration, at the same time as he felt disconcerted by the growing divergence of his music from that of younger, more fashionable, avant-garde composers. Stephen Terry noted that he was 'a tired man, incredibly busy'. The pressures only increased when his own *Festspielhaus*, the Maltings Concert Hall, burnt down in 1969; he was involved in frantic fund-raising to rebuild it. But there was one more principal boy in his life story.

When Joan Magill approached Britten out of the blue in the mid-1960s to ask him to teach her son Ronan, his natural inclination was to say no. Certainly those around him at that late stage in his career were trying to protect him from needless intrusions, and manage his precious time. But they had reckoned without the persistence and sheer nerve of Mrs Magill.

Her letter from Dublin in October 1966 was presumptuous. She asked if Britten would have Ronan to live with him as a pupil, 'even if it were only for one week a year'. Britten's refusal was prompt but polite. But Mrs Magill noticed that it did leave the door open: 'I am afraid I cannot really offer to have him here until we have met and seen how we get on, and also frankly to see whether such a step would be right for the boy'. Further pressure from both Ronan's parents led eventually to a meeting. Three years after the initial contact, Britten agreed to see their son at his agent's house in Islington.

A handsome, rather wild, passionate youth of fifteen with long unkempt black hair arrived at the front door at the appointed hour, nine o'clock in the morning, to find pandemonium inside. A soprano soloist had just withdrawn from performances of Mozart's *Idomeneo* that Britten was to conduct, and Ronan Magill found himself intruding upon the hue and cry of the hunt to replace her. The boy was told he could have fifteen minutes with Britten, or at most half an hour.

He found the composer in his dressing gown in the living room. 'He took a look at some pieces I had composed, and I played for him – and before I knew where we were three hours had passed. Then I joined them for lunch. I kept thinking I ought to be going, but he made no attempt at that. I played him one piece which I had written, which I am pleased to say he liked. I then played Beethoven [the *Waldstein* Sonata] and some

Brahms for him – I didn't know about his hang-ups about those composers at that time. I just played, and we talked and talked and that was that.'

Britten wrote to Ronan's mother in fulsome terms: 'We were all enchanted by him, and I was amazed at his general musicality and intelligence, and his is a remarkable pianistic gift. [. . .] I will see him as often as possible, help him with his composition, make arrangements here for him to have general theory tuition, and discuss his piano playing too.' Mrs Magill reacted by presenting Britten with a silver bowl, the first of several expensive gifts, some of which the composer felt obliged to return. Britten was true to his word: Ronan stayed with him in Aldeburgh for several days in November, and shortly afterwards his mother, now separated from her husband, moved the family home from Dublin to Suffolk. To begin with, the Magills lived in Saxmundham, but later they moved to a house in Aldeburgh, within walking distance of the Red House. At least it absolved Britten from providing Ronan with accommodation.

Ronan was unusual in Ben's long catalogue, in that he never knew him at the important age of thirteen. He was already well into adolescence and experience by the time they met. But he was another boy with an absent father, with a wide-eyed sense of wonder. Ben found time to engage with more than the musician in him. As he had done with many of his young friends, he went for walks with Ronan on the beach, delighted in watching a whirlwind,* went for drives in the lanes of Suffolk, wandered through the woods to find nightingales. He responded to Ronan's fervent nature, and within a few weeks of knowing him had nicknamed him 'Tyger', after the poem 'Tyger, tyger, burning bright' which he had set in his *Songs and Proverbs of William Blake* four years before. 'Hope to see the old Tyger when he's let out of his cage next holidays', he wrote. Ronan was, in his own words, 'a lively, rather indisciplined, wild-haired young boy, or young man – a wild, lusty youth. And I

---

* In the field outside Britten's rural retreat at Horham.

was firing on all cylinders, and I suppose he liked that kind of boyish behaviour.' They talked about Britten's music, particularly the Cello Symphony. They played music together: the Mozart two-piano sonata, one of the Tchaikovsky piano concertos – and Britten's own Piano Concerto. 'He wrote in the flyleaf of the miniature score: "I'm looking forward to hearing a very Tygerish interpretation of this" – meaning, "go and give it everything". He never wanted to stop that side of me. He wanted to discipline it, but he didn't want to get rid of it.'

Six months after their first meeting, Britten felt he had the measure of his new pupil:

> He is a boy of considerable talent, great musicality, and aptitude for the piano, and for composition, and a dedicated and passionate young man. These gifts however need to be disciplined, and in my view as soon as possible. On the other hand, it seems to be essential that he leave school with some scholastic credentials.

He recommended that Ronan leave school (Ampleforth College) at the end of the academic year, to join the Royal College of Music (as he himself had done at the same age).

This was the first of three years or so of intermittent guidance. Ben's piano lessons were more about the meaning of the music than about technique, which he left to others. They took up time he could hardly spare: he was under the compositional lash of two operas, *Owen Wingrave* and then *Death in Venice*, and his health was deteriorating. Ronan's frequent appearances at the Red House caused consternation among Britten's closest associates. Colin Graham, for one, remembers 'Ronan was around an awful lot and Ben pitied him for being pushed so much by his mother. If he knew Ronan was coming, he would start saying, "O God, Ronan again", which isn't exactly welcoming with open arms. He was clever and he was a sweet kid. But his mother was a typical theatre mother. Ben was expected to help, he was expected to declare the boy a genius, expected to write piano concertos for him and all those things, you know.

It was just pressure, pressure, pressure.' Magill, now a professional pianist, can still bridle at suggestions that he was in the way. 'I might have been conceived as a nuisance – well tough on them, they can think what they damn well like. I enjoyed being there, I learnt a huge amount, I will never forget it. It's all locked away in the memory and it stays there.'

Whatever Britten said to others, he encouraged Magill with his customary profusion of letters, including a travel diary during his tour of Australia and New Zealand in 1970 – just as he had done with Roger Duncan years before. The tone is always affectionate, but usually paternal, with a dose of patient admonition. Ronan responded with letters that were ardent, often incoherent. It was perhaps the most extreme example of the emotional extravagance that Britten seemed to provoke. 'You see, Ben', Ronan wrote to him a year after their first meeting, 'when I am with you I am very excited, *all* of me is excited – my body – my hands and my brain – and at the concert I wasn't excited at all – yes I loved the music but the person I was with was just a nice, kind girl. I realised I loved you very much in a way I don't quite understand. Please don't think I am being disrespectful to you but you have become very important to me, and I seem to need you very much. I tried to explain this to Mummy this morning but I'd hate to tell anybody else.'

Ronan's obsessive devotion, which became almost intemperate, did not seem to alarm Ben, who seemed torn between wanting to curb it and willing him to express himself freely. When Ronan returned some money Britten had given him for Christmas, Britten told Pears: 'Tyger has written a very mad letter, returning the tip I sent him – he is in a strange state, & I'm not sure exactly what to do with him'. He drafted an exasperated reply, because Ronan had asked for the money in the first place: 'Then you return the little present I give you, because it isn't money you want, but that you want to feel dependent on me! It is all a bit dotty, isn't it?' But, after sleeping on it, the letter he actually sent was much gentler, suggesting they met up for a 'good talk'. He added: 'There is not much we can't talk about, is there?' It may have been a more sensitive course than anger or silence in handling a somewhat neurotic teenager. But perhaps, as he approached sixty, he was also secretly pleased to find that, in all Ronan's letters, what he might have called 'the old feelings' were still there.

At the time of writing these replies, Britten was in Germany, halfway through writing the first act of *Death in Venice*. Thomas Mann's novella about the writer Gustav von Aschenbach and his obsession with Tadzio, the beautiful Polish boy he encounters on holiday in Venice, had long fascinated Britten. Even though Aschenbach was a widower with a daughter, Britten clearly identified closely with him. 'I'm getting rather attached to Aschenbach, not surprisingly!' he wrote at one stage. The opera laid bare the turbulence in his own mind which for most of his career had so enriched his music. He followed Aschenbach's struggle between admiring youthful beauty and feeling physical desire, and he felt both the pain and the delight every step of the way.

There had been many Tadzios in Britten's life, from Piers Dunkerley and Wulff Scherchen through to Roger Duncan and Ronan Magill. Wulff himself had been aware that younger boys caught Benjamin's eye. After seeing a Sophocles production in Cambridge, he told Britten: 'You would have enjoyed Antigone too. He was absolutely adorable. Now I understand why the Greeks always made boys play the parts of girls.' A few months later, Wulff wrote to him in Canada: 'How are the girls? Pardon the faux pas. How are the dear little choir-boys? Have they been wheedled yet, or are they steel in their dear little tom-sheets.??'

Casting Tadzio has always proved difficult for the producers of *Death in Venice*. The real-life Tadzio, with whom Thomas Mann became infatuated in Venice in 1911, was only eleven years old, whereas in Mann's story he is supposed to be fourteen. Britten's decision to make Tadzio a dancer rather than a singer means, almost inevitably, that the stage character is well developed physically, and probably in his late teens. This risks changing the intended dynamic of the story, so that Aschenbach falls in love with a young man, rather than with a boy on the cusp of adolescence. The dancer who created the role for Britten was Robert Huguenin, and he set a standard that others found hard to emulate – as Pears realised in New York, when he made his début at the Metropolitan Opera in the role of Aschenbach.

> I miss Bob Huguenin <u>very</u> much. This boy Bryan is a much better dancer [. . .]. But he has <u>not got IT</u> at all!! Oh dear! I wouldn't dream of looking at him for more than 5 seconds. A sweet chap and all that, 19 or 20 years old, blond from N. Carolina, but no Bob.

Britten sets Aschenbach's (and his own) dilemma in the ancient Greek context of a tussle between Apollo, representing the orderly, objective aesthetic, and Dionysus, the god of uncontrolled passion. The moment of first communication between them is near the end of Act I, when Tadzio, the newly crowned victor in the beach sports (the Games of Apollo), approaches Aschenbach. The ageing writer decides to speak to him ('we will become friends') but falters at the last minute. 'Don't smile like that', Aschenbach pleads internally with Tadzio: 'no one should be smiled at like that'. Immediately we are aware that the boy's smile may not be entirely innocent, but that he may in some way be complicit in the man's struggle. The pure milk of innocence is once more on the turn, just as it was with the boy in the hotel bedroom in *Emil and the Detectives* forty years before. Tadzio's smile provokes a Dionysian turmoil leading directly to Aschenbach's declaration of love – which marks the start of his self-destruction.

Britten's music for Tadzio is masterly in representing the ambivalence enveloping the boy. The children are associated throughout with pitched percussion, and Tadzio in particular with vibraphone and glockenspiel. The fall and rise of his five-note phrase casts an instant aural spell. All is apparently innocent, and yet in their insistent repetition here Britten's sounds of childhood have an obsessive, cloying sweetness which puts their purity in question.

Britten makes the relationship between Tadzio and Aschenbach less immediately suggestive than in the book. Mann's original has the boy walking past the writer's table closer each day, so that eventually he almost brushes him as he passes. There is never any direct contact in the opera, but Tadzio becomes increasingly aware of Aschenbach following him. Colin Graham, the opera's first producer, is struck by the man's feeling of revulsion after leaning on the boy's hotel bedroom door. 'He is disgusted with himself that he'd gone so low as to be stalking the boy as close as that. This may have been a feeling of Ben's too.' But the libretto indicates that Aschenbach was 'excited' as well as 'shaken', and after his self-reproach the man smiles to himself as he reflects on the power that Eros has, even over heroes. Tadzio demonstrates, just as the handsome young sailor Billy Budd did before him, that beauty has a destructive force.

In balancing the tensions of this story, Britten's 'extraordinary outpouring of music is all the better', according to Michael Berkeley, 'for having been created by a mind in turbulence because it was struggling to deal with these things itself'. It was the very contest that W.H. Auden had warned Britten about thirty years earlier – between order and chaos, between 'bourgeois convention' and bohemianism. Perhaps Britten, for all his dislike of bohemianism, still bridled at Auden's presumption that he would always side with 'bourgeois convention', with his symptomatic attraction to 'thin-as-a-board juveniles, i.e. the sexless and innocent'.*

---

* Auden added the warning that 'bourgeois convention alone ends in large unfeeling corpses'. Perhaps this lies at the root of Britten's conversation with Eric Crozier (recounted in the latter's 1966 memorandum, after his departure from Britten's inner circle) when he referred to Montagu Slater, the librettist of *Peter Grimes*, as one of his 'corpses'. He then told Crozier 'with a queer kind of pleasure' (and prophetically): 'You'll be one too, one day'. Crozier was 'puzzled' at this 'destructive impulse', but perhaps Britten's smile was one of embarrassed self-awareness rather than of self-satisfaction, as Crozier suggested.

At one point Britten was nearly led astray by his librettist. Myfanwy Piper suggested that, in the Games of Apollo, all the child athlete-dancers should compete like the ancient Greeks – naked. Britten thought the idea was 'excellent, & could be wonderfully beautiful, Hellenically evocative'. But he rejected it in case it attracted unwelcome publicity. It would indeed have made the opera notorious, let alone very difficult to dance. It would also have destroyed the subtle balance of the story as Britten tells it. From his own close vantage-point, Ronan Magill – who himself was forty years Ben's junior – is sure of that. 'It's all in the yearning, it's all in the look, the angst of wanting and can't having – or being incapable when you're actually in front of the person to say anything.' He says that Aschenbach's failure of nerve corresponded with Britten's own experience. 'It's the proof of why there was nothing ever dirty or bad about this. It was entirely pure. I think when he was very young, the idea of thin little boys was very beautiful – in the Greek sense.* But I wasn't aware of any of this. I suppose the secret was not to be aware of things. Innocence can be more beguiling than knowledge, so for an older person to see a ruddy, lusty youth making a whole lot of uncontrolled gestures could be attractive, I don't doubt that.' Asked if that was what Britten felt about him, Magill is unabashed: 'If he did, then I'm glad that he did – if I could make him think that way for even five seconds'.

He stopped having lessons when Britten became seriously ill in 1973. He had noticed Ben was increasingly worried and lost in thought (even at the wheel of his beloved Alvis) but he had been unaware of the gravity of his condition. He had noticed the strange, thudding heartbeat the composer had in 1972, when he was staying with him at Horham: he says now that he will remember it to the end of his days. 'It was as though those hollow thuds embodied the origin of all the slings and arrows

---

* The Red House bookshelves do contain a photographic celebration of pre-pubescent boyhood, which is also represented in the garden in the form of a bronze sculpture by Georg Ehrlich.

he had suffered in his life.' After Britten's heart operation, Ronan sent a message to Peter Pears.

Ben's illness has affected me very much. All his good friends would want to give him presents, as a token of their affection (flowers in his room every morning, or perhaps baskets of fresh and rare fruits delivered to him every day). I am not in a position to do any of these things, much as I would like to, but I've made him a present which can't be bought in any shop. I have written this cello piece for Ben. Please give it to him when he is recovering. Everything I feel for Ben is in this piece.

The composer was too weak to attend the première of *Death in Venice* at the 1973 Aldeburgh Festival. So a private performance was staged for him at the Snape Maltings in September – his first chance to hear and see the work which had so consumed him. Ronan, now nineteen, was privileged to be one of the few invited guests. He wrote to Pears afterwards: 'When I saw Ben in the auditorium I was too full up. I couldn't bear it. He looked so well and strong, and pleased with the performance. He looked so much better than I was led to believe – and so young. [. . .] Please kiss Ben for me – and give him my love.'

The close contact with Britten's children always came to an end. It has been suggested that he lost interest in them as they entered puberty, but the evidence is strongly against that. He maintained the friendships in many cases until their middle or late teens. The best clue to the breaking of the spell lies in the decline of the relationship with his 'lost son', Roger Duncan. In 1962, E.M. Forster asked Britten if it was true that he was seeing much less of Roger, whom he described disapprovingly as 'glossy'. Britten's reply indicated that he felt they were growing apart. In what is almost an epitaph to their friendship, he wrote that he had been 'worried about Roger Duncan for some years'.

A natural 'glossiness' has been fostered by Harrow, &, in the losing battle I've been fighting, there was no help

<u>at all</u> from father or mother – as you could imagine. It has been a real sadness for me, as he was a lively, intelligent & tender little boy. Still, there's always hope & whenever I can I try to sow little seeds of doubt.

As with Piers Dunkerley a quarter of a century earlier, he seemed to be finding it hard that Roger had matured and become 'more adult than adults themselves', with the self-assurance that entailed. In other words, Roger had grown up.

His letters from the sixth form at Harrow had still been to 'my darling Ben', but a distance had clearly developed. In one, he apologised for not having written for some time.

> It isn't that I haven't been thinking of you Ben because I <u>have</u> more than my letter-writing can say. [. . .]
> It feels very odd, Ben, and cold not having been in communication with you for so long. I mean that you have had <u>no</u> idea what I've been doing and, until I got your gay letter this morning, I what you've been doing.

After nine double-sided pages in his elegant handwriting, Roger concluded:

> I'm sorry that I was <u>so</u> pensive when I was last at Aldeburgh,* but I know you understood and understand.
> All my love, Ben. Longing to see you soon. I'll ring over weekend (?) Roger xxxxxxxoxoxoxoxoxxxoxx

For most of their friendship, Roger had been unaware of other young friends of Ben's. So it came as quite a shock when one day at around this time Ben visited the Duncans in Devon, with another companion in tow. Briony remembers Roger being upset that he had been 'passed over'. Even today, Duncan is tight-lipped about this occasion, but admits it was 'a bit hurtful' to see Ben with another boy in the position he

---

* Duncan believes this is a reference to the time he told Britten he was not homosexual (see page 226).

had occupied. 'But it was as if, in a heterosexual relationship, someone had a new girlfriend – so what?'

Roger was no longer the wide-eyed little boy, with an enquiring and impressionable mind. He was also leaving school, which would rupture the context in which Ben envisaged his young friends. He frequently visited them there, and he spotted the tell-tale signs of schoolboys, whether caps or tuck-boxes, wherever he went. He told Pears that, on a train journey, he had been distracted by schoolboys from Pangbourne College – particularly by 'a heavenly meeting between two flowers on Reading Station – such pleasure at re-uniting after the holidays was heart-warming – the Greek Anthology level'. Without the scholastic context, he could not make up for his own abbreviated schooldays. There would be much less of the 'boys-together' camaraderie, each one an Emil teaming up with the Detectives. There would be no sports fields, no school showers, no algebra.

While Ben turned his time and attention to new young friends, the older ones were not altogether discarded. As well as arranging a number of reunions with Humphrey Maud, he went out of his way to help Paul Rogerson after he left the religious life. David Spenser lost contact with him in the 1950s and went into the acting world. But one day, as he was out walking with a friend in north London, they had an accidental reunion. 'We walked round the corner and my friend said, "Isn't that Benjamin Britten and Peter Pears?", and I looked, and said, "God, so it is". He said, "Didn't you used to know them? Go over and say hello", and I said, "I wouldn't dream of it. They wouldn't even recognise me." But as we drew nearer Ben suddenly put out his arms and said, "David, dear David" – and they were on the other side of the road! That was really one of the most moving moments ever. It's a lovely memory to have and I treasure it because it was unexpected.' Spenser still holds him in the highest regard because of his encouragement. 'He gave me a feeling of "I can stand on my own two feet, I can tackle life". Whenever I went into the doldrums, I always heard this voice saying, "You've done very well so far and you'll survive everything". '

Stephen Terry, in his early twenties, took the trouble to look back, and wrote Britten a touching testimonial. In understanding the power of the spell each had cast on the other, he could have been speaking for all Britten's children.

My dear Ben,

I've just listened to the War Requiem for the first time in over a year, and wanted to write to you. That single work produces more turmoil in me than all others, and more gratitude than I can convey, and not solely for the music. Perhaps it was because I loved and admired you when I was younger, or perhaps for other reasons, but your music remains the most direct and immediate artistic experience which I can undergo. There is so much in my life that I can find 'felt' or portrayed in your music. So much.

It is also only now that I am really beginning to appreciate the kindness and love which you showed me when I was younger, as a result of which I feel myself to have been allowed access to a world of experience denied to so many. [. . .]

I have much more I could say, but not at the moment; my love to you and Peter, and gratitude.

Stephen Terry

CHAPTER 17

A time there was . . .

Among the ephemera stored in the Britten–Pears Library is a music manuscript pocket-book. The label on the front is inscribed in pencil 'E.B.Britten, Form V, Rough Work', though this has been partly rubbed out. Inside the front cover are various jottings in pencil, including the little rhyme familiar to generations of childhood autograph hunters:

> By hook or by crook
> I'll be first in this book.

Britten has written his name variously as 'E.B. Britten, Edward Benjamin Britten, B.Britten, Benjamin Britten' and given his address (the family home) as '21 Kirkley Cliff Road, Lowestoft, Suffolk, England, Europe, The Western Hemisphere, The World, The Universe'. Then he has envisaged himself in different guises in years to come:

> Admiral Sir Edward Britten, KCVO, HMS Warspite
> The Rt. Rev. Bishop Britten, DD, The Palace, York
> The Right Hon. Benjamin Britten (Home Sec.)
> Benjamino Bretini – 1° Tenore (La Scala)
> Benjamin Sarum [the bishopric of Salisbury]
> Benjamin Britten, OM, Poet Laureate

It seems, at first sight, the typical japes of a thirteen-year-old schoolboy. But, on closer examination, the pocket-book is American, published by Schirmer's, and would not have been available to him at his Suffolk prep school. It contains ideas and sketches for *Paul Bunyan*, the *Michelangelo Sonnets*, and the *Sinfonia da Requiem* (all begun in 1939–40). Some of the writing is in Peter Pears's hand, and one of the would-be titles, 'Lord

Benjamin of Snape', refers to a place that (like Pears) had come on to Britten's radar only in 1937. The book can have no connection with his schooldays, except in his mind. It was all contrived after he had turned twenty-five, when 'the strain of becoming a quarter of a century' was 'bearing hard' upon him.

When Lord Britten of Aldeburgh died in December 1976 at the age of sixty-three, he had been a peer of the realm for not quite six months. His death was the main story on the BBC news bulletins that day, complete with a substantial extract from his *Serenade*, sung by Peter Pears. I happened to be driving when I heard the announcement on the radio, and pulled the car off the road to digest the significance and emotion of the moment. It is inconceivable now to imagine the death of any composer leading the news. But the name of Benjamin Britten, helped a little perhaps by its alliteration and by the homonymic way it identified him as a national composer, had become implanted in national consciousness. The extraordinary success of the recording of his *War Requiem* (200,000 copies bought in five months), not long after the Cuba crisis and at the height of the Cold War, had brought his music to a wide public. But so had the continual performances of much smaller works in school halls – *Psalm 150*, or 'Old Abram Brown', or his folksong arrangements, let alone *A Ceremony of Carols* and *Noye's Fludde*. Parents who would never have sought out his music had encountered it through their children. They may not necessarily have liked it, but they had become aware of its distinctive character and significance. When Dudley Moore had sung 'Little Miss Muffet', his pastiche of a Britten song in *Beyond the Fringe*, it may have been cruel, but it was a sure token of recognition.

Two years before his death, Britten wrote his *Suite on English Folk Tunes*. The long, haunting melody for the cor anglais ('Lord Melbourne') with which it ends speaks to the work's subtitle *A time there was . . .* This quotation from Thomas Hardy is a reminder of what Britten had lost as a result of his heart operation the previous year. At first, when he was too weak to compose, he sat reading the scores of Haydn symphonies as if they were detective stories. It was the same small boy, who liked to show off just a little and hear his contemporaries saying, 'Britten's at it again!' But other aspects of childhood were beyond his reach. No longer could he leap around the tennis court at the Red House with his cunning slices, no longer could he plunge into the North Sea five times a day, or race with young friends around the Suffolk lanes in his open-topped Alvis. His incapacity might have meant that the youthfulness he had worshipped, and maintained in himself all his life, withered into old age. But the music tells a different story.

At this time, he was planning a Sea Symphony,* and had begun to choose and arrange the poems he wanted, much as he had almost thirty years before for his *Spring Symphony*. He made his notes in an old exercise book from South Lodge. It may have been a candle-end economy typical of the wartime generation, but it was also a freshening of the link to childhood. Another work he had in mind was a Christmas opera, based on the Chester Miracle Plays, for the comprehensive school in Pimlico of which his friend Kathleen Mitchell was the headmistress. Nearly twenty years on from *Noye's Fludde* he was looking for a fresh challenge for child performers. He did extensive work on the libretto, which consisted of five scenes, starting with the Angel's Salutation of the Virgin Mary, and ending with King Herod's massacre of the Innocents, interspersed with carols for the audience – in the style of *Saint Nicolas* and *Noye's Fludde*. Community music-making was the spur for his final completed work, *Welcome Ode*, written for Suffolk young people to greet the Queen during her Silver Jubilee tour. And two of the movements in the *Suite on English Folk Tunes*, 'Cakes and Ale' and 'Hunt the Squirrel', show that, whatever his physical constraints, the love of speed and sport was still alive in his mind.

---

* He had programmed Vaughan Williams's *A Sea Symphony* at the 1972 Aldeburgh Festival, alongside his own *Four Sea Interludes and Passacaglia* from *Peter Grimes*.

He had, of course, set Hardy's poem 'A time there was . . .'
before. Under the title 'Before Life and After', it concluded his
1953 Hardy cycle *Winter Words*. The poem inspired one of
Britten's greatest songs, in which words and music conjure up a
time of purity and innocence unsullied by the frailties and failings of the human condition. The pianist's hands are three
octaves apart for most of the song – four at the climax – a picture in sound of the 'great gulf fix'd' between a place of human
suffering and a Garden of Eden where no fruit has been eaten.
The major and minor triads which throughout plod away
murkily in the bass suggest the grim trudge of human experience, while the soaring octaves in the right hand, in duet
with the lyrical vocal line, express the primal beauty of life and
feeling, before experience began. This summed up Britten's lifelong yearning to return to that nascent sensibility, before the
pains and problems of adulthood – of life – intruded, before
questions of guilt and innocence even arose. Even earlier than
innocence, there was nescience – the state of not knowing –
and perhaps, perhaps, there can be again. It was his heartfelt
answer to the gossips, to the sniggerers, to the worriers, even to
himself, whether or not he knew in his heart there could be no
going back.

> A time there was – as one may guess
> And as, indeed, earth's testimonies tell –
>   Before the birth of consciousness,
>   When all went well.
>
> None suffered sickness, love, or loss,
> None knew regret, starved hope, or heart-burnings;
>   None cared whatever crash or cross
>   Brought wrack to things.
>
> If something ceased, no tongue bewailed,
> If something winced and waned, no heart was wrung;
>   If brightness dimmed, and dark prevailed,
>   No sense was stung.

But the disease of feeling germed,
And primal rightness took the tinct of wrong;
Ere nescience shall be reaffirmed
How long, how long?

Britten was pleased at how 'relaxed' this song was. He told Imogen Holst, shortly after finishing the cycle in the wake of his opera *Gloriana*, 'I couldn't have written that a year ago'. But he revealed how intimate these Hardy songs were when he said 'he couldn't face' having them published, because 'they were so personal and he didn't want everyone doing them badly'. It was particularly appropriate, therefore, that *Winter Words* turned out to be the last song-cycle Britten and Pears performed in public – an epitaph to their long musical partnership, and in the end to their life together.

The recording of that recital was broadcast in November 1974, just as Britten was completing the folk tune suite. Pears was away in New York, singing the role of Aschenbach in *Death in Venice*. Ben had at last come to accept that he would remain an invalid, and was eagerly waiting for Peter to return home. He listened to *Winter Words* on the radio, and was overcome. He poured out his devotion to Peter as both artist and man in a touching love-letter, and told him he had had to switch the radio off before the end of the recital, because he wanted nothing more after hearing Pears's passionate, anguished cry: 'How long, how long?' at the close of his Hardy cycle. 'How long?' Britten asked his absent partner. 'Only till Dec. 20th – I think I can just bear it.'

Two years later, a fortnight before illness at last claimed him in Pears's arms, Britten received a final letter from Wulff Scherchen. Over the years there had been no more than the occasional polite note. Now, in November 1976, Scherchen knew the end was near, and his mind went back to his tears of thirty-eight years before, and all that had flowed from them. 'Dearest Ben', he wrote, 'I wonder if you still recall the first evening I spent at the Old Mill, with you playing the piano?'

Ben was too ill to respond. But Peter did on his behalf.

> Dearest Wulff,
> Ben was so touched to have your letter. He is slowly fading,
> taking his time, uncomfortable but not in great pain, calm
> and loving all the time, drowsier each day but surprising us
> too with sudden questions. All there, as one says.
> My love to you –
> Peter.

Wulff Scherchen visited Aldeburgh for what he said would be
the last time in spring 2003, on the brink of his 83rd birthday.
As he entered the Britten–Pears Library, he stopped short with
an involuntary cry at the sight of the magnificent bust of Britten
by Georg Ehrlich on the table. He was a man transfixed. 'I have
of course seen this bust before, but only as an illustration, as a
photograph. I'd no idea it could be so striking, so vivid in the
impact it makes. That's Benjamin, that's Benjamin, conceiving
something in his mind. Even that vein in his forehead, always so
prominent . . . Quite amazing, utterly amazing, deeply moving.'
He paused, lost in thought, and breathed deeply. 'Such a strong
face.'

As he spoke, his right hand moved forward to brush the
bronze vein. Almost seventy years before, Benjamin Britten had
been mesmerised by a beautiful boy called Wulff Scherchen.
Now, as an old man, Scherchen was spellbound by the presence
of the young Ben. In a poignant reversal of roles, he had become
Aschenbach to Ben's Tadzio. This time, they touched.

There was a long silence. 'Nothing else to say', he murmured.
'I've said it all.'

Acknowledgements

I am most grateful to the Trustees of the Britten-Pears Foundation for allowing me to quote from the correspondence, diaries and other documents of Benjamin Britten and Peter Pears, held at the Britten-Pears Library in Aldeburgh, and to reproduce photographs of which they hold the copyright.

I must also thank the British Broadcasting Corporation for agreeing to the use of extracts from my filmed interviews for the television documentary *Britten's Children*, of which it holds the copyright – also (as with the Canadian Broadcasting Corporation) from radio and television programmes in which Britten took part. I am grateful to Isolde Films for permission to quote from interviews (some untransmitted) filmed for Tony Palmer's 1980 documentary for London Weekend Television, *A Time There Was*, and to Decca Records for allowing me to quote from the surreptitious recording of Britten as he prepared to commit the *War Requiem* to disc.

I am grateful to the following for interviews given me, and/or for permission to quote from their letters and other copyright material: Michael Berkeley, Merlin Channon, Basil Coleman, Roger Duncan, Barbara Dunkerley, John Elwes, Maureen Garnham, Jonathan Gathorne-Hardy, Colin Graham, Marcus Hearn, David Hemmings, Gábor and Zoltán Jeney, Richard Kihl, Bridget Kitley, Philip Langridge, Briony Lawson, the Hon. David Layton, Sir Charles Mackerras, Ronan Magill, Sir Humphrey Maud, David Owen Norris, Sue Phipps, Basil Reeve, Paul Rogerson, Bob Rothman, Robert Saxton, David Spenser, Humphrey Stone, Rosamund Strode, Adrian Thompson, John Woolford and Benjamin Zander. The translation of 'Antique' in *Les Illuminations* is by Joseph Allen.

I am also indebted to those who administer the Estates of the following for their kind permission to reproduce copyright material: W.H. Auden, Lennox Berkeley, James Bernard, Russell Burgess, William Coldstream (William Coldstream Trust), Eric Crozier, Ronald Duncan (Ronald Duncan Literary Foundation), Piers Dunkerley, E.M. Forster (in this case, the Society of Authors as agent for the Provost and Scholars of King's College, Cambridge), David Hemmings (permission granted by Curtis Brown Group Ltd), Imogen Holst, Christopher Isherwood, Joan Magill, Elizabeth Mayer, Arthur Oldham, Myfanwy Piper, William Plomer (the William Plomer Trust), John Pounder, Enid Slater, Montagu Slater and William Soutar (the Trustees of the National Library of Scotland). In one or two other cases it has not been possible to trace the appropriate people to secure permission, but if they make themselves known to the publishers future editions of this book can be amended accordingly. I apologise for any inadvertent omissions.

Select Bibliography

Paul Banks (ed.) *Benjamin Britten: A Catalogue of the Published Works*
(Britten-Pears Library 1999)
Alan Blyth *Remembering Britten* (Hutchinson 1981)
Beth Britten *My Brother Benjamin* (Kensal Press 1986)
Humphrey Carpenter *Benjamin Britten: A Biography* (Faber & Faber 1992)
Peter Evans *The Music of Benjamin Britten* (J. M. Dent 1979)
Christopher Headington *Peter Pears: A Biography* (Faber & Faber 1992)
David Herbert (ed.) *The Operas of Benjamin Britten* (Hamish Hamilton 1979)
Michael Kennedy *Britten* (The Master Musicians: J.M. Dent 1981)
Paul Kildea (ed.) *Britten on Music* (OUP 2003)
David Matthews *Britten* (Haus Publishing 2003)
Donald Mitchell *Britten & Auden in the Thirties* (Boydell Press 1981)
Donald Mitchell, Philip Reed, Mervyn Cooke (ed.) *Letters from a Life*
volumes 1–3 (Faber & Faber 1991, 1991, 2004)
Christopher Palmer (ed.) *The Britten Companion* (Faber & Faber 1984)

Sources

The following abbreviations refer to the most-frequently quoted sources in the book:

A Time There Was	Television documentary directed by Tony Palmer (London Weekend Television 1980)
Author's interview	Interview during 2003–4 for *Britten's Children*, television documentary by John Bridcut (Mentorn for the BBC, 2004) or subsequently for this book
BPL	Britten–Pears Library, The Red House, Aldeburgh, Suffolk
Carpenter	Humphrey Carpenter *Benjamin Britten: A Biography* (Faber & Faber 1992)
Crozier memorandum	Eric Crozier *Notes on Benjamin Britten* (unpublished, 1966)
Diary	Britten's diary (Britten–Pears Library)
Holst journal	Imogen Holst's journal (unpublished, Britten–Pears Library)
Kitley memorandum	Memorandum by Bridget Kitley published in Donald Mitchell's essay on Montagu Slater in *Benjamin Britten: Peter Grimes*, ed. Philip Brett (Cambridge University Press 1983) pp 29–30
Letters from a Life	*Letters from a Life* volumes 1–3, edited by Donald Mitchell, Philip Reed and Mervyn Cooke (volume 3 only), (Faber & Faber 1991, 1991, 2004)

Sources are identified by page number and the first relevant words in the text. Where two or more passages from the same source follow each other, only the first passage is identified. But where there is risk of confusion, a repeated source is indicated by the word '*ibid.*'

The words '*op.cit.*' indicate that the source is the same as previously listed in that chapter under the named author.

All letters are either to or from Britten unless otherwise indicated. Square brackets signify that the date of the letter was not stated, but has been deduced.

CHAPTER 1: It's because I'm still thirteen

CHAPTER 2: Britten's at it again!

15 'long delicate' Reminiscence of Paul Azor-Smith, who shared a study
   with Britten at Gresham's (BPL)
   'for those days' Undated post-war memorandum by Britten (BPL)
16 'Layton is' Author's interview
   'One visitor' Interview with Marian Walker by Rosamund Strode 1985
   (BPL)
   'rather a waste' Interview by Joseph Cooper for *The Composer Speaks*,
   BBC 7.7.57
   'he was grateful' Letter to Hubert Hales, Greatorex's successor as
   director of music, 8.12.45
17 'I spend' Diary 27.7.30 and 31.7.30
   'a most excellent' School Report, Summer Term 1930
   'He is such' Letter to Mrs Britten from J.R. Eccles, 21.6.30
19 'I'm always' Author's interview with Rosamund Strode
   'while his anthem' Diary 9.7.30
   'If he was' Author's interview with Sir Humphrey Maud
   'He delighted' Information from David Hemmings
   'colossally' Author's interview
   'One of his composer' Interview by Donald Mitchell with John Lindsay,
   friend of Arthur Oldham 1990 (BPL)
20 'One of his schoolfriends' Private information from Molesworth's
   daughter, Jenifer Rohde
   'Imogen Holst recorded' Holst journal 30.10.52 and 26.10.52
21 'really fruity' Kitley memorandum
   'He spoke' Author's interview
   'arpI harpavarpn't' 25.10.55
   'ArpI larpove' Letters 14.1.72, 20.1.72
   'On one cliff' Author's interview with Roger Duncan
23 'At home' Diary 18.4.30, 25.4.30
24 'The work' Letter 17.3.48
25 'It lays out' Author's interview
   'jumping about' Michael Gordon's memoir quoted in *Letters from a
   Life* volume 3 p172
   'During what' Author's interview

CHAPTER 3: Towards a world unknown

26 'the most perfect' Diary 28.3.33
28 'uncongenial' Undated post-war memorandum by Britten (BPL)
   'the schoolfriend' Author's interview with Basil Coleman
31 'in that rather' Interview for BBC *The Week Ahead* 6.6.69
33 'Britten had himself' Diary 2.8.37
34 'wonderful' Diary 1.6.32
   'glorious' Diary 6.1.33 and 7.1.33
35 'piles of' Author's interview
   'sit and laugh' Author's interview

36 'But he was still' Holst journal 27.11.52
   'Of course' Letter 7.1.71
37 'He probably' Author's interview
   'of course very' Preface to published score (Faber Music 1969)
   'musical grandmother' Interview with John Alston (son) by Donald
   Mitchell 1988 (BPL)
   'a dear' Letter 3.1.34
38 'you have only' Letter 6.5.37
   'the sins' Letter 14.4.36
   'Once upon' Recording by New Symphony Orchestra of London,
   conducted by Eugene Goossens (LW 5163)
39 'Observing that' Preface to published score of *Five Walztes (Waltzes)*,
   Faber Music 1970
   'Of course they' Britten's 1955 sleeve note for Decca's recording of his
   Simple Symphony (LW 5163)

CHAPTER 4: The wider world of man

41 'In a loud' Interview with John Pounder by Donald Mitchell 1989
   (BPL)
   'that is almost' Diary 11.6.36
42 'There's quite' Letter 2.1.37
   'for a long' Diary 17.4.37
   'We have had' Diary 4.4.37
   'he felt sure' Holst journal 27.11.52
43 'very nice' Diary 3.2.36
   'very fond' Diary 15.4.36
44 'and referred' Letter to John Pounder 14.4.36
   'riotously' Diary 12.9.35
   'Please thank' Letter [probably 1936]
   'But what' Diary 16.1.36
   'which was a' Letter 14.4.36
45 'Bloxham seems' Diary 7.4.36
   'Life is' Diary 5.6.36
   'Kit & Piers' 6.9.36
46 'He's a charming' Diary 30.7.37
   'the boy has' Diary 23.4.37
   'charming kid' Diary 6.5.37
   'Harry was a' Information from Timothy Morris (Harry's son)
   'Harry died' *ibid.*
47 'It is grand' 4.8.37
   'the little boy' Diary 3.7.36
   'a very good' Diary 6.5.37
   'He gives me' 25.6.37
   'He is a' Diary 26.6.37
   'for ages' Diary 3.7.37

48 'Very pleasant sensations' *ibid*.
'tried to bring' 1980 letter from Christopher Isherwood, quoted
in Humphrey Carpenter *W.H.Auden* (George Allen & Unwin 1981)
p188
'Well, have we' Interview with Basil Wright in Christopher Headington
Britten (Eyre Methuen 1981) p35
'Christopher Isherwood has' Diary 9.7.37
'They are charming' Diary 17.7.37
'young Harry' Diary 22.7.37
'He is an' Diary 29.7.37
'he struck up' Diary 23.7.37
'they certainly' Diary 25.7.37
49 'Lovely walk' *ibid*.
'Young Brown' Diary 26.7.37
'We get on' *ibid*.
'He takes me' Diary 30.7.37
'adolescent efforts' Diary 2.8.37
'Harry has a' Diary 13.8.37
50 'It is exhilerating' *ibid*.
'No quarrels' Diary 14.8.37
'Harry is terribly' Diary 18.8.37
51 'It is a' 23.8.37
'Robert said later' Untransmitted section of interview with Robert
Britten for *A Time There Was*
'I to a' Diary 23.8.37
'I think I was' Untransmitted section of interview with Robert Britten
for *A Time There Was*
'either end' Untransmitted section of interview with Beth Welford for
A Time There Was
'Split is' 24.8.37
'our section' Diary 25.8.37
'In later life' Information from Beryl Morris, August 2003
53 'Beth Britten refers' Beth Britten *My Brother Benjamin* (Kensal Press
1986) p107
'I am surprised' Diary 11.10.37
'architect' Diary 24.2.38
'I want to' Letters written from Bloxham School [1938]
54 'simply dying' Letter (undated, as are all Dunkerley's letters as a
schoolboy)

CHAPTER 5: Full marks for that boy!

56 'Another guest' J. Allan Pearce quoted in *Letters from a Life* volume 1,
p333
'There was no' Author's interview
'It pours' 6.4.34

57 'He opened' Author's interview
   'always seemed' Interview by Donald Mitchell 1978 (BPL)
58 'The rather' Communication from Wulff Scherchen, March 2003
   'Dear Wulf' 25.6.38
59 'Dear ?' 26.6.38
60 'It's a good' Author's interview
   'My dear Wulf' 9.7.38
61 'In the years' Author's interview
62 'an enchanted' ibid.
   'Ben turned' Communication from Wulff Scherchen, March 2003
63 'My back' Author's interview
   'did you play?' Undated letter (Berg Collection, New York Public Library)
   'Well, old thing' Undated [probably 24.7.38]
64 'I'm sure' 21.7.38
   'a thousand' Letter 1.8.38
65 'I can assure' 29.8.38
   'Then you won't' [undated, probably 24.7.38]
   'He'd suddenly' Author's interview
   'He briefly flared' Letter from Wulff Scherchen 13.7.41, and author's interview
   'I think she' Author's interview
66 'I've got to' 21.9.38
   'On the back' Letter from Wulff Scherchen 9.9.38
   'enjoyed being' Letter 3.10.38
   'You have a' ibid.
67 'Sturm &' Letter to Wulff Scherchen 10.10.38
   'all my works' Letter 19.1.39
68 'proud as' Author's interview
69 'but otherwise' 22.11.38
   'My dear Wulff' 17.10.38
70 'In fact, Pears' Information from letter to Lennox Berkeley 1.1.39

CHAPTER 6: Lost to the worlds

72 'Now, my dear' Undated, but pre-Christmas 1938
   'Just on the' Author's interview
73 'By the way' Letter 21.9.38
   'very successful' Letter from Lennox Berkeley 20.12.38
74 'uncommonly nice' Undated letter
   'My dear Lennox' 1.1.39
76 'Although I' Author's interview
   'There they found' ibid.
   'there was a' Interview by Donald Mitchell 1989 (BPL)
77 'certainly he' Interview by Donald Mitchell 1987 (BPL)
78 'our little' 10.1.39

79 'I must admit' Author's interview
'A propos' 10.1.39
'Christopher's new' William Coldstream's Notebooks, 17.1.39,
reproduced in *Letters from a Life* volume 2, p1337
'He just said' Author's interview
'entranced' Memorandum by Wulff Scherchen 1989 (BPL)
80 'I'm beginning' 19.1.39
81 'I'm awfully' 22.1.39
'It was all' Author's interview
82 'My darling' 28.1.39
'Your eternal' 29.1.39
83 'Beware!' 8.2.39
'It'll be heaven' Letter 17.2.39
'If you're coming' Letter 16.3.39
84 'Am I looking' 13.3.39
'sprung the' Letter 16.3.39
'might drive' Letter 19.3.39
85 'which didn't' Pears speaking in *A Time There Was*
'I got heavily' Letter to Aaron Copland 8.5.39
'one relationship' Interview by Donald Mitchell, 1981 (BPL)
'It came as' Author's interview
87 'I wanted it' Conversation with author
'Wulff darling' 22.4.39

CHAPTER 7: So young Apollo anguish'd

89 'One of Pears's' Interview by Donald Mitchell 1987 (BPL)
'The freedom' Letter to Peter Pears 16.3.39
'It just seemed' Author's interview
90 'eat, sleep' 1.5.39
'as usual' Letter 3.5.39
'let me have' Conversation reported in letter from Trevor Harvey to
Wulff Scherchen 1.5.39
'What a fool' 1.5.39
91 'We may spend' 16.5.39
'a heavenly' Letter 22.5.39
92 'I longed' Letter 4.5.39
'I have lost' 30.5.39
93 'I've just had' 6.6.39
94 'Dear Wulffchen' 9.6.39
'I still feel' Letter 27.6.39
'Just got' 21.6.39
95 'Talk about' 13.7.39
'I feel worse' 20.6.39
'I still feel' 27.6.39
'I was delighted' 13.7.39

95 'mad with' Letter, May 1939
'may be the' 20.6.39
'Unless anything' 13.7.39
96 'all right' 1.9.39
'I think of' 29.9.39
'Of course I' Author's interview
'He fostered' Letter from Pears to Britten 21.11.74
97 'I had been' Letter 14.10.39
'once or twice' 7.11.39
98 'Desolate' 8.12.39
'My darling Wulff' 8.12.39
99 'It is very' 29.7.39
'Soon wild' John Keats 'Hyperion', last lines of Book III
(unfinished)
100 'I am playing' 8.12.39, before the second performance
'Wulff was' Letter 6.8.39
'I'm afraid' 21.8.39
'You wonder' Author's interview
101 'very Romantic' Letter to Hedli Anderson, probably in October 1939
'a halo-like' Author's interview
102 'Graceful son' Translation by Joseph Allen 1971
103 'Who, by the way' 12.4.40
'He was trying' Author's interview
'It went' Letter, September 1939
'have the privilege' Letter 19.10.39
104 'The performance' Letter 7.11.39
'bound to' Letter from Ralph Hawkes 21.12.39
'Wulff-sick' Letter to Wulff Scherchen 29.9.39
105 'Petersickness' 24.1.72
'Dein B.' 20.1.72
106 'You can rest' 5.12.39
'A voice' Book II
107 'the placing' 22.1.40
108 'We seem to' Letter 5.4.40
109 'One begins' Letter 20.5.40
'may need it' Letter to Beth, Kit and Sebastian Welford 30.6.40
'mental perplexities' Interview with *High Fidelity Magazine*
December 1959

CHAPTER 8: Peter and the Wulff

111 'being so sweet' Letter 7.4.40
'so much older' Letter 23.5.40
'I find' 12.12.40
'urged on' Information from Wulff Scherchen
112 'on the day' Letter 26.7.40

112 'At last' Britten wrote this letter on 15.8.40. At the top is a date in
     Scherchen's handwriting: 3.9.40, presumably the date of receipt
113 'It is tragic' 26.8.40
     'Don't think' 10.9.40
114 'really pretty' Letter to Enid Slater 13.3.39
     'squelch' Information from Wulff Scherchen
     'enforced separation' 24.11.40
     'overlook the past' Letter 13.7.41
115 'I was beautifully' *ibid.*
     'dear old Wulff' 9.9.41
116 'I'm told' 25.9.41
117 'a warm nest' Letter 31.1.42
     'Ben excitedly' Letter to Beth Welford 25.8.40: map reproduced in
     Letters from a Life volume 2 p850
118 'like a sack' Letter to Bobby Rothman 24.6.42
     'and this I' Author's interview with Bobby Rothman
119 'the grand kid' Letter to David Rothman 12.11.41
     'I don't think' Letter to Ruth Rothman 12.9.41
     'that rapscallion' 15.9.41
     'It was just' Author's interview
     'Please give' 11.4.75
120 'He entered' Author's interview
     'Well, what kind' Letter to Bobby Rothman 29.9.42
     'How could' Letter 22.5.43
121 '& Wulff' Letter 10.3.42
     'It was a letter' Now part of the Elizabeth Mayer collection at BPL
     'My dear Benjamin' 1.5.42
     'There is really' Letter 1.6.42
122 'My dear old' 14.5.42
123 'God – you blighter' 1.6.42
124 'He was rather' 5.6.42
     'my real' Letter 30.9.42
     'We never got' Author's interview
     'impossible' Letter 25.9.42
125 'Thank you' Letter 24.6.42
     'He did indeed' Information from Wulff Scherchen

CHAPTER 9: The happy dirty driving boys

126 'the key' Author's interview
127 'Ben then' Untransmitted section of interview with Robert Britten for *A
     Time There Was*
128 'scared of' Composer's note in the 1965 study score (Boosey & Hawkes)
     'relegated' Letter to Peter Pears 18.12.47
129 'which is quite' Author's interview
     'sang (but not' Letter to Paul Rogerson 25.6.52

130 'fighting it out' Information from John Elwes, who (as John Hahessy) sang in the first performance of *Missa Brevis*

131 'chesting up' Author's interview
'we now have' Letter 6.11.72

132 'A friend of' Information from Lindsay Nance

133 'It was a' Author's interview
'Roger Duncan's sister' Author's interview with Briony Lawson
'I can remember' Kitley memorandum

134 'They sang' Television interview about the 1967 Aldeburgh Festival, BBC *Music International* 9.6.67

135 'It is a bit' *ibid.*
'They'd learnt' Author's interview

136 'quickly scribbling' Letter to Elizabeth Mayer 8.12.43

138 'It was all' Author's interview

139 'To me' *ibid.*
'mammoth' Talk on BBC *Music Programme* 9.1.66

140 'never ever' Author's interview
'rather exciting' Radio interview in January 1969, broadcast on BBC *The Week Ahead* 6.6.69
'a very grisly' Letter to Osian Ellis 31.3.69

141 'very downcast' Author's interview
'the splendid sound' Radio interview for BBC *The Week Ahead* 6.6.69
'were completely' Author's interview with Adrian Thompson
'assinine pomposity' Letter to William Plomer 22.5.69

143 'I just remember' Author's interview
'We had a' Author's interview

144 'any guitars' Letter to Russell Burgess 5.2.74
'You couldn't' Author's interview

CHAPTER 10: His undying friends

148 'it was nice' Author's interview

149 'poor kid' Letter to Peter Pears 4.9.47
'He had exactly' Author's interview with Sir Humphrey Maud

150 'who would not' *ibid.*
'very, very much' 22.8.48
'I'm sure' 18.1.49
'and he replied' Author's interview
'superb operas' Letter 23.10.[48?]
'a sense' Letter from Marion and Humphrey Maud to Peter Pears 5.12.76
'There was a bit' Author's interview
'a very fetching' Carpenter p348

151 'perhaps it wasn't' Author's interview
'He said that that' *ibid.*

152 'quite a lot' Interview by Donald Mitchell 1981 (BPL)

153 'terribly funny' Author's interview with Robert Saxton, who recounted
a conversation with Crozier
'She went berserk' Author's interview with David Spenser
156 'Little David' 4.9.47
157 'I never took' Author's interview
'I made it' Carpenter p342
158 'to stop him' Interview with Eric Crozier, Carpenter p342
'I said no' Author's interview
159 'not when a third' Carpenter p344
'bad-tempered breakfasts' Interview by Donald Mitchell 1998 (BPL)
'quite bitchy' Interview with Oldham's friend, John Lindsay, by Donald
Mitchell 1990 (BPL)
'furious rows' Author's interview
'impressed by' Kitley memorandum
'terrified' Information from Bridget Kitley 2004
'not an altogether' Jonathan Gathorne-Hardy *Half an Arch* (Timewell
Press 2004) p96
'Britten was most' Letter to Eric Crozier 28.1.50
160 'facetious' Gathorne-Hardy *op.cit.* p96
'at once aware' *ibid.* p115
'brown all over' Carpenter p349
'with all my' Undated letter
'they had each' Gathorne-Hardy *op.cit.* p114
161 'It was lovely' 27.4.52
'badly' Conversation with author
'Ben told him' Letter 20.4.52
'magnificence' Article by Britten in *Sunday Telegraph* 17.11.63
162 'Hold it up' Letter-card [July 1952]
'I thought' Postcard 26.5.52
'My dear' 10.5.52
163 'I was glad' 3.6.52
'the most wonderful' Postcard 5.7.52
'Oy!' Postcard 11.7.52 [?]
'she didn't even' Author's interview with Paul Rogerson
164 'We will certainly' Letter-card [July 1952]
'My dear old' 25.8.52
165 'to cheer' Holst journal 17.11.52
'bathing suit' Letter 4.12.52
'Everything is' Letter 3.2.53
'Found Paul' Holst journal 8.2.53
'I look forward' Letter 8.6.53
'very depressed' Holst journal 22.7.53
166 'was coming' *ibid.* 11.8.53
'Peter came' *ibid.* 14.8.53
'bandaged' *ibid.* 17.8.53
167 'Got to Miss' *ibid.* 18.8.53

168 'My dearest Paul' 6.9.53
'They are very precious' Letter to Mamie Rogerson 25.11.53
169 'everything in my power' Letter to Paul Rogerson 6.9.55
'in quite' Author's interview
'Do you know' Holst journal 8.2.53
170 'on one occasion' Letter 25.8.52
'looking so beautiful' Holst journal 20.1.53
'You will be' 6.3.51
171 'I have never' Letter from Piers Dunkerley, December 1951
'the several big' Letter to Piers Dunkerley 6.11.54
'He had never even' Author's interview 8.3.05
172 'ridiculous jealousy' Information from Barbara Dunkerley
'The one exception' *ibid.*
'In a discursive' This 1970 conversation is detailed in the lengthy
footnote on Piers Dunkerley in *Letters from a Life* volume 1 pp401–8
173 'in awe' Author's interview 8.3.05
'It didn't worry' Carpenter p408

CHAPTER 11: Go play, boy, play

175 'very boyish' Author's interview
176 'He was what' Author's interview
'Ha! That was' Author's interview
'I was actually' Author's interview
'We fought' Holst journal 1.3.53
'When I got' Kitley memorandum
177 'most people' Author's interview
'helping him' Article by Britten in *Sunday Telegraph* 17.11.63
'Get your first' Britten quoted by Sir Humphrey Maud during interview
by Donald Mitchell 1998 (BPL)
'long rallies' Author's interview
'Bit of tennis' Diary 12.9.37
'He lifted' Author's interview
178 'I'll bring' 7.9.72
'absolutely none' Author's interview
'something almost' Jonathan Gathorne-Hardy *Half an Arch* (Timewell
Press 2004) p96
'I was no' Crozier memorandum
'how he enjoyed' Holst journal 27.2.53
'glorious Indian' Letter to James Bernard 18.10.51
179 I'd love to' 12.1.50
'cunning bowling' Author's interview
'Ben was delighted' Author's interview
'he and Peter' Holst journal 10.8.53
'only quite' Britten's 1955 sleeve note for the Decca recording of *Simple
Symphony*

179 'he wasn't much' Author's interview
     'Do you know' 9.2.30
180 'getting quite' Letter 22.2.30
     'your wretched' Letter 25.6.52
     'Glad you're' Letter to Paul Rogerson 3.6.52
     'Glad, in a way' Letter 25.6.52
     'He always wanted' Author's interview
     'a bad kick' Letter to Humphrey Stone 16.10.56
181 'he had a nervous' Author's interview
183 'This enjoyment' Crozier memorandum
     'through almost every' Author's interview
184 'It wasn't scientifically' Author's interview
185 'convincing fast' Author's interview
186 'I would say' Author's interview
     'a certain dash' Author's interview
     'tea and trains' David Hemmings *Blow-Up . . . and Other
     Exaggerations* (Robson Books 2004) p54
     'It was absolutely' Holst journal 11.8.53
187 'It was the proper' Author's interview
     'like a schoolboy' Letter 16.3.39
     'Everything is going' Letter 30.3.39
     'the blackest' Untransmitted section of interview with Beata
     Sauerlander (née Mayer) for *A Time There Was*
188 'he did not really regret' Letter to his aunt, Florence Britten 20.1.48
     'The waves' Undated letter [September 1947]
     'all the little' Letter to Peter Pears 26.7.56
     'At night' Author's interview
189 'Our bodies' Author's interview
     'You'd say' Author's interview
     'We used to' Author's interview
     'We rushed in' Author's interview
     'The climax' Diary 19.7.36
     'Beth came along' Author's interview
190 'we never' Author's interview
     'It was a lovely' Untransmitted section of interview for *A Time There
     Was*
     'It was quite' 7.9.55
     'When they were' Holst journal 11.8.53
191 'three-inch' Author's interview
     'designed to wake' Author's interview
     'feel dead' Diary 1.11.36
     'healthy mind' Author's interview
192 'slipping' Author's interview
     'an awfully soft' Letter to Ursula Nettleship 21.4.44
     'in wonderful' Letter from Peter Pears 21.7.64
     'a very copious' Author's interview

CHAPTER 12: *Malo . . . than a naughty boy*

194 'He looked' Author's interview
'he had such' Author's interview
'Thank you' Author's interview with David Hemmings
'rather depressing' Author's interview
'without thinking' Author's interview with David Hemmings

195 'Please, Sir' *ibid.*
'blue-chintz' David Hemmings *Blow-Up . . . and Other Exaggerations* (Robson Books 2004) p56

196 'It was fascinating' Author's interview

197 'David Hemmings was' Author's interview
'loved David' Interview by Donald Mitchell 1987 (BPL)
'really smitten' Carpenter p356

198 'Hemmings later felt' Author's interview
'Ben got very' Author's interview
'Noone could have' Maureen Garnham, *As I Saw It: Basil Douglas, Benjamin Britten, and the English Opera Group, 1955–57* (St George's Publications 1998) p20

199 'He was not' Author's interview

200 'Ben patted' Hemmings *op.cit.* p56

201 'But it was' Author's interview

202 'Malo is full' Author's interview

204 'an underlying' Author's interview
'too suggestive' Letter to Myfanwy Piper 26.4.54

205 'Thank God' 3.12.64
'the worst' Letter from Plomer to Britten 21.11.64
'He got a great' Author's interview
'I like Miles' last' 31.1.54
'I wasn't exactly' Author's interview

207 'This may be emotional' *ibid.*

208 'David is lovely' Letter to Basil Coleman 25.9.55
'remembering perhaps' Britten's 1955 sleeve note for the Decca recording of *Simple Symphony*
'I would like' 18.11.54

209 'Dear Ben' 23.1.55
'extremely disappointed' 20.3.55
'remarkable performance' Garnham *op.cit.* p14

210 'An awkward silence' Information from David Hemmings
'I was Spanish-' Author's interview

CHAPTER 13: *For I am but a child*

212 'true innocence' Ronald Duncan *Working with Britten* (The Rebel Press 1981) p91
'really wonderful' Letter to Peter Pears 18.7.57
'sinking rapidly' Communication from John Elwes 2005

213 'fear and worry' *ibid.*
214 'worth a million' Carpenter p305
'clear, resonant' Britten's description in his programme note for the
1955 Aldeburgh Festival
'an E flat' Author's interview
215 'the boyish' Britten's essay in *Kathleen Ferrier: A Memoir*, edited by
Neville Cardus (Hamish Hamilton 1954)
'almost anti-' BBC radio interview 7.7.57
216 'not important' Letter to Elizabeth Mayer 6.4.43
'a naïve' Letter to Jonathan Gathorne-Hardy (then aged 18) 10.1.52
'enjoying' Diary 16.10.37
217 'which bleeds' Letter to John Pounder 4.5.38
'for ages' Holst journal 7.10.52
'a sneaky' Carpenter p286
'Britten was very' Information from Paul Rogerson
218 'desperately' Author's interview
'he said, Well' Author's interview
'I think he really' Author's interview
'Roger needs' Author's interview
'just very caring' Author's interview
'Please give' 2.10.58
219 'I expect' 21.1.55
'David H' Letter to Basil Coleman 3.2.55
'little David' 9.6.55 and 19.5.55
'It was rotten' 9.6.55
'I hope the back-hand' 19.5.55
220 'I want to be' Duncan *op. cit.*, p132
'But I think' Author's interview
'I had little' Letter to Basil Coleman 25.9.55
'I like the' 7.9.55
221 'pretty tearful' Letter to Basil Coleman 25.9.55
'Roger is going' 22.11.55
'knocked sideways' 18.1.56
'The air is' 8.2.56
'most of it' 11.3.56
222 'So your voice' *ibid.*
'My Darling Ben' Letter from Roger Duncan [March 1956]
'He is terribly' Good Friday [30.3.56]
223 'I know exactly' 10.5.56
'it was a pity' Information from Merlin Channon
'seems to be' Letter 16.5.56
'Roger was a' Letter 12.6.56
'Give my love' Letter 15.4.58
'Roger is a' Letter 16.4.58
'more & more' Letter 31.1.57
224 'very sweet' Letter 18.7.57

224 'flipping' Author's interview
'Roger Duncan readily' *ibid.*
225 'My darling Ben' [Summer Term 1956]
'I am longing' 26 May [1960?]
'a strong bond' Author's interview
'Ben just had' Author's interview
'he used to' Author's interview
226 'It was just' Author's interview
'very proper' Author's interview
'I think my father' *ibid.*
227 'You must know' 10.12.76
'But he declined' Letter from Roger Duncan to Peter Pears 3.5.78

CHAPTER 14: The coming of the fludde

228 'On one occasion' Author's interview with Rosamund Strode
'giving his second' Information from the American conductor
and author Frederik Prausnitz, recorded in *Letters from a Life*
volume 3, p13
229 'all the photographs' BBC radio interview with Britten by Joseph
Cooper for *The Composer Speaks* 7.7.57
'Well, it's not' Author's interview
'I heard' Letter 7.3.49
'I like' Interview for BBC *Radio Newsreel* 21.11.63
231 'It was like' Author's interview
'the pleasure young' Benjamin Britten *On Receiving the First Aspen
Award* (Faber & Faber 1964)
'He was about' 'Working with Britten' by Imogen Holst, from *The
Britten Companion*, edited by C. Palmer (Faber & Faber 1984) p48
232 'Once we've had' Author's interview with Robert Saxton
'Ben conducted' Kitley memorandum
'happy and' Crozier memorandum
'He was so struck' Untransmitted section of interview with Imogen
Holst for *A Time There Was*
233 'a gift' Author's interview with Colin Graham
'as adults' *ibid.*
234 'Quite a bizarre' *ibid.*
'Normally Ben' Author's interview
'even if they' BBC radio interview by Lord Harewood for *People
Today* 23.6.60
235 'It was unadulterated' Letter to Peter Pears 21.7.59
'His mind' Author's interview
236 'During what' Interview with Pam Wheeler and Anne Surfling,
Carpenter p581
'Some of us' Author's interview
237 'Ben suddenly' Author's interview

237 'I had a message' Author's interview
238 'By means of' *ibid.*
239 'Everybody's in' Author's interview
'perhaps the most' 15.5.63, transcribed in *Britten on Music* by Paul
Kildea (OUP 2003) p241ff
'I think they get' Interview with John Schlesinger for BBC *Monitor*
22.6.58
240 'He knew that' Author's interview
'children really' Author's interview

CHAPTER 15: Keep on writing

241 'The singer' Interview in *The Hidden Heart*, Channel 4 television
documentary by Teresa Griffiths 2001
'if he didn't' Holst journal 6.4.53
'such an extraordinary' Author's interview
242 'You either have' Britten quoted in Arthur Oldham *Living with Voices*
(Thames Publishing 2000) p16
'my session' Letter from Oldham to John Lindsay, April 1948, quoted
in Oldham *op. cit.* p22
'Imogen Holst' Holst journal 7.8.53
'very pushy' Author's interview
243 'Dear Mr Britten' 2.2.63
'Thank you' 8.2.63
'I enclose' 17.7.63
244 'splendid' Letter 28.7.63
'She was impressed' Author's interview with Robert Saxton
245 'It is a little' Letter 12.10.63
246 'If anybody' Author's interview
'If you' Postcard [September 1964]
'Good luck' October 1965
'Sounding right' Undated
247 'Thank you for' Letter 18.4.67
'If it worries' Letter 20.4.68
248 'Dear Mr Britten' 26.5.69
'My dear Toss' 31.5.69
'It was lovely' Author's interview
249 'What we want' Letter, March 1965 (in draft)
250 'Sometimes things' 23.10.68
'Your large-scale' Letter from Zoltán Jeney senior 22.12.70
'abusing' Letter to Zoltán and Gábor Jeney 15.7.71
'Although he did' Letter to RVW Trust 10.9.71 and author's
communication with Gábor Jeney
251 'Of course you' 4.6.50
'to help in' Letter to Walter Zander (his father) 6.4.52
252 'seems to be' Letter to Walter Zander 25.5.52

252 'Hope all goes' 1.2.52
'Benji is such' Letter to Grete Zander 6.2.53
253 'I already' Interview by Marcus Hearn for Hammer Films 1999
254 'Love to all' 18.7.43
'Your experiences' Letter 23.2.48
'Jim, he said' Hearn *op. cit.*
'It has also' Letter 18.10.51
255 'would stay' Hearn *op. cit.*
'Jim, now' *ibid.*
'drinking coffee' Holst journal 10.8.53
'I think you have' Letter 26.3.58
'I look forward' 26.11.58
256 'with boys' Letter 25.6.59
'My dear Jim' Letter to James Bernard 3.11.59
257 'I am truly' 5.11.59
258 'two or three' Letter 11.4.71
'It is not easy' Letter 29.7.71
259 'made great strides' *ibid.*
260 'frightened' Interview with Britten by Donald Mitchell for the
CBC 1969
261 'He fondly remembers' Author's interview
264 'Dear Robert' 31.12.69
265 'I can't say' Author's interview

CHAPTER 16: No one should be smiled at like that

266 'He took great' Author's interview
'At the time of' Carpenter p335
267 'Every single hour' Merlin Channon's memoir *Benjamin Britten and
opera at Woolverstone 1958–1962* (unpublished)
'bowled up' Conversation with author
'It was something' Author's interview
268 'people like' Memorandum by Joy Bowesman, *Letters from a Life*
volume 1 p104
'My dear Joy' 12.4.54
269 'anything wayward' Author's interview
'It was never' *ibid.*
271 'passionate yearning' Author's interview
'Little John' Letter to Peter Pears 17.11.64
272 'My dear Johnnie' 19.1.65
'a serious' *ibid.*
'one a baby' 24.1.65
273 'I have been writing' Letter to John Newton 1.2.65
'It has been' Letter to John Newton 1.3.65
'Johnnie went' 19.1.66
274 'quite OK' Letter 26.6.64

274 'because of the' Carpenter p466–7
     'Ben was so' Author's interview
275 'strange fascination' Interview with Britten by Donald Mitchell for the
     CBC 1969
     'There were two' 19.1.30
276 'a tired' Carpenter p467
     'even if' 14.10.66
     'I am afraid' Letter 18.10.66
     'He took' Author's interview
277 'We were all' 18.9.69
     'Hope to see' Letter to Ronan Magill 3.2.70
     'a lively' Author's interview
278 'He is a boy' Letter to Joan Magill 24.4.70
     'Ronan was around' Author's interview
279 'I might have' Author's interview
     'You see' 15.12.70
     'Tyger has' Letter 24.1.72
     'Then you return' Letter (not sent) 8.1.72
280 'good talk' Letter (sent) 9.1.72
     'I'm getting' Letter to Peter Pears 19.2.72
     'You would have' Letter 11.3.39
     'How are the' 15.6.39
281 'I miss Bob' Letter to Britten 12.10.74
282 'He is disgusted' Author's interview
     'extraordinary outpouring' Author's interview
     'bourgeois convention' Letter 31.1.42
283 'excellent' Letter to Myfanwy Piper 6.2.72
     'It's all in' Author's interview
     'It was as though' Conversation with author
284 'Ben's illness' Letter from Ronan Magill to Peter Pears 8.4.73
     'When I saw' 13.9.73
     'glossy' Letter 19.4.62
     'worried about' Letter to E.M. Forster, Easter Saturday 1962
285 'a bit hurtful' Author's interview
286 'a heavenly' Letter 29.1.50
     'We walked' Author's interview
287 'My dear Ben' 25.9.72

CHAPTER 17: A time there was . . .

289 'the strain of' Letter to Wulff Scherchen 22.11.38
292 'I couldn't have' Holst journal 6.2.54
     'How long' 17.11.74
     'Dearest Ben' 16.11.76
293 'Dearest Wulff' Letter 25.11.76
     'I have of course' Author's interview

Index

INDEX